OTHER TITLES IN THE

LIBRARY OF
HIDDEN KNOWLEDGE

The New Master Key System

The New Science of Getting Rich

Natural Abundance

The New Game of Life and How to Play It

As We Think, So We Are

Coming in October, 2013

The Spiritual Science of Emma Curtis Hopkins

Praise for

ONE LAW

"Dr. Miller is a teacher of teachers, with an inestimable gift for translating large weighty subjects into wisdom that is accessible to modern spiritual seekers. She simplifies what could be complex concepts with gentleness and good humor, making the path of self-realization an enjoyable journey under her care. In *One Law*, she gets to the heart of arcane yet timeless truths of another era, weaving science and spirituality with insights and tools that are hugely relevant today."

Claire Sierra, MA, director of the Bliss Breakthrough Program and author of *The Magdalene Path*

"In *One Law*, Henry Drummond tells us that it is 'altogether unlikely' that humanity's spiritual life and being would be separated 'into two such incoherent halves.' This statement written seven generations ago, provides all the insight we need for dealing with today's ecological and subsequently, social and economic crises. The prophesies by those who have understood *One Law* in the depths of their souls for centuries are coming true today. Dr. Ruth Miller's profound writings lead us to ask who are these people, what are their practices, how do their languages connect them to the energies of the planet, and how might we look to them for a type of leadership so foreign to we who have been isolated in one of those incoherent halves?"

Milt Markewitz, chair of the Earth & Spirit Council of Portland, OR and author of *Three Worlds*

ONE LAW

Henry Drummond on
Nature's Law, Spirit, and Love

includes excerpts from *Natural Law in the Spiritual World*
and
The Greatest Thing in the World

edited by RUTH L. MILLER

LIBRARY OF
HIDDEN KNOWLEDGE

ATRIA BOOKS
New York London Toronto Sydney New Delhi

BEYOND WORDS
Hillsboro, Oregon

ATRIA BOOKS
A Division of Simon & Schuster, Inc.
1230 Avenue of the Americas
New York, NY 10020

BEYOND WORDS
20827 N.W. Cornell Road, Suite 500
Hillsboro, Oregon 97124–9808
503-531-8700 / 503-531-8773 fax
www.beyondword.com

Managing editor: Lindsay S. Brown
Editor: Gretchen Stelter
Copyeditor: Sheila Ashdown
Proofreader: Jade Chan
Design: Devon Smith
Composition: William H. Brunson Typography Services

First Atria Books/Beyond Words hardcover edition June 2013

Manufactured in the United States of America

10 9 8 7 6 5 4 3 2 1

Library of Congress Cataloging-in-Publication Data

  One law : Henry Drummond on nature's law in spiritual life (includes the Greatest Thing in the World) / edited by Ruth L. Miller.
    pages   cm
  1. Drummond, Henry, 1851–1897.   2. Religion and science.   3. Natural theology.
4. New Thought.   I. Miller, Ruth L., 1948–.   II. Drummond, Henry, 1851–1897.
Natural law in the spiritual world.   III. Drummond, Henry, 1851-1897. Greatest thing
in the world.
BL240.3.O54   2013
289.9′8—dc23
                                                                              2012048697

ISBN 978-1-58270-421-0
ISBN 978-1-4767-1606-0 (ebook)

The corporate mission of Beyond Words Publishing, Inc.: *Inspire to Integrity*

CONTENTS

A Note from the Editor

Welcome to the sixth volume of the Library of Hidden Knowledge. In this series we translate the essential inspirational works of our great-grandparents' generation into a form that's accessible to the twenty-first-century reader. The writers of the nineteenth and early twentieth centuries were encouraged to use a flowery prose with long sentences, a masculine gender bias, and casual references to other writers' works. We've used more modern language, removed the masculine bias, organized the text into shorter sections, and added modern examples and explanations from both the sciences and world religions. We've also included the original text so the reader can experience both versions.

This volume is based on two of the most beloved English-language texts of the last decades of the nineteenth century: *Natural Law in the Spiritual World* and *The Greatest Thing in the World*, both by Henry G. Drummond. In them, Drummond integrates rational thought and the scientific method with some of the most profound ideas of Christianity, the only religion familiar to most Europeans and Americans at the time, and for many made spirituality an intellectually sustainable experience for the first time.

Natural Law was wildly popular when published in 1884, selling nearly half a million copies in its first year. I remember seeing it on my grandmother's bookshelf, and I'm sure many other baby boomers recall seeing it as well. It not only made sense of religion for readers but it also helped members of that generation integrate their spiritual life, with all its power and potential, into their working life, giving them hope and guidance during two world wars and the Great Depression.

The second piece in this book, *The Greatest Thing in the World*, has also been very popular and has never been out of print since it was first published as an extended "Christmas card" in 1889. Even today it's a beloved gift to share with another seeker on the path. We've included it here not just because it was so popular but also because it's a fitting conclusion to the ideas presented in the essays we've selected from *Natural Law*. Presented in combination, the texts establish that there is continuity between our natural life and our spiritual life, and Drummond provides us with clear guidelines for succeeding in both.

GETTING THE MOST FROM THIS BOOK

As with all books in the Library of Hidden Knowledge series, we've included the author's original text in the second section, so you can move back and forth between our version and his. For most readers, it works best if you read the interpretations in the first section, perhaps do some of the exercises, and then scan the originals for phrases and sentences that leap off the page. In doing it this way, many find that they can go back and forth between our interpretation and the original work and grasp the author's meaning much more easily.

A NOTE ABOUT SCRIPTURAL REFERENCES

It's worth noting here that Drummond was an intensely evangelical Christian. He was raised in Scotland in the mid-nineteenth century, in a place and time where to choose not to be Christian meant having no morals and no hope of a spiritual life. He didn't have much access to the religious works and ideas of other traditions, nor the experience of "living saints" like Gandhi, Mother Teresa, and Nelson Mandela, who have so graced our lives in the twentieth century. As a result, he was unaware of the many parallels in teaching, much less the power, to be found on other spiritual paths. So while our interpretations include examples from many traditions, his originals make no distinction between spirituality and Christianity. Drummond made liberal use of the King James Version of the New Testament in his writing, with few citations. We've maintained many of his quotes in our interpretation but have used whichever translation seemed clearest, indicating in the endnotes which translation was used if not the King James.

Beyond those, we're acting on the assumption—based on who Drummond was and what he taught—that had he known some of these other truths, he would have embraced them fully. Therefore, we've included a number of quotations from the sacred texts of other traditions, using the translation that makes the point most clearly.

We trust you'll find the following pages to be as powerful and as inspiring as we have.

Ruth L. Miller
Gleneden Beach, Oregon

INTRODUCTION

The word "science" is derived from the Latin word *scientia*. It means "knowing" or "knowledge" and has evolved into a particular way of knowing, based on a process called the scientific method. It involves carefully observing the natural world, asking questions about how the observed phenomena could be the way they are, developing a method for answering those questions, implementing that method, and finally presenting the results to the world for other researchers' input.

This is precisely what Henry Drummond did with *Natural Law in the Spiritual World*. Having observed that his lectures in the natural sciences and in practical religion were beginning to overlap, he asked why and how that could be. Then he came up with a method to explore the question based on analogy, which is what many of the sciences do today when they deal with phenomena that are far too large, much too distant, or way too small for direct observation. Using this method, which he calls "analogical," he tested his ideas and presented them to the reader for consideration and input.

This is also precisely what Albert Einstein did, although Einstein usually included mathematical equations in his publications. And, in his later years, Einstein came to a similar conclusion. He imagined a possibility, tested it against known theories, and delivered new theories as needed.

The further the spiritual evolution of mankind advances, the more certain it seems to me that the path to genuine religiosity does not lie through the fear of life, and the fear of death, and blind faith, but through striving after rational knowledge.[1]

Drummond was a rarity in the world of the mid-nineteenth century, studying both the sciences and the ministry. He taught natural science during the week and religion on the weekends. After a few years of this, he began to feel that the same principles applied to both—and this experience became the basis for the ideas presented in this volume of the Library of Hidden Knowledge series.

BIOGRAPHY

Henry Drummond was born on August 17, 1851, in Stirling, outside Glasgow, Scotland. As a child, he was appreciated for his sunny disposition and sweet temper, and his spirituality was obvious at an early age. His family was very active in Christian missionary circles, and his uncle, Peter Drummond, was the founder of the Stirling Tract company, through which millions of small religious publications were sent to Christian missionaries and evangelistic churches around the world.

Drummond attended the University of Edinburgh, where he was most interested in the physical and mathematical sciences. He was thought to be halfhearted and independent in his schoolwork, but like many students who don't aim to be high achievers grade-wise, he was deeply involved in activities. He excelled in many sports and was a good shot. He began to form a library, his first purchase being a volume of extracts from John Ruskin's works. And he was a member of the theological society of his college, to which he read a paper on spiritual diagnosis, maintaining that preaching was not the most important aspect of ministry, and that dealing with those in anxiety would yield better results. From the beginning, then, he thought that practical religion might be treated as an exact science.

Reading Ruskin's work, especially *On Art and Life*, taught Drummond to see the world around him in a new way—full of charm and loveliness. He next acquired the writings of Ralph Waldo Emerson, who powerfully affected both Drummond's teaching and writing all his life. Both these authors were optimists with a high and noble concept of good but no concept of evil. They taught him to find a joy in Nature that carried over into his religion.

The religious writers he appreciated were Dr. William Ellery Channing and F. W. Robertson. Channing's works taught Drummond to believe in God as the good and gracious sovereign of all things. From Robertson, he learned that we may have fellowship with God because we are the same stuff, and so God sympathizes with humanity.

He thought he might go for the degree of Doctor of Science, but his religious activity was even more powerful, and so, after completing his bachelor's degree, he went to be trained for the ministry in the Free Church of Scotland.

Like many who've been trained in the sciences, his attitude toward much of the theology he was taught was cool—not quite outright denial but kept at a respectful distance.

Still, while preparing for the ministry, Drummond became deeply interested in the mission work of the American evangelist Dwight L. Moody. In 1873 Moody launched his missionary campaign at the Barclay Free Church in Edinburgh and immediately attracted the ablest students to his work. Moody saw that Drummond was his best instrument for attracting other young men and immediately involved him in the work—with almost magical results. Drummond attracted and deeply moved crowds from the very first, and for two years he gave himself to this work of evangelism in England, Scotland, and Ireland. He made himself a great speaker; he knew how to seize the critical moment, and people said that it was the combination of his modesty, refinement, gentle and generous disposition, manliness, and, above all, his profound conviction in what he thought and said that won disciples everywhere he visited.

In the Free Church, a professorship of divinity in a theological semi - nary was considered a higher position than the pastorate of any pulpit, and only the highest and best were offered the opportunity. So it's not too surprising that in 1877 Drummond became a lecturer on natural science in the Free Church College at Glasgow. It was a good choice; there, he could combine all the pursuits he felt called to explore.

His lectureship in Glasgow became a professor's chair, and he occupied it for the rest of his life. During a few months of the year, he lectured on geology and botany and delivered occasional talks on biological problems and the study of evolution. He gave two examinations a year. The first he called the Stupidity Exam, which he used to test the students' knowledge of common things, asking such questions as, Why is grass green? Why is the sea salty? Why is the sky blue? What is a leaf? After this, he began his teaching and then tested his students at the end of the term on the material he had taught them. His classroom was also a museum; he always had specimens to use as examples while lecturing, and he introduced his students to the use of scientific instruments and took them for geological excursions.

This rather light teaching schedule meant that he had seven or eight months of the year at his disposal, and he spent very little of that time in his beautiful home in Glasgow. He wandered all over the world and was so genial that he made his way into the hearts of rich and poor everywhere. He was as much at home addressing a meeting of working people as he was speaking at Grosvenor House, the home of the Dukes of Westminster in London. He had fastidious tastes, was always faultlessly dressed, and appreciated the comforts and luxuries of civilization, but he could throw off those comforts at a moment's notice and be perfectly happy.

While in Glasgow, Drummond was profoundly influenced by the Reverend Marcus Dods, to whom he often said he owed more to than any other person. On many weekends, he worked in a mission for workingmen that was connected with Dr. Dods's congregation, and there he preached the series of addresses that became *Natural Law in the Spiritual World*.

After publishing the book in the summer of 1883, he took off on one of his annual adventures, and when he returned to the college the next year, he discovered that he was famous. *Natural Law* sold about 120,000 copies in England alone, while sales of the American and foreign editions are beyond count.

This is not too surprising, considering the time. Serious readers in both the religious and the scientific communities discovered the common ground they were seeking in Drummond's *Natural Law*. Evolution was becoming more than a theory at that point; it was a movement, and Drummond had integrated the facts of science and some of the main doctrines of Protestant Christianity, repairing what, for many, was becoming an unbridgeable divide.

Drummond used the funds from the sale of his book to finance his annual excursions to other continents. As a traveler in Africa, he visited areas most European explorers had only heard about and cheerfully endured much that many would not accept without complaint. Then in 1888 he completed and published *Tropical Africa*, a valuable digest of his insights and observations from that continent. The book was praised by critics and the public alike.

Drummond paid three visits to America and one to Australia. In 1890 he traveled around the southern continent, and in 1893 he delivered the Lowell lectures in Boston. He had intended to take time to revise the notes for those lectures before publishing them, but an attempted piracy compelled him to publish them before he was quite ready. They appeared in 1894 under the title *The Ascent of Man*. In them, he aimed to demonstrate that altruism, the disinterested care and compassion of animals and people for each other, played an important part in natural selection, which had by then become known as "the survival of the fittest." The book sold more than twenty thousand copies and would have sold more except that he insisted on selling it only at the retail price, with no discounts, which offended booksellers, who didn't carry it as widely as his other titles.

Drummond also delivered talks to social and political leaders in London. He was invited to speak at Grosvenor Hall, where the elite of the elite gathered to discuss the important ideas of the day. His integration of science with religion and his reinterpretation of the accepted Christian doctrines of the day caused a stir both in the Hall and in the news.

His Sunday evening presentations to students at the University of Edinburgh began in 1884 and were the basis of what became known as the "Edinburgh Revival" and "Students Holiday Mission." The substance of these lectures appeared in a series of booklets, beginning with *The Greatest Thing in the World*, which has remained in print, often in gift editions, since its first publication in 1889.

Although he spoke and wrote on Christian themes, few of his lectures and sermons focused on standard theological issues, and Drummond himself was not connected with any church and never attended public worship unless he thought the preacher had some message for him.

The great secret of Drummond's power as a speaker was that he preached nothing except what he believed in his heart of hearts. This was in no way limiting, as his mind was always open. He always maintained an attitude of hopeful anticipation, seeing each person's views as new facts to be estimated on their own merits.

And though he was ordained in the ministry, he used neither the title nor the dress that goes with that role but preferred to regard himself as a layman. He had, like his role model Ralph Waldo Emerson, a disregard for the pulpit and a profound belief in the powers of the human will. Unlike Emerson, however, Drummond believed that people might find the power in Christ to change their lives, and he maintained the absolute conviction that Christ could forever meet all the needs of the soul.

Because of this belief, he continued his work of evangelism throughout his life. He addressed mainly college students, who dearly appreciated him, and for years he went to Edinburgh every week that he was in Scotland to deliver Sunday evening talks at the university. There, he was invariably followed by crowds, the majority of whom were medical students.

He refused to quarrel and had a thoroughly loyal and deeply affectionate personality, but he remained independent. He never married, and he never took on any work that he didn't feel called to do.

Although he had a number of tempting offers from editors, he would not write unless the subject attracted him, and even then he hesitated. He wrote brightly and swiftly and would have made an excellent journalist, but everything he published was edited with the most scrupulous care. Writing, as with all else he did, was apparently done with ease, but there was immense effort behind it.

He seemed to be invariably in good spirits and was always ready to help a friend. Though few people were more criticized or misconceived than he was, Drummond never wrote an unkind word about anyone, never retaliated, was never resentful, and would speak highly of the abilities and characters of his opponents. It's even been said that he privately arranged for one of his loudest critics to receive an important job offer. In fact, based on what was written about him after his passing, it might be said that he had fulfilled his own criteria for a spiritual person:

An inspiration; not more virtuous, but differently virtuous; not more humble, but different, wearing the meek and quiet spirit artlessly as to the manner born. The otherworldliness of such a character is the thing that strikes you; you are not prepared for what it will do or say or become next, for it moves from a far-off center, and in spite of its transparency and sweetness, that presence fills you always with awe.[2]

Drummond had suffered from bone cancer for some years when he was struck down at the height of his professional success. In the process, though, it seemed as if his sufferings freed and revealed the power of his soul. Those who saw him in his illness felt that as the physical life dwindled, the spiritual energy grew. Always gentle and considerate, he became even more careful, tender, thoughtful, and unselfish. He never complained in any way. His doctors found it very difficult even to get him to talk of his illness.

Henry Drummond died on March 11, 1897. He lay on his couch in his drawing room and passed away in his sleep, with the sun shining in and the birds singing at his open window, the world whose glories he had sung nourishing his soul as he passed on.[3]

TITLES

Natural Law in the Spiritual World (1883)
Tropical Africa (1888)
The Greatest Thing in the World and Other Addresses (1894)
The Ascent of Man (1894)
The Ideal Life and Other Unpublished Addresses (1897)
The Monkey That Would Not Kill (1898)
The New Evangelism and Other Papers (1899)

FOREWORD—DISCOVERING THE NATURALNESS OF THE SUPERNATURAL

The most certain thing there is in our lives—our consciousness—is the one thing that science cannot explain. It's easier to explain how hydrogen evolved into other elements—how those elements probably gathered together to form living systems, how those living systems evolved, how our bodies work. All of that is easier than explaining why we ever have one single thought, or experience, or feeling.

Peter Russell, twentieth-century noetic researcher

Books and articles dealing with science and spirituality receive more suspicion—more derision, even—than any other body of work. Both scientists and philosophers are the leading critics. Scientists are tired of people trying to reconcile two things they think never should have been compared; spiritual philosophers are offended by the requirement to meet the standards of the scientific community, whose ideas they aren't sure they accept anyway. Both groups have discovered that when science is compared to spirituality or fused with it, the arguments are too often based on some fatal assumption about both approaches.

But that need not be the case. We should not try to fuse them or compare them. The question is really simple: Is there reason to believe that, even though we think of them as separate, the laws of the spiritual world are simply extensions of the laws of the natural world?

This suggests a second question: Can we identify any currently accepted laws of science at work in the spiritual realm?

THE EXPLORATION

I came to this inquiry quite unexpectedly. For some years I've had the privilege of addressing two very different audiences. On weekdays, I've lectured to college students on the natural sciences and on Sundays to a church audience on religious subjects.

At first, it seemed necessary to keep the two sets of information entirely separate; they seemed at opposite poles of thought. And for a time I succeeded in keeping them in two separate compartments of my mind. But gradually, the wall between them began to give way. The two fountains of knowledge slowly began to overflow, and finally their waters met and mingled.

The greatest change was in the compartment holding spirituality. I began to hear myself stating spiritual laws as if they were the same as the laws of biology and physics.

Now, this was not simply a scientific coloring given to spirituality; I wasn't simply illustrating theology with natural facts and examples. It was an entire recasting of their truth. Then when I seriously considered what was happening, it seemed that I was actually introducing natural law into the spiritual world.

Some would say that such a thing is impossible, that the natural sciences cannot be applied to other disciplines. To them I would reply that this has not only been allowed in other fields but has also achieved results as rich as they were unexpected. What are the physical politics of Walter Bagehot[2] or Marx and Engel[3] but an extension of natural law to the political world? What is the biological sociology of Herbert Spencer[4] or E. O. Wilson[5] but the application of natural law to the social world? Are the splendid achievements of such thinkers mere hybrids of things meant to remain apart?

Nature usually solves such problems for herself: any inappropriate hybridism is made sterile—as in the case of mules and modern commercial seeds—but these developments in knowledge have been far from sterile. The application of biology to politics, economics, and sociology has revolutionized those sciences and led to the emergence of other fruitful disciplines. So if the introduction of natural law into the social realm is a genuine and permanent contribution, should its further extension to the spiritual realm be considered unacceptable? Doesn't the principle of continuity demand its application in every direction?

AN UNEXPECTED DISCOVERY

When I began to follow these lines of reasoning, I had no idea where they would lead me. I was having great success using parables and analogies in my teaching, and I was prepared, at least for the time, to continue on that line, regardless of the consequences.

Then, in almost every case, after stating what appeared to be the truth gathered directly from the results of scientific exploration, I was soon startled by how similar it was to something I had heard before—often, and when I was least expecting it, from some familiar religious doctrine.

I wasn't looking for this result. I didn't begin by listing the spiritual doctrines, as we do the laws of Nature, and then proceed to try to match them. In fact, the majority of the doctrines of spirit seemed too far removed from the natural world even to suggest this. Nor did I begin with religious doctrines and work downward to find their relations in the natural realm. In fact, it was exactly the opposite process: I extended the natural law as far as it would go, with the appropriate spiritual doctrine rarely appearing relevant till I had gone as far as I could, at which point it suddenly became clear that there was an application.

When that happened, I really did not know whether I was more thankful that Nature was so much like spiritual revelation or more awed that revelation was so like scientific observation of Nature. It came as a surprise to me that our inherited theology, with all the old-fashioned language that has gathered around it, should be so faithful a description of what we call "the truth as it is in Nature."

SCIENCE AND FAITH

We all recognize that educated young people find it hard to accept or retain the forms of religion they grew up with, and this is especially true of those trained in the sciences. The reason is clear: no one can study science without questioning the ideas they were told were true when they were children.

Only those who've been through it can appreciate the radical change the practice of science makes in a student's mental framework. Having learned to use it, the integrity of the scientific method claims our loyalty so fully that all other ways of seeking truth seem comparatively unstable. This is because when we observe the natural world as scientists, we focus on measurable things among fixed laws. Before we studied the sciences, we didn't know that any form of truth could feel so stable. As a result, we now find all other approaches to discovering truth unacceptable. For most of us, this change happens in spite of ourselves; we struggle against it, yet, to our alarm, we find that we're drifting into what philosophers call "pure positivism"—a total reliance on the senses for knowledge. This is the inevitable result of scientific training.

Still, it's not possible for science to undermine a faith that's based on understanding rather than a blind adherence to the voices of authority from our childhood. No truth of Nature can successfully oppose any spiri - tual truth that has been personally discovered and logically supported.

Science cannot overthrow that kind of faith, but its study inevitably shakes it. Scientific doctrines, based as they are on observations of Nature, are so certain that the truths most people were taught in churches and temples seem strangely ungrounded. The difficulty that the scientifically minded have with spirituality is therefore real and inevitable, and their doubt is entitled to respect. What most of them really long for is a spirituality that is as intellectually rigorous and satisfying as the sciences. The great physicist Albert Einstein said it well: "Science without religion is blind; religion without science is lame."[6]

While the process of questioning past beliefs and ultimately finding a new spiritual resolution may be inevitable, it's by no means easy, for the scientist must fight the tendency to accept doctrine as truth every step of the way. This means that *the one hope for a scientist's spiritual life is more science.* To quote Sir Francis Bacon, the man who virtually invented the scientific method in the late sixteenth century,

This I dare affirm in knowledge of Nature, that a little natural philosophy, and the first entrance into it, doth dispose the opinion to atheism; but, on the other side, much natural philosophy, and wading deep into it, will bring about men's minds to spirituality.[7]

No one who knows the splendor of scientific achievement or cares for it, no one who feels the solidity of its method or works with it can remain neutral with regard to spirituality. On the other hand, no one who knows the peace of mind to be found in the religious traditions or feels the very human need of a spiritual life can stand idly by while the intellectuals of our age slowly divorce themselves from it.

A POSSIBLE RESOLUTION

It's not enough to say that there's no controversy between spirituality and science. What's needed now is to draw science and spirituality together again, as they once were understood—hand in hand, leading humanity to a higher way of life and greater experience of possibility. And we can only do so by demonstrating the supreme naturalness of the supernatural. We must either extend the scientific method into spirituality or eliminate spirituality completely—and in our heart of hearts we know that elimination would be intolerable. To quote Albert Einstein again, "Science can only be created by those who are thoroughly imbued with the aspiration toward truth and understanding. This source of feeling, however, springs from the sphere of religion."[8]

The first step, therefore, is not to reconcile science and spirituality, as so many have tried and failed; instead it is to demonstrate the natural laws of science working in spiritual experience. Then, and not till then, will people see that to be loyal to the whole of Nature we must also be loyal to the part of the whole that is defined as spiritual. Then we'll see that the contribution of science to spirituality is the demonstration of the supreme naturalness of what's been called the supernatural, and the gift of spirituality to science is the demonstration of the "supernaturalness" of the natural. In this way, our experience of the supernatural slowly becomes natural and the natural slowly becomes supernatural.

Essential Points

- When science is either pitted against spirituality or fused with it, most authors are basing their argument on some fatal assumption about the scope and province of both.
- The application of biology to politics, economics, and sociology has revolutionized those sciences and led to the emergence of other fruitful disciplines.
- No one can study science without questioning what they were told was true when they were children.
- It's not possible for science to overthrow a faith based on understanding. No truth of Nature can successfully oppose any single spiritual truth that is personally discovered and logically supported.
- What's needed now is to draw science and spirituality together again, as they once were understood, hand in hand, leading humanity to a higher way of life and grander experience of possibility.
- The first step is not to reconcile science and spirituality but to demonstrate the natural laws of science working in spiritual experience.

Exercises

Religion, as Drummond suggested, encourages us to see the world through the eyes of the authorities who teach us, while science encourages us to make personal observations and test what we observe. Attempting to maintain both approaches to knowledge can lead to what psychologists call "cognitive dissonance," which causes internal conflict and may lead to an unwillingness to go forward with either. But Drummond found a way. He was a devout Christian, a teacher and supporter of Christian missions all over the world who worked through the questions of evolution and an expanding universe to find an understanding that was compatible with his religious beliefs. He did so by learning as much as he could about both his religion and science—and each of us can benefit from doing the same, no matter what our religious beliefs are or have been.

You can start to do so with the following exercises. Start a Science and Spirituality notebook and write your responses to the following:

1. Think back to the first time you realized that what you were learning in school was different from what you were being told in church, synagogue, mosque, or temple. How did you feel then? What did you do about it? Did you throw both ideas out? Try to reconcile them? Choose one over the other? How did you feel about what you did? Where are you now in that process? You might find reading a book like J. C. Pedigo's *Views from the Pew: Moving Beyond Religion, Discovering Truth Within* helpful if you're having difficulties with this process.

2. Watch a science documentary on television or the internet, get a copy of *What the Bleep Do We Know!?* or read a popular book about the new biology, like Bruce Lipton's *The Biology of Belief*, or physics, like Danah Zohar's *The Quantum Self* or Amit Goswami's *Physics of the Soul*. Compare what they're saying to what your religious beliefs have been. If you've taken the Creation description in your religion literally, how does this material support it? Contradict it? Can you find a way to merge them? If your idea of God is a person sitting on a throne somewhere above the earth, how do the photographs of far-off galaxies relate to that idea? Is it possible that both are true? How? If you've discarded the idea of God, how do these ideas suggest that there may be a way to define divinity that makes sense to you?

I

The Role of Law in Science (Introduction: Part I)

Scientific Law: a phenomenon of nature that has been proven to invariably occur whenever certain conditions exist or are met; also a formal statement about such a phenomenon; also called natural law.

dictionary.com

To lightly touch on the definition of natural law, we'll take it in its most simple and obvious form: an observed and measured sequence of events or consistent order among observed phenomena.

Natural law is the most magnificent discovery of science. Before the birth of science as we know it, the world was only seen as chaos—a collection of single, isolated, and independent facts. Individual phenomena were studied separately, without any consistent way to link them. Deeper thinkers saw that relationships and patterns must link these facts, but the presence of any coherent law was a far-off vision. They heroically sought to organize the individual objects of the universe into a logical form in their philosophies (most obviously those of the Greek stoics and Pythagoreans), but there's no evidence that they succeeded. We see today the grandeur of the harmony they experienced in their mysticism, but they failed to reach that in their science.

Copernicus and Galileo in the sixteenth century, and Johannes Kepler a century later, began to describe the modern understandings of the universe. Their methods were consistent and replicable. When Isaac Newton published his description of the laws of gravitation in the late seventeenth century, his work was less important to his colleagues as a new fact than as proof of the existence of an incontestable law. Since then, the search for individual phenomena has given way to the larger study of their relationships; the pursuit of consistent laws has become the passion of science.

We can't begin to estimate what the discovery of consistent natural law has done for science. Charles Darwin's theory of evolution, regardless of whether one accepts it or not, transformed biology from a catalog of life-forms to an actual science. It provided the basis for generations of biological theory, describing and predicting developmental processes and prolonging health and well-being for millions of people as a result. Albert Einstein's search for a unified theory of physics in the early twentieth century was taken up by succeeding generations and has yielded myriad understandings of Nature's law at work, providing accurate predictions of form and behavior from subatomic levels to the astronomical.

The natural laws, then, are great lines of reason running through the universe, organizing it into intelligent order. In Nature's laws, one stands face-to-face with truth, solid and unchangeable. Each single law is an instrument of scientific research, simple in its adjustments, universal in its application, and nearly infallible in its results. And despite its limitations, natural law is still the largest, richest, and surest source of human knowledge.

Natural Law and Causation

It's important to understand *law* as simply a description of order, for the idea is often misapplied as rules of cause and effect. In its truest sense, natural law implies nothing about causes. The laws of Nature are simply statements describing the orderly conduct found in Nature by a number of competent observers. These laws do not, in truth, cause anything, nor even actually act. They are simply consistent and reliable descriptions of observed conditions.

Natural laws are the constant expression of what we may expect to find in the world around us—but they have no causal connection with the things around us. They originate nothing; they sustain nothing; they are merely responsible for uniformity in sustaining what has been originated and what is being sustained. The laws of gravity, for instance, speak only of processes observed. They are modes of operation, not operators; they are processes, not powers.

It's fair to say that we do not fully understand exactly what these laws are. We don't even know for sure that they have any absolute existence, since we can describe them only through human perception. Newton did not discover gravity. He discovered the consistent pattern that we call the law of gravity, but he tells us nothing of gravity's origin, essence, or cause.

THE ROLE OF METAPHOR, PARABLE, AND ANALOGY

Science has usually advanced through the use of metaphor and analogy. Plato stated his doctrine in the parables of the cave. Almost two thousand years later, Blaise Pascal and Alfred Lord Tennyson offered their "Pensées" and "In Memoriam," respectively, as explanations of their deepest insights. Our modern understandings of singularities as "black holes" or computer hard drives as "memory" are examples of this approach, as are comparisons between magnetic fields and the quantum field. The mystical writings of spiritual traditions follow suit: Jesus the Nazarene spoke in parables to teach the deepest principles of social and individual well-being. The early Christian philosopher Plotinus wrote of the world as an image. In the eighteenth century, Emanuel Swedenborg, an engineer, described his discovery of a world beyond this one as filled with angelic beings and crystalline forms. So it's been common with all deep thinkers that "the invisible things of God from the creation of the world are clearly seen, being understood by the things that are made."[1]

Clearly, parables are essential for teaching and, when used by the greatest of teachers, must always be honored simply because our limited language requires that we use this method of presenting truth. Analogies have also helped scientists comprehend the underlying principles and processes of Nature. And if the analogies explaining natural law can be extended to the spiritual realm, then, as Thomas Huxley, the creator of *The Encyclopedia Britannica*, suggested, the whole study and experience of spirituality enters the domain of science.

> By science I understand all knowledge which rests upon evidence and reasoning of a like character to that which claims our assent to ordinary scientific propositions; and if anyone is able to make good the assertion that our theology rests upon valid evidence and sound reasoning, then it appears to me that such theology must take its place as a part of science.[2]

NOT ANALOGY BUT IDENTITY

The position I'm taking here, then, is not that the spiritual laws are *analogous* to the natural laws, but that *they are the same laws*. It is not a question of analogy but *identity*. The natural laws are not the shadows or images of the spiritual. It's not necessary to use them in the way a poet might, using autumn as a metaphor for decay or the falling leaf as a symbol of death, because they are the same laws.

The natural laws do not stop with the visible and give place to a new set of laws when we can no longer see them working. The laws of the invisible must be the same laws as those we can see. The similarities between spiritual experience and natural phenomena exist not because they are governed by parallel laws but rather because they are governed by the same laws in a continuum. At one end, they may be dealing with matter; at the other end, with spirit. As Emerson tells us,

> The universe becomes transparent and the light of higher laws than its own shines through it. It is the standing problem which has exercised the wonder and the study of every fine genius since the world began; from the era of the Egyptians and the Brahmins, to that of Pythagoras, of Plato, of Bacon, of Leibnitz, of Swedenborg.... A Fact is the end or last issue of spirit.[3]

Thus spirituality clearly can be brought within the realm of the laws of science.

THE DEVELOPMENT OF THE LAWS OF SCIENCE

The laws of science have been developed over time. One by one, slowly through the centuries, the sciences have evolved into their current form. The law of gravity had to be understood before the speed of light could be calculated. The laws of inorganic phenomena had to be worked out over the eighteenth and nineteenth centuries before the life sciences could begin to establish theories of organic processes in the last half of the twentieth century.

The botany that Linnæus developed in Sweden in the 1740s was a splendid contribution to human knowledge. It did more in its day to enlarge the view of the vegetable kingdom than all that had gone before. But the great Linnæus himself knew that his system was a temporary structure; it was a purely artificial system he had invented based on his own ideas, and all artificial systems must pass away. Nature must be interpreted by observation, not by extending our ideals.

Nearly a hundred years later, the classification system developed by Augustin Pyrame de Candolle,[4] based on observations of plant material from around the world, slowly emerged in Switzerland and banished the Linnæan system forever. Then in the 1860s we had Darwin's contribution, while the gardener-monk Gregor Mendel discovered the processes by which different species were formed and modified, which took botany beyond categories and into process. The work of Ludwig von Bertalanffy in the 1920s established the inter-connectedness within and between life-forms as systems. Then James Watson and Francis Crick in the 1950s defined the structure and function of the DNA molecule in the nucleus of every living cell, taking the science a giant leap closer to a full set of laws. And most recently, the understanding of cell function based on membrane receptors, offered by Candace Pert, Bruce Lipton, and their colleagues, gives us a working principle for further development.

Likewise, the laws of quantum physics, astrophysics, psychology, and immunology had to be worked out over the past century before the time could come for applying them to spiritual phenomena—and the time for that is now.

Understanding in Spirituality

Spiritual philosophy and theology also go through necessary stages of progress. Theology currently relies on ancient philosophic doctrines and forms dependent on the time and place they were developed, as the sciences did prior to the 1600s. Like the sciences in their early days, the present understanding of spirituality, especially in the field of theology, generally depends on authority rather than on demonstrated laws. And this is why there are so many radically different spiritual traditions.

But now that the method of science is fully established, it will soon be seen whether it is possible to discover consistent laws. Applying it to the realm of spirit, though, the scientific method will find the essential similarities among different spiritual traditions and approaches, without abolishing the radical distinctions that currently exist between them. We can be sure of this because, in fact, science has led to increasing subdivisions of every field it's been applied to.

Within the unity of the whole, there is always room for the different characteristics of the parts. Science will be complete when all known phenomena can be arranged so that a few well-known laws at once separate and unite—separating into particular groups yet uniting all to a common center. So we can expect the same as we apply science to our understanding of spirituality.

Essential Points
- Before the birth of science as we know it, the world was chaos, a collection of single, isolated, and independent facts, and individual phenomena were studied separately.
- When Isaac Newton published his description of the laws of gravitation in the late seventeenth century, his work was less important to

his colleagues as a new fact than as the revelation of the existence of an incontestable law.

- The laws of Nature do not, in truth, cause anything, nor even actually act. They are simply consistent and reliable descriptions of observed conditions.
- The great thinkers have declared that all that we see and hear—all the phenomena of Nature—are actually metaphors and analogies demonstrating our individual and collective thought.
- Like the sciences in their early days, the present understanding of spirituality depends on authority rather than on demonstrated laws.
- The laws of Nature had to be worked out through the sciences before the time could come for applying them to spiritual phenomena—and the time for that is now.

Exercises

Again, take out your Science and Spirituality notebook as you consider and write your responses to the following:

1. Drummond tells us, "Natural laws are the constant expression of what we may expect to find in the world around us—but they have no causal connection with the things around us." Draw a circle representing the earth and then draw a larger circle around it, with a small circle representing the moon (or the space station) on that circle. Imagine them moving in space. What would happen if the moon (or space station) and earth were not attracted to each other? What would the moon do?

2. Draw a line representing what the orbiting object would do if it weren't attracted to the earth. Is your line curved or straight? We use the word "gravity" to describe the tendency of a smaller object to move toward a larger one. Even though the normal movement of an object like the moon (or space station) tends to go in a straight line, it gets pulled toward the earth, so it ends up going in a circle.

3. Now draw a line representing what the orbiting moon (or space station) would do if it didn't keep moving forward but were only

pulled toward the earth. We see it happen every now and then when satellites fall from the sky; they run out of power and can't keep going forward—and so get pulled toward the earth.

4. Imagine the solar system and the galaxy all working in the same way. There's a tendency to go outward and a tendency to come toward the big objects, and together these tendencies form all the orbits of all the planets, moons, and asteroids. Why do you think the balance between these tendencies is what it is?

II

MANY FIELDS, ONE LAW
(INTRODUCTION, PART II)

Matter is (though it may seem paradoxical to say so)
the less important half of the material
of the physical universe.
Balfour Stewart, nineteenth-century physicist

THE LAW OF CONTINUITY

The law of continuity furnishes the fundamental argument for the position we're attempting to establish in these essays. This law states that what's occurring at one level of matter or activity can be expected to occur—or something like it can occur—at other levels and in other fields. For example, the process of cell replication—mitosis—occurs in all beings made up of cells, from the tiniest microbe to the largest whale. Likewise, gravity can be counted on to operate throughout the visible universe, not just when we're climbing a tree or knocking a glass off a table.

It's not likely, therefore, that one set of principles guides our experiences in the natural life of the body and then suddenly gives place to another set of principles altogether in the realm of spiritual experience. It's equally unlikely that the spiritual person would differ in all the conditions of growth, development, and life from the natural person. Nature has never led us to expect such a disconnect. She has not prepared us for it anywhere. As Bertrand de Jouvenal reminded us, *Nunquam aliud natura, aliud sapientia dicit.* "Nature never says one thing while wisdom says another."

If we think about it, no one person can be separated into two such incoherent halves—in thought, word, or action. There's a consistency and continuity across all of Nature, which we find in all the fields of science and can expect to find as we extend the principles of Nature into the realm of spirit.

Granted, the spiritual person must be studied in a different field of science from the natural person, just as the living organism is studied in a different field from the mass of atomic matter that is the body. But that's why science is made up of multiple fields of study and multiple approaches to understanding, with different areas of focus. The universe is the harmony, the whole in which the different fields of science focus on different parts. And the harmonies of the parts depend on the harmony of the whole.

We must never forget that the different sciences are merely compartments created by human beings to organize knowledge—they are how we reduce Nature so we can understand it. Science's breaking up of observed natural phenomena into groups, as well as the allocation of certain prominent laws to each, is artificial. We must be careful not to break up Nature except for this purpose. And the law of continuity helps us in that.

CONTINUITY IN THE NATURAL WORLD

Probably the easiest way to appreciate the principle of continuity is to try to imagine the world without it. The opposite of a continuous universe would be an incoherent universe—chaos—with no consistency from one moment or location to the next.

There once was a children's book with the fascinating title *The Chance World*. It described a world in which everything happened by chance. The sun might rise or it might not, or it might appear at any hour, or the moon might come up instead. When children were born, they might have one head or a dozen heads, and those heads might or might not be on their shoulders—there might not even be any shoulders—but arranged about the body in all sorts of ways. If someone jumped up in the air, it was impossible to predict whether they would ever come down again. That they came down the last time they jumped was no guarantee that it would happen the next time. Gravity and everything else changed from hour to hour. One day a child's body might be so light that it was impossible for it to descend from its chair to the floor, but the next day, the movement might drive it through a three-story house and dash it to pieces somewhere near the center of the earth. In this chance world, predictable cause and effect were abolished. Law was annihilated. And the effect on its residents was that reason was impossible. It was an insane world with a population of lunatics.

That's what the world would be without the principle we call Continuity—the law that ensures that we can expect essentially the same kind of structure and process no matter when or where we look at Nature. George Douglas Campbell, the Duke of Argyll, explained this wonderfully.

> If there were no other indication of unity than this, it would
> be almost enough.... The structure of our own bodies, with
> all that depends upon it, is a structure governed by, and there-
> fore adapted to, the same force of gravitation which has
> determined the form and the movements of myriads of worlds.
> Every part of the human organism is fitted to conditions
> which would all be destroyed in a moment if the forces of
> gravitation were to change or fail.[1]

A good example of the law of continuity is the application of a method called spectrum analysis. An astronomer can use a mass spectrometer, a tool invented by a chemist for use with rocks and minerals, to determine what elements are present in the stars being observed. A biologist can do the same to determine what's locked within a cell. The same elements are present everywhere in the universe and may be tested with the same piece of equipment in the earth or in a plant or body or hundreds of light-years away. Its use in biological laboratories is well illustrated in the film *Medicine Man* with Sean Connery, which tells the story of a researcher struggling to find out why a particular flower eliminated tumors in members of a remote tribe in the Amazon.

The law of continuity says that biological laws apply to all forms of life, wherever they are, just as gravity describes the attraction of all forms of matter to each other. And yet this law seems to break as we move, for example, from living systems to other phenomena. When we pass from the lower realm of inorganic substances to the higher realm of organic systems, we use a new set of laws. This also happens when we shift our focus to the subatomic or quantum level of matter.

But the reason why the lower laws sometimes don't seem to act in the higher realm is not that they're annihilated but rather that they're overruled in the more complex interactions of the organic system. And the reason the higher laws are not found operating in the lower realms is not because they don't apply everywhere but because inorganic systems lack the genes and nerves and other mechanisms that make up living systems. Consider the fact that plants and humans seem to defy gravity by growing and moving upward. It's not that the law fails but that higher principles are overriding it—and, as we saw in the previous quotation, the very structure of the living organism is defined by it.

Which is not, please remember, saying that laws actually work or act on anything. Laws are only our way of describing orderly patterns; they do not themselves operate. Gravity does not keep the moon in orbit; gravity is simply the word we use, or the equation that applies, to describe the process.

Continuity from the Natural to the Spiritual World

For the same reason that the same principles don't seem to apply as we shift our focus from the material to the living, many people think that the law of continuity no longer applies when the natural passes into the spiritual. But that can't be so. It's like saying that the propositions of geometry apply when figures are drawn with chalk on a blackboard but fail when applied to structures of wood or stone. Or that electricity and radiation can't work according to known laws because we can't see them.

In the same way that geometry is continuous for the whole universe, the laws of life are continuous for the whole universe. Wherever there is life, we may expect to find it arranged, ordered, and governed according to the same set of laws. Consider, for example, the principle of biogenesis (which we'll discuss in detail in a later essay); it's the law that natural life can only emerge from preexisting natural life. Everywhere in the world, life emerges from life—which is to say that without the living molecule we call DNA, there is no living organism.

Applying the law of continuity, this means that spiritual life can only come from preexisting spiritual life. That is, without a spiritual equivalent to DNA, there can be no spiritual organism.

So there aren't two laws; there's one—one law working across a spectrum or continuum of existence. At one end, the law deals with inanimate matter; toward the middle, it deals with living organisms; and at the other end, it deals with spiritual experience. The qualitative terms *natural* and *spiritual* make no difference except in the degree they may affect the form.

NATURAL LAW IN THE SPIRITUAL REALM

Since in Nature we generally come upon new laws as we pass from lower to higher kingdoms, the newer laws one would expect to meet in the spiritual realm would transcend the laws of the physical. As gravity is largely overcome when we pass from the domain of objects into the domain of life, so other laws might seem to be lost as we enter the spiritual realm. This would explain why both analogy and experience confirm that, in the spiritual realm, there are different forms of being, with a wider range of abilities.

Based on their experience, some people may suggest that some of the laws of the natural world—gravity, for instance—have no application at all in the spiritual realm. But isn't it possible that just as it is in the case of a plant, which grows upward, away from the earth, when gravity would hold it down, gravity need not be suspended for spiritual forms? There's a principle of growth at work in the plant that overrides the attraction of gravity. Likewise, the spirit may rise regardless of gravity. Or if spirit is not material, it's not the law of gravity that no longer applies; instead, there would be no matter that would be affected by gravity.

So just as fewer of the mechanical laws apply in the plant and animal realms, if we apply the law of continuity across all realms of existence, we can expect to see less of the vital principle of biological life that enables a plant or animal to get up from the earth at work in the spiritual realm. It would be as obscure there as gravity is in the activity of living systems, because it is overridden by something higher, more potent, and more characteristic of the spiritual realm.

The vital principle of living systems is called *bios* (the Greek term for the energy of living things). It's a different thing from the vital principle of the spiritual life, which the Greeks called *pneuma* (meaning "breath" or "spirit"). The Chinese call this spiritual principle *chi* or *qi*, and the Sanskrit texts of Buddhism and Hinduism call it *prana*.

One interesting example of how this might work is when a martial arts practitioner intentionally uses qi to anchor his or her body to the earth. Over and over again, it's been demonstrated that two much larger and stronger people can't lift that person off the ground. Thus the laws of the spiritual realm, in the form of intention, can override the laws of the natural realm. Another is the phenomenon of psychokinesis. Numerous controlled experiments have demonstrated that people can change the way that usually randomly distributed balls fall into place.[2] This may also help explain how spiritual healing works.

Since the law of continuity is true, the only way to refute the conclusion that the laws of natural life are exactly the same as the laws of spiritual life is to say that there is no spiritual life—which is exactly what the young scientist is prone to do. Only with the maturity that comes with many observations, as Francis Bacon indicates in the quotation in the previous essay, does the scientist begin to accept that while the spiritual realm as described in childhood is not real, both natural and spiritual life must be real. In his later years, Albert Einstein was more likely to talk about spirituality than physics. Amit Goswami, the preeminent author of textbooks on quantum mechanics, published *Physics of the Soul* when he retired from teaching. And early twentieth-century mathematician Arthur Eddington stated his transformed realization as "something unknown is doing we don't know what."[3]

This statement, that the laws of natural life apply to spiritual life as well, does not exclude the possibility that there are also new laws within the spiritual realm. Nor, as we've seen, does it imply that the old laws will work in the same way within that realm. It simply asserts that whatever else may be found, the familiar natural laws must be found at work among spiritual beings; that they must be there though they may not be seen; and that they must project beyond there, if there is anything beyond what we call the spiritual realm.

Spiritual Laws and the Natural World

We've established that, as the upward thrust of the growing plant appears to overcome gravity, which is the primary defining law of the mineral realm, any new laws of the spiritual realm would appear to overcome the laws of the lower kingdoms. Therefore, in all probability, if any such totally new and foreign set of laws existed in the spiritual realm, they could never be defined with our current language and concepts. Where would the language to frame them come from? How can we, knowing only the natural world, describe the processes of the spiritual?

Yet if they could be of any practical use to us, we may be sure that clues to them can be found in some way in the natural world. And in fact, the greatest among the spiritual laws are the laws of Nature in disguise. The time has come for that fact to be explained.

Understanding the natural laws, which are based on our perceptions, makes it possible for us to read the unseen universe beyond our normal perceptions, as well as to think and live in fuller harmony with it. Indeed, as Balfour Stewart, author of *The Unseen Universe*, points out, "the physical properties of matter form the alphabet [of science] . . . the study of which, if properly conducted, will enable us more perfectly to read that great book which we call the 'universe.'"[4]

Yet there's nothing especially exalted in the natural laws themselves to make us anxious to relate them to the spiritual. It's only because they're more accessible to us and only "because they are at the bottom of the list—are in fact the simplest and lowest—that they are capable of being most readily grasped by the finite intelligences of the universe,"[5] as Stewart points out.

The natural laws now known give a fair rendering of the facts of Nature. Projecting them into the spiritual realm may give us a fair idea about that realm, or at least of the few aspects of it that we can begin to understand. After all, the true greatness of all law lies in its vision of the unseen. Still, to impress the laws of this small world of ours onto all other realms of being, to speak of all laws as natural, is to act as if what we can see defines all that is—both seen and unseen. It's defining the unseen only in terms of the part of the universe that has been described and measured by our five senses. And that may not give us the truth we seek.

ALL LAW IS EXTRASENSORY

Law in all its forms is the invisible in the visible—whether applied in an organism, a community, or a galaxy. Law is great not because the phenomenal world is great but because the vanishing lines of possibility they point to are avenues into an eternal order.

If we take a wider view, then, we realize that all law is an abstraction. It is extrasensory—beyond the senses—and so, essentially, spiritual. And this is what the sciences have begun to demonstrate.

Both metaphysical philosophy and quantum mechanics prove that matter is fundamentally immeasurable, a nonentity. Einstein demonstrated mathematically that matter is interchangeable with energy with his famous equation $E=mc^2$. The Copenhagen group, working with the subatomic units that make up matter, found only probabilities where they expected to find objects. As Arthur Eddington put it, "Penetrating as deeply as we can by the methods of physical investigation into the nature of a human being, we reach only symbolic description."[6] He goes on to explain that:

The mind-stuff of the world is, of course, something more general than our individual conscious minds. . . . The mind-stuff is not spread in space and time; these are part of the cyclic scheme ultimately derived out of it."[7]

The demonstration in 2012 of the existence of the Higgs boson was the final nail in the coffin of a matter-based universe. When the Higgs field of organized energy coalesced for an instant into the precursor to matter and then fell back into its normal energy state, the whole of quantum theory was demonstrated to be law, and matter will never be thought of as "real" again.

Matter derives from mind-stuff. Energy, the sciences of the twentieth century tell us, comes into particle form as a function of the consciousness of the observer.[8] This is beautifully illustrated by Berkeley-based physicist Fred Alan Wolf in "The double-slit experiment" segment of the film *What the Bleep!? Further Down the Rabbit Hole*. It's the premise of physics professor Amit Goswami's *The Self-Aware Universe*: Matter can only exist in the presence of an observer.

Matter has no separate existence without thought. This is not a new concept. It's been woven into metaphysical writings for centuries. The Hindu Vedas describe matter as "malleable, changeable" in the word *maya*, which is usually translated as "illusion." Emma Curtis Hopkins, the teacher of the founders of the American New Thought movement in the early twentieth century, tells us in her second lesson that "matter is transient, changeable, the result of thinking we are separated from our Source."[9]

NATURE AS SYMBOL OF THE SPIRITUAL

The great nineteenth-century British historian-philosopher Thomas Carlyle understood that "all visible things are emblems. What thou seest is not there on its own account; strictly speaking it is not there at all. Matter exists only spiritually, and to represent some idea and body it forth."[10]

In short, the great thinkers across time—both scientific and spiritual—have declared that all we see and hear—all the phenomena of

Nature—have no reality apart from our thought. They are symbols, metaphors, and analogies demonstrating our individual and collective thought. As the eighteenth-century Swedish engineer Emanuel Swedenborg put it,

> In our doctrine of representations and correspondences, we shall treat . . . of the astonishing things that occur . . . throughout Nature, and which correspond so entirely to supreme and spiritual things, that one would swear that the physical world was purely symbolical of the spiritual world.[11]

Ralph Waldo Emerson, the great nineteenth-century American philosopher, tells us,

> Every natural fact is a symbol of some spiritual fact. Every appearance in nature corresponds to some state of the mind, and that state of the mind can only be described by presenting that natural appearance as its picture.[12]

The natural or material world, therefore, is only a thing that teaches—but really, it's not even a thing; it's a show that shows, a teaching shadow. Plato described it as a cave where people inside see shadows dancing on the wall and believe that's all there is, even when they have the possibility of stepping outside and learning more. The whole function of the material universe lies in this one purpose—it helps us solve the riddles of life.

Many spiritual traditions also suggest that the physical world we experience is a "shadow" of spiritual reality, which helps us learn about and begin to experience our spiritual nature. Helen Schucman's *A Course in Miracles* says that what we perceive has no meaning in itself; we "make our world" by projecting our beliefs and thoughts onto the real Creation, which has always been a formless, heavenly field of light. The Taoist Chuang Tsu suggested that this world experience is a dream that we're dreaming in another reality. A number of twentieth-century spiritual teachers, ranging from Werner Erhard to Wayne Dyer, have said that "if you want to know what you believe, look at your world."

But thought is not material; it's the opposite: it is spiritual. And the fact that matter results from thought means that the spiritual (thought) existed first, and the natural world is best described as a visible representation, a working model, of the spiritual. Therefore, since it has no meaning in itself, we can treat it just as the mathematician treats x—as an unknown quantity.

It is very well for physicists to speak of "matter," but for people generally to call this "a material world" is an absurdity. Should we call it an x-world it would mean as much, namely, that we do not know what it is.[13]

And so we come to see that the reality we truly live in is not a well-defined natural world; it's the spiritual—and we know very little, indeed, about either.

Essential Points

- The law of continuity states that what is occurring at one level of matter or activity—or something like it—can be expected to occur at other levels and in other fields of study.
- It's not likely, therefore, that one set of principles guides our experiences in this material life and then suddenly gives place to another set of principles altogether in the realm of spiritual experience.
- Plants and humans seem to defy gravity by growing and moving upward; yet it's not that the law fails but that higher principles are overriding it.
- The law of continuity says that biological laws apply to all forms of life, wherever they are, just as gravity describes the attraction of all forms of matter to each other.
- There aren't two laws; there's one law working across the spectrum of existence. At one end, the law deals with inanimate matter; toward the middle, it deals with living organisms; and at the other end, it deals with spiritual experience.
- Matter has no separate existence without thought.

- The spiritual (as thought) existed first, and the natural world is best described as a visible representation, a working model, of the spiritual. It's a thing that teaches—but really, it's not even a thing; it's a show that shows, a teaching shadow.
- The reality we truly live in is not a well-defined natural world; it's the spiritual—and unknown.

Exercise

To understand the idea that the world around us is a reflection of our thought, we need to compare the two.

1. In your Science and Spirituality notebook, make a list of twenty things in the world you can perceive around you right now. Consider: If they were a set of symbols for your beliefs, what would they tell you? If you need help interpreting them, a book about dream symbols may be useful. If there are animals or birds in your world, the book *Animal Speak* by Ted Andrews is useful as well. In your notebook, write about what the things you see tell you about your beliefs about good and evil, about what you can and can't do, about what people are like. Are there other important symbols or metaphors in your world—in your workplace, your family, your vehicle(s)?

2. If one set of laws is at work in both the natural/physical world and in the spiritual/metaphysical world, the spiritual beings people of all cultures describe, called *angels* or *devas* or *light beings*, must move and grow and develop, too. What evidence in your spiritual tradition do you have for that? In another place in your notebook, write down any specific stories, texts, or verses that might apply. What does this mean for your own development? For the development of people you know who have passed on?

III

BIOGENESIS

---

*As the web issues out of the spider and is withdrawn, as plants sprout
from the earth; As hair grows from the body, even so, the sages say, this
universe springs from the deathless Self, the source of life.*
Mundaka Upanishad 1.1.7

Omne vivum ex vivo. [All life from life.]
William Harvey, seventeenth-century physiologist

An Old Scientific Debate

For two hundred years, the scientific world was engrossed in the grand
problem of the origin of life. Two major schools defended exactly
opposite views: one said that matter could spontaneously generate life;
the other held that life could only come from preexisting life.

The doctrine of spontaneous generation, as the first is called, was
held most publicly by Henry C. Bastian. After a series of elaborate
experiments, he concluded that "both observation and experiment
unmistakably testify to the fact that living matter is constantly being
formed *de novo*, in obedience to the same laws and tendencies which
determined all the more simple chemical combinations."[1] Life, he said,
is not the gift of life. It is capable of springing into being of itself. It can
be spontaneously generated.

This announcement enticed many observers into his laboratory,
and the highest authorities in biological science worked intently on the

problem there and in their own labs. The experiments to test the hypothesis can be followed or repeated by anyone.

Glass vessels are three-quarters filled with solutions of water mixed with hay or any organic matter. They are sealed to exclude the outer air and boiled to kill all germs of life. The air inside, having been exposed to the boiling temperature for many hours, is supposed to be likewise dead, so that any life that may subsequently appear in the closed flasks must have sprung into being of itself. In Bastian's experiments, after every effort to secure sterility, life did appear inside in great quantities. Therefore, he argued, it was spontaneously generated.

But many of the observers found two errors in this conclusion. John Tyndall repeated the same experiment, but after every care, he thought there might still be undestroyed germs in the air inside the flasks. If the air were absolutely germless and pure, would the myriad forms of life appear? He manipulated his experimental vessels in an atmosphere that, having been tested for optical purity—the most delicate known test—was sure to be absolutely germless. Here, not a vestige of life appeared. He varied the experiment in every direction, but matter in the germless air never yielded life.

The other error was detected by William H. Dallinger in 1888. He found the most surprising and indestructible vitality among the bacteria and molds. Many could survive much higher temperatures than Bastian had applied to annihilate them. Some germs almost refused to be annihilated—they were all but fireproof!

For almost a century afterward, people believed that life required a carbon-hydrogen base and the energy of sunlight for survival, but then deep-sea submersible research vessels identified life-forms based on sulfur that use the heat of volcanic vents as their source of energy. These new life-forms had evolved to survive in previously unsurvivable conditions. In recent studies, documented in David Wilcock's *The Source Field Investigations*, researchers have found crystalline life-forms emerging from sand that has been heated to almost melting temperatures and placed in an electrically conductive high-carbon salt solution. Still, just as in the experiments of more than a hundred years ago, we don't know if there were living forms in the crystals that survived the process. The law of continuity says we must assume so until proven otherwise.

So the attempt to get the living out of the dead has so far failed. Spontaneous generation had to be given up, and now it's recognized everywhere that life can only come from the touch of life—a law that is known as *biogenesis*. So far as science can settle anything, this question is settled: "All really scientific experience tells us that life can be produced from a living antecedent only."[2]

A SPIRITUAL PARALLEL

For far longer than two hundred years, a similar discussion has dragged on through the religious world. Two great schools again have defended exactly opposite views: one group says that spiritual life can only come from preexisting spirituality; the other holds that it can spontaneously generate itself.

Effectively, we might say that one small school has persistently maintained the doctrine of biogenesis. The other, larger and with greater pretension to philosophic tradition, has defended spontaneous generation. The weakness of the naturalistic biogenesis school comes from holding the extreme view that spirituality is not dependent on one's natural life. The weakness of the latter comes from the view that human beings are created as worshiping beings and so can be expected to maintain certain relations to their creator. While this fundamental assertion was conceded to some extent by members of the naturalistic school, they could not accept the idea that spirituality itself is spontaneously generated by the evolution of character in the course of life.

The difference between the two positions is radical. Translating from the language of science into that of spirituality, the spiritual theory of spontaneous generation is simply that human beings can become gradually better and better until they reach that quality of character known as spiritual life—with no previous spirituality present in their experience or being.

Spiritual biogenesists oppose this way of thinking, saying that spiritual life must be derived from a preexisting living spirit, and that a spiritual person is no mere development of the natural person but rather a new creation, existing in a new realm. In short, we might as well expect a brick to become gradually more and more alive until it becomes a living being as to expect a human being to attain the eternal life of a spiritual being by becoming better and better behaved. It's not unlike the story of Pinocchio, the puppet who could only become a boy by a power outside himself.

So far, the advocates of spiritual biogenesis have based their argument almost completely on the sacred scriptures of the world's many religious traditions. They've paid no attention to Nature. What they offered, therefore, was seen solely as dogma, valid only for those who chose to accept religion, or at least the supernatural and its traditional interpreters.

It's not too surprising that this has happened; it's rarely easy to argue from experience, and spiritual teachers have always had difficulty meeting the challenge of humanists on this subject. All that's really possible is an analogy, and up to now there hasn't been one. There was no known parallel in Nature for the spiritual phenomena in question.

But now things are different. Understanding biogenesis as a scientific fact, it may be that spiritual biogenesis can reshape its argument in this new light.

THE BARRIER

Let's remember first that the passage from the mineral realm to the plant or animal realm is only possible if a plant or animal reaches into the mineral and absorbs it, transforming it in the process. It's totally blocked on the mineral side. Nothing, no change of substance, no modification of environment, no chemistry, no electricity, no other form of energy, nor any evolutionary process can endow any single atom of the mineral realm with the attribute of life. Only by integration into some preexisting living form can atoms be gifted with vitality. Without this preliminary contact with life, they remain fixed in the inorganic realm forever.

In brief, unless a mineral is born "from above"—is pulled and transformed from the kingdom just above it—it cannot enter the kingdom above it. The plant stretches down to the dead world beneath it, touches minerals and gases there with its mystery of life, and brings them up, transformed, to the living realm.

Those who contemplate Nature have been fascinated by this extraordinary dividing line. Those who watch the progress of science have seen barrier after barrier disappear—between star and galaxy, between plant and plant, between animal and animal, and even between animal and plant—while this gulf of life versus non-life expands with every advance of knowledge. These observers may tend to consider the law of biogenesis and its analogies more profound than any other fact or law in Nature. As the early-nineteenth-century biologist James Hutchison Stirling said,

> We are in the presence of the one incommunicable gulf—the gulf of all gulfs—that gulf which Mr. [Thomas] Huxley's protoplasm is as powerless to efface as any other material expedient that has ever been suggested since the eyes of people first looked into it—the mighty gulf between death and Life.[3]

Nature stands broken in two. The physical laws may explain the inorganic realm; the biological laws may account for the development of the organic. But regarding the point where they meet, that strange borderland between the dead and the living, science is, at present, silent. As Thomas Huxley wrote in his article on biology in early editions of *The Encyclopædia Britannica*, "the present state of knowledge furnishes us with no link between the living and the not-living."

There are researchers associated with the Massachusetts Institute of Technology and the Santa Fe Institute who are in the process of designing what they call "protocells." These are collections of molecules that may have the capacity to do some of the things that living systems do under the right circumstances. The researchers are using lessons learned from artificial intelligence and molecular biology to combine just the right factors in just the right way to possibly generate structures that act like living systems or that could develop into living systems. If they succeed, they will have proven our point: all life comes from life; a living system (in this case, humanity) must reach down into the mineral and imbue it with the characteristics necessary to become part of a living system.[4]

TRANSCENDENT QUALITIES

What's the difference between a crystal and an organism, a stone and a plant? They have much in common. All are made of the same atoms. All display the same properties of matter. All are subject to the physical laws. All may be very beautiful.

But besides possessing all that the crystal has, the plant has something more—a mysterious something called life. This life is not something that existed in the crystal only in a less developed form. There is nothing at all like it in the crystal. There is nothing like the beginnings of it in the crystal, not a trace or symptom of it. The plant has something new, an original and unique quality emerging over and above all the properties that are common to both it and the stone. In the previous essay, we referred to it by the Greek term *bios*.

When from vegetable life we rise to animal life, here again we find something original and unique. That something permits movement and direct involvement with offspring, to name just two defining characteristics.

From animal life, we ascend again to spiritual life. And here also is something new, something still more unusual. Those who live the spiritual life have a distinct kind of life added to all the other aspects of life—a kind of life far more distinct from animal life than the active life of a plant is from the inertia of a stone.

THE SPIRITUAL BARRIER

Yet as the door from the inorganic to the organic is shut and no mineral can open it, so the door from the natural to the spiritual is shut and no human being can open it. Just as the brick cannot bring itself to life, the human being cannot become spiritually alive from within. The passage from the natural realm to the spiritual realm is hermetically sealed on the natural side.

As the mineral cannot enter the plant kingdom and the plant cannot enter the animal kingdom without being pulled "from above," unless we human beings are born "from above," we cannot enter the kingdom just above us. The breath of spirit, the *qi*, the *prana*, is the essential element. Blowing where it will, it touches people with its mystery of life and bears them across the gulf between the natural and the spiritual, between the spiritually inorganic and the spiritually organic.

No organic change, no modification of environment, no mental energy, no moral effort, no evolution of character, no progress of civilization, can endow any single human being with the attribute of spiritual life.

SPIRITUAL REVELATION ON THE SUBJECT

Both science and the spiritual traditions have much to say at this point. Let's first ask what spiritual revelation has to say with reference to this spiritual biogenesis. Then we'll discover whether science may not also have some further support. After all, what is science but what the natural world has said to natural people? And what is revelation but what the spiritual realm has said to spiritual people?

In the Hindu tradition, seekers, or *chelas*, cannot decide when or how they will find their teacher, called a guru, or when or how they will experience *Samadhi* (union with the divine). Yet how many struggle to maintain a perfect practice? And if the films of Bollywood are any indication, how many upper-caste Brahman households struggle to keep up the daily rituals in today's world, believing that only by doing so can they earn the right to a better life after this? In the Hindu text that most clearly describes humanity's relationship with a deity (Brahman), we read that

As long as the individual self thinks it is separate from Brahman, it revolves upon the wheel in bondage to the laws of

birth, death, and rebirth. But when through the grace of Brahman it realizes its identity with him, it revolves upon the wheel
no longer. It achieves immortality.[5]

In the Muslim tradition, it's clearly stated in the Qur'an that only
Allah gives life eternal. In the Qur'an, we read, "To Allah belongs the
sovereignty of the earth and of the heavens, and to Allah all shall
return."[6] Still, the commentaries in the global media make it clear that
too many middle-class families simply go through the motions,
expecting to earn the eternal life promised to them, and far too many
young people have been persuaded that becoming martyrs will earn
them that life.

The Sufi leader Hazrat Inayat Khan tells us,

> It is not religion, orthodoxy, outer forms, or a certain kind of
> life which means spiritual life: it is to be conscious of the spirit
> that makes one spiritual. . . . The ideal of God is a bridge con-
> necting the limited life with the unlimited; whoever travels
> over this bridge passes safely from the limited to the unlimited
> life. . . . Make God a reality, and God will make you the truth.[7]

In shamanic traditions, Western observers say that "mystical union
with the Divinity" is "typical for the ecstatic experiences."[8] Practitioners
may not always fully realize personal encounters with the divine, even
with a lifetime of preparation and a variety of rituals employed; still,
such encounters are understood to be innate potential in everyone. So
across indigenous cultures, the shamanic teachings—even those with no
body of sacred literature—explain this great law. In the Lakota tradition, for example,

> The *nagila* is not based on one's personal experiences, but is
> similar to an impersonal aspect of the "collective self" or a
> "transpersonal self." It is the "self-not-self," "part-of-me-but-
> not-part-of-me" part of who one is; it is the *nagila*, which

participates in communing with the highest entity in the spiritual hierarchy.[9]

In Judaism, mature adults who seek union with the divine are, more and more, encouraged to study the mystical tradition known as Kabbalah. Here they focus on a model of creation that helps them shift their mental and emotional perspective from "Creator God outside of me" to "spiritual oneness with the Creator." The study and practice typically takes decades, yet it is only "by God's grace" that one may actually experience that unity.[10]

So in the sacred writings of the spiritual traditions, there is agreement: the great barrier is fixed. The spiritual realm is guarded from the realm beneath it by a spiritual law of biogenesis: there must first be life.

In some ways, the problem is that of the choice between studying and living the inner teachings or following some ritual practice that someone else has handed us. The ritual cannot impart spiritual life.

Describing the means by which the natural becomes spiritual, the New Testament reports Jesus's words:

> Except a man be born of water and of the spirit he cannot enter into the kingdom of God. That which is born of the flesh is flesh; and that which is born of the Spirit is spirit. Marvel not that I said unto you, ye must be born again.[11]

These teachings have probably suffered more from those who have misunderstood them than from those who have opposed them. How many of the multitudes who confess Christianity these days are clear about the distinction its founder made between "born of the flesh" and "born of the spirit"? By how many teachers of Christianity is this fundamental postulate persistently ignored or misunderstood?

In the Christian tradition, the attitude of the natural person, with reference to the spiritual, is a subject on which the New Testament is quite pronounced: "To be carnally minded is death."[12] "You have a reputation of being alive, but you are dead."[13] "But she who gives herself to self-indulgent pleasures is dead while she lives."[14] "And you he hath given life which were dead in trespasses and sins."[15] Not only in our relation to the spiritual person but to the whole spiritual realm the natural person is regarded as "dead" just as a stone is to an organism. And the same idea holds true in Islam and in Hinduism, where people who have broken religious law, who have not made the necessary connection with the divine, are considered "dead" to the spiritual community—not out of social expectation but rather as the expression of a fact.

In short, the natural realm is to the spiritual as the inorganic is to the organic.

Scientific Models

Life, both science and spirituality say, depends upon contact with life.

Some well-meaning people who are ignorant of the spiritual realm make misplaced efforts to show that it's not possible to make the shift from natural to spiritual. Their attempts are doomed to fail. Can the rocks explain animal life? No; they really do not know. On this principle, the New Testament statement could not be more truly scientific: "Now the natural man doesn't receive the things of God's Spirit, for they are foolishness to him, and he can't know them, because they are spiritually discerned."[16]

This is not a dogma of theology but a necessity of science. And science, for the most part, has consistently accepted the situation. It has always proclaimed its ignorance of the nonmaterial realm.

The biologist Herbert Spencer affirms, "Regarding science as a gradually increasing world, we may say that every addition to its surface does but bring it into wider contact with a surrounding nescience [unknown]."[17] And from our standpoint, he is quite correct. The more we explore, the more we begin to understand, and the more questions there are to be answered. The natural world is limitless in its shapes and forms, and the tools of science continuously come up against their own limitations.

As scientists, we insist that our understanding is based on our observations of Nature. But Nature can't show this particular process to us—she can't even supply all the elements of it. If science were to insist that its tools could explain spiritual birth, the thoughtful person must part company with such science. After all, if the tools of science are not yet able to pinpoint the process by which the egg becomes a living, breathing organism, how can they address this next birth?

The process of birth, which is the first step in bringing people into both the natural world and the spiritual world, is virtually miraculous. But there's no more mystery in the second, spiritual birth than in the first, natural birth; the second birth is scarcely less perplexing to the theologian than the first is to the embryologist.

How can a scientist who knows nothing other than the chemical and physical laws judge the principles of biology? How can a scientist who knows of nothing other than material processes judge the principles of semantics, sociology, or spirituality? And when some root from a living tree, penetrating the soil around it, honors the mineral with a touch and brings it into the realm of the living, will it explain its form and purpose? Until the organism has done its gracious work, can the mineral even know that it's being touched? Clearly, any communication from the kingdoms above it to the mineral realm could only be called a "revelation from above."

So it's clear that a remarkable harmony exists here between the organic realm described by the sciences and the spiritual realm described by revelation. There are not two laws of biogenesis, one for the natural world, the other for the spiritual; there is one law for both. Wherever there is life of any kind, this same law holds; there is continuity.

THE FUNDAMENTAL DISTINCTION—
BEYOND RELIGION AND SCIENCE

What now, let us ask specifically, distinguishes a spiritual person from a non-spiritual person? Is it that one has certain mental characteristics not possessed by the other? Is the spiritual person merely an ordinary person who happens from birth to have been surrounded with a peculiar set of ideas? Is our spirituality merely that peculiar quality of the moral life defined by Matthew Arnold as "morality touched by emotion"?[18] Does the possession of a high ideal, a generous nature, a reverent spirit, and a favorable environment account for our spiritual life?

The distinction between the moral natural person and the spiritual person is the same as that between the inorganic and the organic, the dead and the living. The moral natural person is endowed simply with a high quality of the natural animal life. But this life is of so poor a quality that it's almost not life at all. As the passages quoted above indicate, the non-spiritual person "has no life"; but those who have the quality we call spirituality have a new life—a new, distinct, and supernatural endowment. They are not of this world. They are of the timeless state of eternity: "it does not yet appear what he shall be."[19]

The difference between the spiritual person and the natural person is a distinction of quality, not of quantity. If we were to construct a scientific classification, science would compel us to arrange all natural people, moral or immoral, educated or ignorant, sane or insane, as one family. One might be high in the family group, another low; yet, practically, they are marked by the same set of characteristics—they eat, sleep, work, think, live, and die.

But spiritual people are removed from this family so completely by the possession of an additional characteristic that a biologist wouldn't hesitate a moment to classify them elsewhere, other than genus *Homo* and species *sapiens* ("knowing, mental mankind"). In fact, some modern scholars have suggested that a new species is emerging within the genus *Homo*, one they've called *spiritualis* ("spiritual mankind"—A. K. Muk-hopadhyay); *luminous* ("light-radiating mankind"—Alberto Villoldo); or *spiritus* ("spirit mankind"—David Hawkins).

The spiritual person is the mental or moral person plus something else. There's been the infusion into the spiritual person of a new life, a quality unlike anything in Nature. As the plant endows minerals with the qualities of life, the spirit endows souls with its own high qualities and develops within them new and secret faculties. Through these new senses, people who are born into this new realm, or "born again," are said to "see the kingdom of the Father" in Christianity, to "travel other worlds" in shamanic traditions, to "rise above the human condition of suffering" in the Vedic traditions of Buddhism and Hinduism, and to experience "union with the Source of All"—each according to the spiritual tradition they operate in.

THE NATURE OF SPIRITUAL LIFE

What is this something extra that constitutes spiritual life? What is this strange, new endowment? It's not ordinary vitality, it's not intellectual, it's not moral, but something beyond. It's the state of consciousness that Buddhists call "Buddha Nature," that Hindus call "Atman," that Christians call "Christ" or "the Son," that Jews call *Shekinah*, and that Sufis (mystical Muslims) call "the Beloved." In all cases, it's something to be found not "out there" but within. The esoteric, or inner core teachings of the world traditions—(in chronological order) Hinduism (including Jains and Sikhs), Zoroastrianism, Taoism, Buddhism, Wicca, Sufism, Judaism, Christianity, and Islam, as well as the far older shamanic traditions—are in agreement:

- The new kind of life in spirit is real, not rhetoric.
- It's not "out there" but found by learning to go within, through the experience of the natural person into a different kind of mental state.
- The spiritual force or life is not the same as the electromagnetism operating in matter or the life energy that sustains living organisms.

In these traditions, the spiritual life is something one learns to experience over time and with the help of a trained teacher.

In the Christian tradition, however, the assumption is that accepting Christ as one's source and guide (or "savior," which is what the name Jesus (Joshua) means in Hebrew) is the first step in becoming a Christian and is sufficient to experience this new life—the rest of one's life in the body is to figure out how to make this new state normal. As a result, the Christian New Testament offers many sentences where the nature of the spiritual life is made clear: "Tend to your souls, or are you not aware that Yeshua the Messiah is in you?"[20] "At that day you shall know that I am in the father, and you in me, and I in you."[21] "He will come unto us and make our abode with us."[22] "I am the vine, you are the branches."[23] "It is no longer I who live, but Christ lives in me."[24]

They're not just figures of rhetoric; they are explicit declarations—if language means anything, these words announce a literal fact. They tell us that the Christ (or in other traditions, the Buddha-nature, the Great Spirit, the One) is not in some place called heaven that we must stretch outward to reach, and there is not some mysterious ability to connect with out there; rather, it is living within us.

They make it clear that the spiritual life is a new aspect of the soul, a mysterious presence and power that was not there before. It's a new kind of force, not just a visit from a force. Spiritual life is a change in essence.

And beyond these qualities, we find that none who are spiritually alive ever claim their spirituality as their own. This is especially true in the mystical traditions. "[T]he Father that dwells in me, he does the works,"[25] Jesus the Nazarene tells us in the New Testament. "Not self, but Atman (OM) is the power," say the Hindu priests and Buddhist teachers alike. "Not for me, but to Allah be all praise," says the devout Muslim when praised for good deeds.

THE SOURCE OF SPIRITUAL LIFE

A hundred questions now rush into the mind about this life: How does it come? Why does it come? How is it manifested? What faculty does it employ? Where does it reside? Is it communicable? What are its conditions?

One or two of these questions may be vaguely answered, but the rest bring us face-to-face with mystery. Fear not, though: a path of knowledge without mystery is an absurdity. Science has taught us to expect mystery, and now we find it.

Science cannot say what spiritual life is. In fact, what natural life really is remains unknown to the scientific mind, and the word "life" still wanders through the sciences without a definition. Science observes Nature, and Nature is silent on the subject of spiritual life; therefore, science must also be silent as to spiritual life. Science, therefore, has not eliminated the true mysteries from faith—only the false. And it's done more; it's made true mystery scientific.

So, in the absence of clarity from the study of Nature, we fall back on that "higher source" that must inform the lower realm. We turn to the revelations shared by spiritual minds in the sacred scriptures.

We open the Torah, the Hebrew Bible, and ask with Moses when he encountered a bush that glowed with unquenchable light, "Who shall I say sent me?" And he heard, "I am that I am."[26] And in the New Testament, we ask with Paul when this life first blinded him with its light on the Damascus road, "Who art thou?" And he heard, "I am Jesus."[27] Mohammed, too, asked and was told, "I am Gabriel," and his uncle, a Christian who had transcribed Hebrew Bibles, told him, "This is Namus, whom Moses met in the wilderness."[28] Likewise, Arjuna, hero of one of the oldest sacred texts, asks the luminous being called Krishna who has appeared before him, "What shall I do?" and the being tells him that whatever he does, all is well, and he will be free as long as he remembers this being who says, "I am the taste of water, the light of the sun and the moon, the syllable ॐ (om) in the Vedic mantras; I am the sound in ether and ability in man."[29]

Life can only come from life: "I am that I am."

A SUBTLE SHIFT

Spiritual life seems to be not as real to us as our natural life, and it's certainly unfamiliar. Many of us therefore retreat from the experience, calling our withdrawal reverence. Doing so, we think we are justified by the command to go "thus far and no farther," as found in ancient scriptures.

For example, the average member of an indigenous tribe may neither know nor care what the shaman does or how he does it—and may even be a little frightened—and so declares the shaman's space "sacred" or "taboo." Some intellectual Jews or Buddhists will claim to be drawn to the philosophy or psychology of the system, rather than outwardly acknowledging the deep inner peace and satisfaction that comes with the experience of that higher form of consciousness abiding in and with them. Similarly, although "Christ as life" has been the primary doctrine in the Christian church, from Paul to Augustine to John Paul II in the Catholic tradition, and in the Protestant from John Calvin to Joel Osteen and Bishop Jakes, when self-described spiritual people are cross-examined, their deeper uncertainty is amazing. They state the doctrine adequately and unhesitatingly, but when pressed with the literal question of whether the Christ lives within them, they, too, often shrink from the answer. Most Christians do not really believe that the living Christ has touched them, much less that the Christ consciousness abides in them. Like most people of most traditions, they still see the spiritual life as something "out there" that they must strive to achieve.

Yet we must make sure that, in making reverence a virtue, we're not merely excusing ignorance, nor simply evading the truth. It is, after all, a truth that's been stated in the many sacred scriptures a hundred times—often in the most literal form and with almost monotonous repetition: "the kingdom of heaven is within," "look within," "in the stillness within," and so on. Reverence is no excuse for not acknowledging and learning to live in terms of the spiritual life within.

THE SCIENCES' UNDERSTANDING OF LIFE

Are we forsaking science in saying these things? Yes and no. Science has drawn the distinction between natural life and spiritual life for us and has said that the spiritual is different from any other topic it deals with.

What more does science tell us of life? Nothing. It knows nothing further about its origin. It knows nothing about its ultimate essence. It can't even really define it. There's a kind of helplessness in scientific texts here, and a continual confession that, to thoughtful minds, is almost touching.

To apply what we do know from science, consider this: Vegetable life is not contained in a reservoir somewhere in the skies, to be measured out at certain seasons. Life is *in* every plant and tree, inside its substance and tissue, and continues there until it dies. This localization of life in the individual is precisely where vitality differs from the other forces of Nature, such as magnetism and electricity.

Or consider this: The laws of conservation and transformation of energy don't seem to hold for the power we call vitality. For example, an electrician can demagnetize a bar of iron; that is, he can transform its magnetic energy into something else—heat, motion, or light—and then re-form these back into magnetism, with only a little loss (in the form of heat) through the laws of entropy. But the biologist cannot completely kill a plant or an animal and bring it back to life. Modern technology, to be sure, allows the skilled practitioner to restart a heart or transfer organ function to a machine for some time, but once the cells are no longer alive and working, the body cannot be revived through physical means.

Energy is, by definition, nonlocal, for the electromagnetic forces have no root, no individuality, no fixed indwelling. Heisenberg's uncertainty principle tells us that energy's waves and fields are everywhere, and so their location can't be determined. The life we call *bios* is not like that. It's not something that spreads out through space or that can be gathered like electricity from the clouds and dissipated back again. Life is definite and resident; either cells have it or it does not exist.

GROWTH AND DEVELOPMENT OF LIFE

The gradualness of growth is a characteristic that strikes the simplest observer. It's well known to those who study Nature that things mature more and more slowly as we rise in the scale of life. Growth is most gradual in the highest forms. Human beings, for example, attain their maturity after nearly two decades, while the mayfly completes its whole life cycle in a day.

In addition to being gradual, the processes of growth are secret. Life works in the invisible. Roots form underground before branches spread above; the embryo develops in the womb or shell.

But when the new life manifests itself, it comes suddenly; it's a surprise. This is the only way it can come! Life cannot come gradually—health can, structure can, but not life.

Applying the analogies of biology to spiritual life, we should expect three things:

1. The new life should dawn suddenly.
2. It should develop unobserved.
3. It should develop gradually.

In the case of spiritual birth, there may be cases—probably in the majority—where the moment of contact with the living spirit, though sudden, has been obscure. But the real moment and the conscious moment are two different things. The moment of birth in the natural world is not a conscious moment—we don't know we're born till long afterward. Yet there are people to whom the origin of spiritual life in time has been absolutely clear: Mohammed's first meeting with Gabriel, or Saul the Jew when he became the Christian apostle Paul, or Gautama's enlightenment and transformation into the Buddha (which simply means "awakened one"). And this is certainly, in theory, at least, the normal origin of life, according to the principles of biology.

The difference, then, between the living and the dead is a sharp line. When dead atoms of carbon, hydrogen, oxygen, and nitrogen are seized upon by life, suddenly something entirely new exists. Then the organism begins to form and at first is very lowly. It possesses few functions; it has little beauty. It takes time to mature.

Growth is the work of time, but life is not. Life comes in a moment. At one moment something was dead matter; the next it lived—both in nature and in spirit.

Essential Points

- It's now recognized everywhere that life can only come from the touch of life, a law known as biogenesis.
- The spiritual theory of spontaneous generation is that human beings can become gradually better and better until they reach that quality of character known as spiritual life.
- Spiritual biogenesists oppose this way of thinking, saying that spiritual life must be derived from a preexisting living spirit.
- Only by integration into some preexisting living form can dead atoms be gifted with vitality. The plant stretches down to the dead world beneath it, touches minerals and gases with its mystery of life, and brings them up, transformed, to the living realm.
- The spiritual person is the mental or moral person plus something (or someone) else. It's the infusion into the spiritual person of a new life, a quality unlike anything else in Nature.
- It's not "out there" but found by learning to go within, through the experiential natural person.
- It's not the same as the electromagnetic energy operating in matter or bios, the life energy that sustains living organisms.
- Life works in the invisible. When the new life manifests itself, it comes suddenly; it's a surprise. Then the organism begins to gradually take form.

Exercises

The processes of growth are so common that we don't usually pay attention to them.

1. To understand how tenacious life-forms are, consider how canned food has been heated and cooled to form a vacuum and then sealed from all oxygen to remain safe from the development of harmful bacteria. Test this by placing an unused plastic bag directly out of the box, without touching the inside of the bag, around an unopened can of food with a pull-top tab. Seal the bag immediately. Then from outside the bag, carefully pull the tab on the pull-top to open

the can without cutting the bag. Now let the can sit in the sealed bag and observe what happens in the can every few hours for a few days. (Warning: Do not eat the food in the can after doing this! It's safe for the composter or garbage only!)

2. To observe inorganic growth, buy a crystal-growing kit from a variety store and follow the instructions. Or make a syrup of one cup sugar to a half cup water (you may have to heat it to totally dissolve the sugar) and set a popsicle stick or bamboo skewer into it and leave it for a few days. Notice how the crystals form on the stick by adding other crystalline material to the outer layer.

3. To understand organic transformation and growth, imagine you are a caterpillar. You're soft and squishy, long and skinny, and you're constantly hungry. All day and most nights, you crawl up and down branches, looking for leaves to chew on. Then the days get longer and the sun gets hotter. You start to slow down and feel very sleepy. You find a nice shady spot among some of your favorite leaves and suddenly you start spitting out a fine thread. This is different! How do you think you'd feel in this situation? Return to the caterpillar's experience: the sticky thread has stuck to the branch and you want to roll over and over, letting it come out of you. Now it's beginning to cover you, and somehow that's OK. You're getting sleepier and sleepier as more and more of you is covered, so you just close your eyes and let the stuff keep coming, until it's all done and you're sound asleep. You dream, and in your dream you're being held in a warm, loving, safe place.

After a very long sleep, you begin to wake up. You realize that you're beginning to get hungry again—not for leaves but for pollen and nectar. That's strange! You start to wiggle and realize there are parts of you that weren't there before. What are they? You're still squishy and soft, but not in the same way. It's all very strange, but you're more and more awake, so you start to push forward, only to find that the silky thread is now a hard case and you have to figure out how to break it if you're going to eat. You decide to treat it like a leaf and start to bite it. Your mouth feels very strange, but it sort of

works, and the case begins to break open. Your old caterpillar movements don't work as well as they used to, but you push forward a
little, break away a little, push a little, and so forth, until suddenly the
case is open and you're free to crawl away—but you can't! Those
parts that you felt before are in the way. Nothing works the same as it
used to, and now you're really hungry! Again you try to crawl and
realize that you're being lifted off the branch instead of inching along
it the way you used to. Your body has legs ... and something else—
something big and floppy and wet, and so big and heavy that you
can't really get anywhere. Now this is a problem: How are you ever
going to eat? So you sit there contemplating, What next? There's no
way to get anywhere; are you going to die here on this branch? You
begin to feel a little frightened. What's happened to you? Then
you become aware that the big floppy things aren't so heavy. They've
dried a little, and when you think about moving, they lift a little off
your back. You think about moving again, and they move again.
Interesting! What's happening to you now? What do you do with
this? You realize that these new legs are stronger, too, and you can lift
yourself completely off the branch. What a strange feeling to have air
flowing under your belly! Then you feel a breeze, and those big
floppy things catch it. Suddenly you're not on the branch anymore!
Oh no! This can't be a good thing! Falling hurts! Surely you're going
to die! But you don't fall. Instead, you float on the breeze, and after a
few stunned moments, you begin experimenting with your new
wings until you see below you a wonderful meal of flowers filled
with pollen. You focus your attention on it and, strangely, you land
safely. You must be in Heaven!

Take a moment to appreciate the experience of being a
butterfly. Now write in your Science and Spirituality notebook
some of the natural laws that were at work in this process and some
of the metaphors that apply to your life as a natural human being.

IV

ENVIRONMENT

Permeating the earth, I support all beings by [My] energy;
and, having become the watery moon, I nourish all herbs.
Bhagavad Gita 15:13

Whatever amount of power an organism expends in any shape
is the correlate and equivalent of a power
that was taken into it from without.
Herbert Spencer, nineteenth-century biologist

HEREDITY AND ENVIRONMENT

In all well-written biographies and biographical novels, the first few chapters concentrate on the context. The character's familial background is clearly understood to be an essential starting point. First, we're introduced to the family. The grandparents and often even the more remote ancestors are briefly sketched and their chief characteristics brought prominently into view. Then the parents are described in detail. We're told about their appearance and physique, their character, their disposition, and their mental qualities. We're asked to observe how much the father and mother have transmitted their unique qualities to their offspring, how faithfully the ancestral lines show themselves in the latest product, how mysteriously the hereditary characteristics of body and mind have blended, and how unexpected yet how entirely natural a recombination is the result.

These points are elaborated throughout the story, and we realize at last how little we are dealing with an independent being and how much with the survival and reorganization of what was already present.

We're invited, then, to consider more external influences: schools and teachers, religious activities, neighbors, home, financial circumstances, scenery, and finally the social and political atmosphere of the time. These, we are assured, have also played their part in making the individual, have molded the mind and character, and have affected the course of the future life.

IN THE SCIENCES

This relationship of the individual, first with parents and second to circumstances, is not peculiar to human beings. These two factors are responsible for making all living organisms what they are. When naturalists attempt to unfold the life history of any animal, they proceed precisely on these same lines. Biography is really a branch of natural history, and the biographer who discusses the subject as the combination of these two tendencies follows the scientific method as rigidly as Charles Darwin in studying "animals and plants under domestication" or Linus Pauling in describing the nature of bacteria.

Darwin pointed out long ago that there are two main factors in all evolution: the organism and the conditions. We focus here on the human species in order to define the meaning of these factors in the clearest way, but it must be remembered that the development of a human being under these directive influences is essentially the same as that of any other organism in the hands of Nature. We're dealing, therefore, with universal law.

Applying the terminology of science to these factors, what biographers describe as parental influences, biologists speak of as heredity, and all the action of external circumstances and surroundings on our lives, naturalists call environment. Heredity and environment are the primary influences of the organic realm. These have made all of us what we are as physical and social beings, and they're still working in our lives.

Those who truly understand what their own heredity and environment have given them and who've made a conscious choice as to how much to allow to each, directing the two influences to cooperate with or counteract one another, have mastered the process of personal development. When we take every opportunity to experience better and higher conditions, balancing an inward lack with a more perfected influence from around us, making our environment while it makes us, we've found the secret of a balanced and successful life.

In Spirituality

In the spiritual realm also, the subtle influences that form and transform the soul are heredity and environment. It doesn't occur to most of us, though, how natural the spiritual is. The utter incomprehensibility of the whole realm prevents us from seeing fully what we already half suspect—how completely we are, more often than not, missing the road.

This is because in striving for some strange transcendent thing "out there," we're seeking to promote our spiritual life by methods as unnatural as they are unsuccessful. The distressing incompetence most of us feel as we try to develop our spirituality is due more to our imperfect knowledge of our conditions than to the lack of will we commonly blame for it. So here especially, where all is invisible, where much of what we feel is real is so ill defined, it becomes vitally important to clarify these conceptions.

Living in the spiritual realm is just as simple as living in the natural realm—and it's the same kind of simplicity. It's the same kind of simplicity because it's the same kind of world. As we've seen, there are not two kinds of worlds. The conditions of life in the one are the conditions of life in the other. The organism and the environment are one whole.

The Relationship between Nature and Nurture

In the social and biological sciences, there's an ongoing debate and exploration regarding the relative importance of heredity and environment, which is often referred to as "nature versus nurture." Fortunately, it's not necessary to balance their importance here.

This is so because what heredity does is determined outside the natural person; no one selects their own parents, but everyone, to some extent, can choose an environment. Even when largely determined by heredity in the first years of our life, our relation to our environment is always changeable. In fact, our control over our environment is so great and its influence over us is so strong that we can even direct it to undo, modify, perpetuate, or intensify the earlier hereditary influence up to a point, as Bruce Lipton and other leaders in the emerging science of epigenetics have demonstrated.[1] This manipulability is why we needn't concern ourselves with how heredity applies to the spiritual organism.

ENVIRONMENT'S INFLUENCE

The influence of environment on our spiritual life, however, is crucial and may be understood in two ways. First, we might discuss the modern and very interesting question of the power of environment to modify the species, to induce what is known to science as variation. A change in the surroundings of any animal, it is now well known, can cause it to change. By the attempt, conscious or unconscious, to adjust itself to the new conditions, an actual physiological change is gradually brought about. In a classic experiment, John Hunter kept a seagull in captivity and fed it only corn. The stomach of the bird, normally adapted to a fish diet, gradually changed until it came to resemble the gizzard of an ordinary grain-feeder such as the pigeon.[2] Alarik Frithiof Holmgrén (1831–1897) reversed this experiment by feeding pigeons for a lengthened period on a meat diet, with the result that the gizzard became transformed into the carnivorous stomach.[3] Alfred Russel Wallace mentions the case of a Brazilian parrot that changes its color from green to red or yellow when fed the fat of certain fishes.[4] Many other circumstances are known to exert a powerful modifying influence upon living organisms, including not only changes of food but changes of climate and temperature, changes in surrounding organisms, and, in the case of marine animals, even changes of pressure, ocean currents, and light. In recent years, whole new species have been observed to develop as organisms are moved to new environments—for example, a new species of sparrow in Italy.[5] These relations are still being worked out in many directions, but the influence of environment as a prime factor in variation is a recognized doctrine of science.

Even the popular mind is fascinated by the curious adaptation of nearly all animals to their habitat. The sandy hue of the sole and flounder, the white of the polar bear with its suggestion of arctic snows, the stripes of the Bengal tiger, as if Nature had printed the actual reeds of its native jungle on the cat's hide—these and a hundred others are marked instances of animal life adapting to its environment.

Carrying the investigation of the effects of environment into morality and spirituality would open a fascinating and suggestive inquiry. We might show how moral people are continuously affected by their surroundings, by the society they're part of, by the company they keep, by their occupation, by the books they read, by Nature herself— by all the habitual atmosphere of our thoughts and the world of our daily choices. Or we might go deeper still and prove how the soul is also modified from outside sources—its health or disease, its growth or decay, all its changes, for better or for worse, determined by our religious and spiritual habits.

These investigations might be fruitful, but we must focus our attention on another aspect of environment that is maybe not so fascinating but definitely more important.

ENVIRONMENT'S PRIMARY FUNCTION

Most discussion of environment revolves around the question of variation, but the primary function of environment is not to modify but to *sustain*. It's true that in sustaining life, the environment modifies the life form. But this latter influence is incidental, while the former essential. Our environment is that in which we live and move and have our being. Without it, we would neither live nor move nor have any being.

Another way to say it is that the principle of life lies in the organism while the conditions of life are in the environment. Without the fulfillment these conditions provide, which are wholly supplied by the environment, life can't be sustained.

An organism in itself is but a part; Nature is the complement that makes a whole. Alone, cut off from its surroundings, the organism simply cannot exist. Alone, cut off from my surroundings, I cannot exist. I exist only insofar as I am sustained; I continue only as I receive. My environment may modify me, but first it has to keep me. All the time that its secret, transforming power is indirectly molding body and mind, it is directly ministering to my many wants and constantly sustaining life itself.

Every living organism normally requires for its development an environment containing air, light, heat, and water. In addition to these, if vitality is to be prolonged for any length of time, especially if there is to be growth and the expenditure of energy, there must be a constant supply of food. When we simply remember how indispensable food is to growth and work, and when we further bear in mind that the food supply is solely contributed by the environment, we realize at once the meaning and truth of the proposition that *without the environment, there can be no life.*

A CONSTANT FLOW

We fail to praise the ceaseless ministry of the great inanimate world around us only because its kindness is not obvious to us. Nature is always freely giving, and all her greatest gifts are given in secret. Everything we eat, wear, live in, move in, work with—everything, in fact, that we see, hear, touch, smell, or taste—is a product of our environment. We too often forget how truly every good and perfect gift comes from the world around us because, normally, no pause in her changeless beneficence teaches us the sad lesson of deprivation.

As long as any organism continues to grow, move, act, think, speak, work, or perform any other function demanding a supply of energy, there's a constant, simultaneous, and proportionate drain upon its surroundings. The environment, therefore, is really an unacknowledged part of the organism. This means that there are three things to keep continually in view:

1. The organism itself consists of only half of what is essential to life.
2. The other half is contained in the environment.
3. Constant exchange occurs in the union between the organism and the environment.

In the case of humans, for example, at least 70 percent of the adult human body is made of pure water. The rest consists of gases and minerals of the earth, and definite amounts are continuously exchanged between the organism and the environment. For example, two pounds of water are released daily from every healthy adult through the pores of the skin, back into the environment it came from.

A Source of Power

The dependence of the organism on its environment is a truth in the physical, and, following the law of continuity, it must also be true in the spiritual. Its significance in biology is self-evident, but to further clarify, let's consider a process in chemistry.

When a gallon of gas is added to an engine or a piece of wood or charcoal is thrown on the fire, we say that it will radiate a certain quantity of heat. This heat, we usually think, resides in the fuel, to be set free during the process of combustion. In reality, however, the heat energy is only in part contained in the fuel. It's contained just as truly in the environment—in the oxygen of the air. That's why carburetors and fuel injectors send a mix of air and fuel into the cylinders of our engines.

The atoms of carbon that compose the fuel have a powerful affinity for the oxygen of the air, so whenever they reach a certain temperature, they rush together with inconceivable speed. At that moment, additional heat appears, which comes neither from the carbon alone, nor from the oxygen alone; they are not transformed into heat. They are really inconsumable and continue to exist after they meet in the fire, in the form of carbonic acid gas. The additional heat is the energy emitted in their chemical reaction, the rushing together of their molecules of carbon and oxygen; it comes, therefore, partly from the fuel and partly from the environment, as Isaac Newton explained in his laws of thermodynamics.

Wood or coal or gasoline alone never could produce heat, nor could their environment alone. The two are mutually dependent. So although in nearly all the sciences we credit everything to the substance that we can weigh and measure, in most cases, like this one, the invisible environment plays a substantial role.

This is one of those great commonplaces we rarely notice simply because they're so familiar and simple. These days, however, every field of knowledge could benefit from a rediscovery of the commonplace.

THE SPIRITUAL ENVIRONMENT

Without environment, the soul is like a fish without water or fuel without oxygen. The soul, a spiritual organism, has a principle of life, like any natural organism, but, as with any natural organism, that life isn't sufficient; it requires an environment to be sustained. Without a nurturing, sustaining context, the soul cannot live or move or have any kind of being any more than our natural bodies could if we were cut off from our natural environment.

And what is the spiritual environment? It's the infinite, the unfathomable, indescribable source and nurturer of all life. It's the ground of being, called in the Muslim tradition Allah the Sustainer, in the Hindu and Buddhist traditions Brahman, and in the Judeo-Christian tradition God, and also known as the Great Spirit, the Great Mother, and the Tao. As Krishna says in the Bhagavad Gita, "With their minds and lives entirely absorbed in Me, enlightening each other and always speaking of Me, they are satisfied and delighted."[6]

THE IMPOSSIBILITY OF SELF-SUFFICIENCY
Without this sustaining context, there is no life, no thought, no energy, nothing. "Without me you can do nothing."[7] To examine ourselves is

good, but it's useless unless we also examine environment. To cry over our weakness is appropriate, but it's not a way to be healed. If we are to benefit, we must investigate the cause as well as the result.

The greatest mistake of those seeking a spiritual life is to attempt to live as if there were no spiritual environment. We search for something we call faith, forgetting that faith is just an attitude; it's an empty hand for grasping all that an environing presence offers. We act as if faith were something we can ask for and receive, not realizing that it's an internal attitude that allows us to experience the supportive environment around us. As a result, when we feel the need for power to overcome the challenges of our world, we try to generate that power within ourselves by some forced process. We act as if it were some emotion that can be generated by some strained activity, but that only leaves the soul in further exhaustion.

Because we don't see the other half of the problem, failing to achieve our desire also fails to teach us. So after each new collapse, we start over on the old conditions, and the attempt ends again in the same disaster.

Not that at times we don't get glimpses of the truth. After much discouragement, with a sense of our own feebleness, we join the Hebrew psalmist David as he insists for the thousandth time, "My soul, wait for God alone,"[8] but the lesson is soon forgotten. The strength that we receive in that moment, we immediately credit to our own achievement; and any temporary success is mistaken for a symptom of our own improved ability.

The Qur'an describes this process as thus:

Now when affliction befalls man, he cries out unto Us for help; but when We bestow upon him a boon by Our grace, he says, "I have been given this by virtue of [my own] wisdom!"[9]

Once more, we declare ourselves self-sufficient. Once more, we go on living as if we were without an environment. And once more, after days of wasting without repairing, of spending without replenishing, we begin to die of hunger, only returning to the source of life again as a last resort, when we have reached a starvation point.

Then, maybe, we'll begin to understand: that it's not faith we seek but the willingness to accept our strength from the source of our spiritual life—to stop believing that we are that source and allow ourselves to rest in the sustaining environment and be energized by it. Until we do, we struggle and suffer.

THE LAW OF THE PERSISTENCE OF ENERGY

Why do we do this? Why do we seek to breathe without an atmosphere, to drink without a well? Why this unscientific attempt to sustain life for weeks at a time without an environment?

It's because, in our culture, we've never truly seen the need for an environment. We have not been working with a scientifically proven principle. We were told to "wait only upon God," to "repeat only Om," to "focus all desire on Allah," but we don't know why. It's never been clear to us that the soul is an essential, living part of us, and without the source of life, the soul will die, just as surely as without food and drink the body will perish.

And this is because we've never comprehended the law of the Persistence of Energy. Instead of being content to transform energy, we've tried to create it. The law of Nature here is as clear as science can make it. In the words of Herbert Spencer, "whatever amount of power an organism expends in any shape is the correlate and equivalent of a power that was taken into it from without."[10] We're dealing here with a simple question of dynamics. Whatever energy the soul expends must first be "taken into it from without."

The source of life, therefore, is our refuge *and strength*. Just as we are nourished in the body only to the extent that we breathe and eat what our natural environment provides, so we are nourished in the soul only to the extent that we receive this ever-present power. Therefore, communion with the divine, by whatever name, is a scientific necessity. It's how we are nourished; it's where we live and move and have our being.

Without environment, we can do nothing—in either the natural or the spiritual world—and no idea will help the defeated spirit struggling in the wreck of its religious life more than a common-sense understanding of this plain biological principle.

In the natural realm, we use this law unconsciously. We absorb heat, breathe air, and all but automatically draw on our environment for our food and drink, for nourishment of the senses, for mental stimulus, for everything that can prolong, enrich, and elevate life.

But in the spiritual realm, we have all this to learn. We are infants in our understanding and must learn to acquire even a bare living. The spiritual person is not taxed beyond the natural; religious life is not a difficult road.

The arrangements for the spiritual life are the same as for the natural life. It's all the same process. What's been missing is the knowledge of an ongoing fundamental principle, broad as the universe, solid as Nature.

Only Half

When we say that the spiritual being, like the natural organism, contains within itself only one half of what is essential to its life, we merely repeat the confession, so worn and yet so true to experience, of our inability to manage the great unfolding of the universe. Who has not come to the conclusion that we are but a part, a fraction of some larger whole?

We know that each of us is but a part, for there is room in us for more. We feel that the source of life or some form of higher power must be the other part because, at times, our need is satisfied without our action. And who doesn't tremble sometimes for lack of spiritual energy?

But now we understand this void in our life, the powerlessness of our natural will. We understand that spiritual power, like all other energy, is in our environment. We find here, at last, the root of all human frailty, emptiness, despair, and even that which is called sin. This is why Allah, Krishna, and Christ tell us, "Without me you can do nothing." Powerlessness is the normal state of *every* natural organism and spiritual being apart from its environment.

Some religionists protest against this doctrine of limitations as the heartless fiction of a worn-out theology. Modern humanists cry out against anything beyond their own rational mind and natural body. Both would have humanity stand alone, apart from our source of nourishment and supply.

But those who oppose this understanding are confused. In their commitment to humanity's greatness, they credit the organism with the properties of environment. They're protesting against the order of Nature. It's as if they complain to the sun for being just a source of energy and not an engine producing goods, to the carbonic acid for being in the air and not feeding the plant. It's as if they would grow grain inside the body and make bread in the digestive organs in order to feed themselves.

All theology, on the other hand, has remained loyal to at least the root idea in this truth, recognizing that there is a source the spiritual being must depend on.

The New Testament, for example, insists on the spiritual person's dependence. In its view, the first step in spirituality is for one to feel helpless. This is why the first beatitude is to the poor in spirit. The condition of entrance into the spiritual kingdom is to be like a child—a state of mind combining helplessness with artless dependence. And in Jesus's farewell discourse we are told, "As the branch can't bear fruit by itself, unless it remains in the vine, so neither can you, unless you remain in me."[11] Bearing fruit without connecting with the source of life, by whatever name, is impossible. We might as well expect the natural fruit tree to flourish without air and heat, without soil and sunshine. Paul also thoroughly grasped this truth; he made the constant confession, "When I am weak, then am I strong."[12]

In Islam, this recognition is fundamental to daily life, particularly in daily communion with the divine through prayer and the study of the Qur'an as a source of wisdom and guidance, reminding the reader that Allah is the source of life and its mercies.

So approach the Qur'an with humility, with a sense of utter dependence upon Allah, seeking His help and support at every step. It is in this spirit of trust, praise, and gratitude that you should let your tongue and heart, in mutual harmony, begin the recitation:

Bismi illahi 'r-Rahmani 'r-Rahim, "In the name of Allah, the Most-merciful, the Mercy-giving . . ." This is the verse which appears at the head of all but one of the 114 Surahs [chapters] of the Qur'an.[13]

And in the Qur'an itself we read, "The hearts of all who have attained to faith should feel humble at the remembrance of God and of all the truth that has been bestowed from on high."[14]

The understanding that the soul is dependent on its spiritual source is also the essence of most of the psalms in the Hebrew Bible and the constant reminders of the prophets. In perhaps the most famous of them, the twenty-third, David sings, "The Lord . . . leads me beside the still waters; He restores my soul . . . He sets a table before me . . . My cup runs over." In a later song, he says, "I will lift up my eyes unto the hills, from which comes my help. My help comes from the Lord, who made heaven and earth."[15] Jeremiah, explaining this to the people of Jerusalem in an effort to abort the coming invasion and Babylonian captivity, said,

This is what the Almighty Lord, the Holy One of Israel, says: You can be saved [meaning free, fulfilled] by returning to me. You can have rest. You can be strong by being quiet and by trusting me. But you don't want that.[16]

The Hebrew people, like so many in this age of empires and cities, often assumed they could do things on their own, that they didn't need a spiritual environment for their spiritual lives to thrive—and they suffered as a result. Only when they remembered the source of their life did they thrive.

In the Buddhist tradition, to begin the spiritual life is to "take refuge." Initiates agree to let go of their former sense of self, to leave behind all notions of personal power and authority, and place their trust in the Buddha (the Awakened One), the *dharma* (the path or way, also translated as "underlying power and purpose"), and the *sangha* (the community of spiritual seekers). There's a clear recognition in Buddhism that the life of the soul requires a kind of nourishment that's different from that required by the life of the body or of the mind, and Buddhist daily practices are designed to help each person experience it.

Buddhism emerged from Hinduism and relies in part on those far more ancient texts. The Bhagavad Gita is a portion of one of the Vedas, the oldest of spiritual texts. In it, Krishna, as the embodiment of the source of all, says,

> That light which residing in the sun, illumines the whole world, that which is in the moon and in the fire—know that light to be Mine.

> Permeating the earth I support all beings by (My) energy; and, having become the watery moon, I nourish all herbs. . . .

> And I am seated in the hearts of all; from Me are memory, knowledge, as well as their absence. I am verily that which has to be known by all the Vedas; I am indeed the author of the *Vedanta*, and the knower of the Vedas am I.[17]

The Upanishads, the priestly commentaries, set the tone and guidelines for Hindu doctrine and practice, and both texts state clearly that a spiritual life that does not frequently and regularly draw on the qualities of the divine for nourishment cannot thrive. For example, in the Chandogya Upanishad, we read, "One should meditate on this Syllable [Om]. . . . United with Om we are united with ALL. This union does not just produce a theoretical or intellectual result, but rather the mastery of life itself."[18]

THE LAW OF DEPENDENCE ON ENVIRONMENT

The world is about as good a world as might be. It's been long in the making, its structure is established, and its laws are in perfect working order. There may be, through evolution or otherwise, finishing touches to add here and there, but it is already, as the book of Genesis says, "all very good." And although people at various times have suggested improvements, there is on the whole a vote of confidence in things as they exist.

It's difficult to conceive anything better of its kind than a lily or a cedar, an ant or an anteater. These organisms, so far as we can judge, lack nothing. It might be said of them, "they are complete in Nature." The wonderful adaptations of each organism to its surroundings—of the fish to the water, of the eagle to the air, of the insect to the forest bed—inspire us as we marvel at the skill of Nature in perfecting her arrangements for each organism. Down to the last detail, the world is made for what lives in it, and regardless of whatever processes formed them, all organisms find their ample, nourishing complement in surrounding Nature.

It may also be affirmed that our environment satisfies humanity. We have good food and drink everywhere. There is no natural want that is not really provided for, apparently in the happiest possible way. There is provision for all capacities, scope to use every ability, room for the indulgence of each appetite, supply that meets every bodily desire. The aim of evolution is clearly not a self-contained and self-sufficient organism, however high on the scale of being, but an organism complete in its whole environment.

Likewise, the spiritual person finds provision in the even vaster spiritual environment—a higher form of provision but just as delicately adjusted to our varying needs. And all this is supplied to us just as the natural environment supplies the natural organisms—in the same simple ways, in the same constant sequence, as appropriately and as lavishly.

The soul's dependence on divinity as its spiritual environment is therefore not an exceptional mystery, nor is the natural person's helplessness, arbitrary or unprecedented. It's the law of all Nature, at all levels of life.

An organism must either depend on its environment or be totally self-sufficient—and to be totally self-sufficient is to run out of resources at some point. Even if an organism, launched into being like a ship putting out to sea, were fully equipped to meet all its needs, its few resources must soon come to an end.[19] Like the chick in the egg that was previously more than adequate, it must break out and find more. But in contact with a large and bounteous environment, its supply is limitless; in every direction, its resources are infinite.

One result of the realization of our natural limitations will be that we'll no longer waste time on the impossible task of manufacturing energy for our souls. Instead, remembering that energy can be neither created nor destroyed, we'll begin to accept that we must receive it. Then, having decided this once and for all, our next step must be to find a new source of energy to maintain our spiritual lives. Based on our understanding of Natural Law, only one course is open to us. We must refer to environment—just as the natural life receives all from environment, so must the spiritual. As Nature is the complement of the natural organism, so divinity, the source of life, by whatever name, must be the complement of the spiritual organism.

It's natural, then, for the soul to find its life in the source of life, also known as divinity, the Great Spirit, God, Allah, Brahma, the ground of being. This is its essence. The source of life as the environment of the soul has been, from the remotest age, the doctrine of the world's deepest thinkers.

COMPLETING THE INCOMPLETE

How does the source of life complete us? How are we incomplete? As we discovered in the natural realm, the body constantly exchanges fluids, minerals, and energy with its environment, so the lower realms of Nature are already complete enough. Then, up to a point, the natural environment supplies humanity's wants, but beyond that it only deprives us. We have all the physical things—food, clothing, shelter, beautiful objects, fabulous work and play with amazing tools and equipment, and opportunities to travel and discover—that we can imagine, but still there's an emptiness that somehow none of these can fill.

How much of us is beyond that point of deprivation? Almost all that makes a person truly human.

THE EXPERIENCE OF INCOMPLETENESS

The moment we pass beyond mere animal life, we begin to come upon our incompleteness. The symptoms are slight at first, only an unexplained restlessness or a dull sense of want. Then the feverishness increases, becomes more defined, and passes slowly into abiding pain. To some come darker moments, when the unrest deepens into a mental agony—moments when the forsaken soul can only cry in terror for nourishment from the source of life.

The first suspicion that we're not self-sufficient and complete comes with intellectual life. There's a solemn moment when the slow-moving mind reaches its mental horizon and, looking over, sees nothing more. Straining to find more makes the emptiness more profound. The mind's cry has no echo. Where is the environment to complete this rational being? People either find it or spend the rest of their days trying to shut their eyes. Thus the alternatives for the intellectual life are to move ahead into spirituality or fall back into agnosticism. The agnostics who trumpet their incompleteness by declaring that it's impossible to know what is true are right. Those who are not complete must be forever incomplete.

The problem becomes more difficult when we begin to explore our moral and social nature. Issues of the heart and conscience are infinitely more perplexing than those of the intellect. Has love no future? Has right no triumph? Is the unfinished self to remain unfinished? Again, the alternatives are two: we slip into a life of spirituality or that of pessimism.

When we ascend further into the inner life, the crisis comes. There, without environment, the void is indescribable. Not having an environment is unthinkable. We feel so isolated at this point in our development that it's been called by mystics "the long, dark night of the soul." The mystery now is so maddening that people are compelled to construct an environment for themselves, whether they call it divinity, Nature, or law.

Understanding this experience, we begin to see that the anguish of atheism or existentialism is an essential stage in the process of human development. The frustration of a life lived without spiritual nourishment is a proof of humanity's incompleteness.

PRAYER AS PROOF

Another evidence of humanity's incompleteness is prayer. Isn't it a very strange thing for a person to pray? Our sense of imperfection, controlled and silenced in our inner being, becomes audible. Our sense of need is so real, and our sense of environment equally so, that we call out to it, addressing it articulately and imploring it to satisfy our need. It's the demonstration of both our littleness and our greatness. Surely there is nothing more touching in Nature than this reaching out! No one would ever so expose the inner heart, so give up all pretexts and self-control, except out of dire necessity. It's the suddenness and unpremeditatedness of prayer that gives its unique value as evidence that we are meant to be connected with a source greater than our normal humanity.

Prayer is a form of question, and humanity puts three questions to our environment. These questions are the three indicators of our incompleteness, coming from three different centers of our being:

1. What is truth? (mental)
2. Who will show us any good? (moral)
3. Where is the one, the complement to my being, whom my soul is seeking? (spiritual)

The first is the question of the intellect: What is truth? The natural environment answers with more questions, driving the seeker ever deeper into the mysteries of matter and energy. Spiritual teachers, sensing this, have said, "Increase of knowledge increases sorrow, and much study is a weariness."[20] Learn of me, says the philosopher, and you shall find restlessness. The Christ/Krishna/Om/Tao replies, "Learn of me . . . and you shall find rest."[21] In this statement, rational thought, which the godless philosopher has made into a curse by sending us on an endless search for answers, finds at last its imperishable blessing; having used it to discover and choose to rest in our spiritual environment, our soul is nourished and our thought is complete.

The second question is sent up from the moral nature: Who will show us any good? Where in this world of woe is there anything to be called good? And in the New Testament, we have "There is none good but God only."[22] And the Qur'an, using the Arabic word that means God (Allah) declares the same. The Hebrew Bible tells us to look at all creation, for "it is good." The Taoist tells us that the Tao, as goodness, is present everywhere.

Finally, there is the lonely cry of the lonely spirit, the deepest and most pathetic of all: Where is the complement to my being whom my soul is seeking? And the yearning is met as before. Rumi, the Sufi poet, seeks understanding and finds the infinite Beloved. The Hebrew psalmist proclaims, "I looked on my right hand, and beheld, but there was no one that would know me; refuge failed me; no one cared for my soul. I cried unto thee, O Lord: I said, you are my refuge and my portion in the land of the living."[23]

THE POET'S EXPRESSION

Much of this awareness has been expressed in poetry, but then, true poetry is only science in another form. Long before it was possible to give scientific expression to the greatest truths, people of insight uttered them in psalms, which could not have been truer to Nature if the most modern scientific research had controlled the inspiration.

Jalāl-ad-Dīn Muhammad Rūmī, the great thirteenth-century Sufi teacher, is one of the world's best-known writers of such poetry. In his "One Whisper of the Beloved" he tells us,

He is the soul of my soul—
How can I escape?
But why would any soul in this world
want to escape from the Beloved?
He will melt your pride
making you thin as a strand of hair,
Yet do not trade, even for both worlds,
One strand of His hair.
We search for Him here and there
while looking right at Him.
Sitting by His side we ask,
"O Beloved, where is the Beloved?"
Enough with such questions!—
Let silence take you to the core of life.[24]

Elsewhere Rumi tells us what happens to us in the experience of discovery.

The real beloved is that one who is unique,
who is your beginning and your end.
When you find that one,
you'll no longer expect anything else:
that is both the manifest and the mystery.
That one is the lord of states of feeling,
dependent on none;
month and year are slaves to that moon.
When he bids the "state,"
it does his bidding;
when that one wills, bodies become spirit.[25]

In another example, the ancient Hebrew poetry is saturated with this high thought, as is clear when we try to conceive of those verses without it. "As the hart pants after the water brooks, so my soul pants after thee, oh God."[26] What a fine use of the analogy of the natural for the spiritual! As the stag seeks nourishment from its environment, so humanity seeks our soul's nourishment; as the water brooks meet the natural wants, so does the source of life fulfill the spiritual need.

It's noteworthy that, in the Hebrew poets, the longing for divinity never strikes the reader as unnatural. It's as natural to them to long for God as for the swallow to seek her nest. Through all their images, no suspicion rises that they might be exaggerating. There's no false note in all their seeking. Even their ceaseless sighing is the lover's weariness for the absent beloved, and if they wish to fly, it's only to be at rest. How joyous a thing it was to the Hebrews to seek their God! These people were true children of Nature. Like the hummingbird among its blossoms, like the mayfly in the sunshine of a summer evening, so they lived their joyous lives. And even a full share of the sadder experiences of life, which came to all of them, simply drove them further into their secret place and led them with more dedication to make "the Lord their portion," as they expressed it.

All that's been said in the Christian tradition, from the Roman philosopher-emperor Marcus Aurelius to the Swedish mining engineer Emanuel Swedenborg, from the early bishop Augustine to the missionary doctor Albert Schweitzer, is but a repetition of the Hebrew poets' faith. And the New Testament has nothing greater to offer us than this. The Hebrew psalmist's "God is our refuge and strength"[27] is only the earlier form, less defined but not less noble, of the Christ's "come unto me all you who are burdened . . . and I will give you rest."[28] A brief phrase of Paul's defines the relationship with almost scientific accuracy: "You are complete in Him."[29] The whole of the New Testament is summed up in this.

The Hindu-Buddhist Yoga tradition is as briefly summarized in this line of Krishna's (who is often called "the Hindu Christ") from the five-thousand-year-old epic poem the Bhagavad Gita: "The same am I to all beings; to Me there is none hateful or dear; but those who worship Me with devotion are in Me and I am also in them."[30] And later, "With their minds and lives entirely absorbed in Me, enlightening each other and always speaking of Me, they are satisfied and delighted."[31] Thus the source of life, embodied as Krishna, who "supervises Nature," encourages the listener to focus on the spiritual environment rather than the small activities and events of daily life.

Taoism, which emerged around the same period as Buddhism, tells us that if we look carefully at Nature, we will observe how to behave effectively and discover all that we need for our soul's nourishment. So it's not too surprising that in the poetry of the Tao Te Ching we have a parallel line of thinking and another expression of the same awareness.

> It is the manner of the Tao that even though continuously used,
> it is naturally replenished, never being emptied,
> and never being as full as a goblet which is filled to the brim
> and therefore spills its fine spring water upon the ground.
> The Tao therefore does not waste that with which it is charged,
> yet always remains a source of nourishment for those
> who are not already so full that they cannot partake of it.[32]

People who have no sense of soul can only wonder at this possibility. People who feel the soul but have little faith can only envy it.

FULFILLMENT AND EVOLUTION

If we ask science or philosophy how life is to fulfill its potential, it will point to evolution. The struggle for life, it assures us, is steadily eliminating imperfect forms, and as the fittest continue to survive, we shall have a gradual perfecting of being; we'll be complete in Nature and in ourselves. Civilization, it's said, will improve the environment step by step, as it improves the organism, and vice versa, in an ongoing reinforcing cycle.

This is good, and it will improve life up to a point. But beyond that point, as we've discovered, it cannot carry us. As the possibilities of the natural life become more defined, its impossibilities become ever more appalling. The most perfect civilization would still leave the best part of us incomplete. Moreover, the time is quickly approaching when people will have to give up the experiment of attempting to live unaware of their environment.

The law for the body, and therefore the soul, is to be complete in its environment. To act as if there is no environment, or as if the influence of environment stops with the natural realm, is death, for neither the soul nor the body can survive, much less perfect itself, in isolation.

How long will it take scientists to follow science's own creed and accept that the material universe we see around us is only a fragment of the universe we don't see? The very use of the phrase "material universe" is a confession of our unbelief and ignorance, since "matter is the less important half of the material of the physical universe."[33]

SPIRITUAL FULFILLMENT

The life of the body may be fulfilled in the physical realm; that is its legitimate environment. The life of the senses may perfect itself in the natural world. Even the life of thought may find a large complement in its natural surroundings. But higher thought, the conscience, and spiritual life can only be fulfilled in the wholeness, or perfection, to be achieved in the spiritual realm. And the perfection to be sought in the spiritual realm is a perfection of relationship, a perfect alignment of what is becoming complete to that which is perfect and complete already.

RECEPTIVITY

This, then, is the third problem: where does the soul, the spiritual organism, and its environment meet? How does that which is being perfected make use of its perfecting environment?

And the answer is, just as for the natural realm, all that's needed is simple receptivity. We easily take in fluids and food, breathe air, and let moisture enter and leave our bodies through the pores of our skin. We allow information to enter our mental awareness and share it without effort in many different ways. We can just as easily allow spiritual life and power to flow through the soul, the spiritual aspect of our being, and share it.

When we no longer identify ourselves as isolated individuals having to toil and scrape to earn our way but perceive ourselves as the natural products of an all-supplying universal process, we begin to become receptive—and abundantly fulfilled. This is the essence of Ralph Waldo Emerson's teachings. This is what Wallace Wattles was trying to communicate.

In the New Testament statement quoted in an earlier essay, Jesus uses the metaphor of a vine to help us understand this, suggesting that we allow ourselves to be nurtured in the same way that a branch is nurtured by the grapevine, so we may develop and become fruitful. When we recognize that both our natural and our spiritual environment are designed to support our fulfillment and evolution, then we begin to experience the benefit of the One Law at work in our lives.

Essential Points

- The great function of environment is not to modify but to *sustain*.
- When we take every opportunity for better and higher conditions, balancing an inward lack with a more perfected influence from around us, making our environment while it makes us, we've found the secret of a balanced and successful life.
- The spiritual being, like the natural organism, contains within itself only one half of what is essential to life; the other half is contained in the environment. Exchange occurs in a union between the organism and its environment.
- When the mind reaches its mental horizon and sees nothing more, people either find the environment that can complete the rational soul or spend the rest of their days trying to shut their eyes; the alternatives of the intellectual life are therefore spirituality or agnosticism.
- For problems of the heart and conscience, the alternatives are again two: spirituality or pessimism.
- Spirituality is not a difficult road. The arrangements for the spiritual life are the same as for the natural life. It's all the same process; what's been missing is the knowledge of the role of environment.
- Without a suitable environment, the darkness at the height of the inner life is indescribable, and to survive, people are compelled to construct an environment for themselves, whether they call it divinity, Nature, or law.

- As we easily take in fluids and food, breathe the air, and let moisture enter and leave our bodies through the pores of our skin, and as we allow information to enter our mental awareness and share it without effort, so we can easily allow spiritual life and power to flow through the soul.
- When we recognize that both our natural and our spiritual environments are designed to support our fulfillment and evolution, then we begin to experience the benefit of the One Law at work in our lives.

Exercises

To understand how the life-forms around us depend on environment for everything:

1. Consider a house cat or dog. In your Science and Spirituality notebook, make a list of all the things that the pet's caregiver must do for that cat or dog to have what it needs to thrive. Now consider the same animal in the wild, look at your list, and write down how Nature does all those things.
2. Take a sprig of mint or basil or ivy, cut a small piece off the end of the stem, and put it in a glass of water, near some light, where you can watch it. In your Science and Spirituality notebook, note how the cutting changes from day to day. Notice when the water needs to be replenished, how the leaves aim for the light, how the new growth of leaves and branches is directly related to the amount of roots below. Consider its process. Is it working hard? Is it straining? Write in your notebook how your life might be different if you lived the way it does.
3. Remember a time in your life when you suddenly, spontaneously started to pray, and describe it in your notebook. What was happening? How did you feel about the situation? How did you feel about the prayer? What happened next? How does what happened then affect your life now?

V

CONFORMITY TO TYPE

How does a cell in the big toe know where it is with respect to the
whole body ... so that the cell can do what is required of it at its
position in the toe? If the blueprint of switching is itself in the DNA
(as materialist biologists would have it), then how does the toe cell
know only to activate the relevant part of the blueprint?
We can see that there has to be a "metaplan."
Amit Goswami, twentieth-century physicist

If botanists were asked the difference between an oak tree, a palm tree, and a lichen, all would declare that the organisms are separated from one another by the sharp line known in taxonomic classification as *genus*. In size and form, in variety of flower and fruit, in the peculiarities of leaf and branch, their structures are as distinct as Eskimo, Gothic, and Egyptian architecture. But if the first young germs of these three plants are placed before even the most learned botanists and they're asked to describe the differences, it would be impossible to do so. They couldn't even say which is which. Examined under the highest powers of a microscope, the organisms at this stage of growth yield no clue. Analyzed with all the equipment of the laboratory, these plants would still keep their secret.

The same experiment can be tried with the embryos of animals. Take the ovule (egg cell) of a worm, an eagle, an elephant, and a human being. Let the most skilled observers apply the most searching tests to distinguish among them, and they will fail.

But there's something more surprising still. Compare the plant and the animal in the earliest stages, and there is still no measurable difference. Oak and palm, worm and human—all start in life as virtually the same. No matter what different forms they may develop into later, no matter whether they will live on sea or land, creep or fly, swim or walk, think or vegetate, in the embryo as it first meets the eye of science, they are indistinguishable. As Lionel Beale, one of the first cellular biologists, tells us,

> There is, indeed, a period in the development of every tissue and every living thing known to us when there are actually no *structural* peculiarities whatever—when the whole organism consists of transparent, structureless, semi-fluid living bioplasm—when it would not be possible to distinguish the growing, moving matter which was to evolve the oak from that which was the germ of a vertebrate animal. Nor can any difference be discerned between the bioplasm matter of the lowest, simplest, epithelial scale of a person's organism and that from which the nerve cells of our brain are to be evolved. Neither by studying bioplasm under the microscope nor by any kind of physical or chemical investigation known can we form any notion of the Nature of the substance which is to be formed by the bioplasm, or what will be the ordinary results of the living.[1]

This stage is when "embryonic stem cells" may be removed and used for healing and repairing organs and other damaged tissues in the body. They have the capacity within them to become any aspect of the adult organism.

And no, it's not just in the genes or heredity. Even at the level of the DNA (the molecules of deoxyribonucleic acid in the nucleus that make up the blueprint of all life-forms), there's virtually no difference between the chimpanzee, the dolphin, and the human being—and the difference between these higher life-forms and a worm is a very small percentage of the total set of DNA molecules in the cell (which is called a genome).

FROM FORMLESS PROTOPLASM TO LIVING BEINGS

If we analyze the material that all life starts from, we find a clear, jelly-like substance resembling egg white. It's made of complex molecules composed of various combinations of carbon, hydrogen, oxygen, and nitrogen. Its name is protoplasm. And it's not only the unit with which all living bodies start in life but also with which they are subsequently built up. "Protoplasm," says the biologist Thomas Huxley, "simple or nucleated [into cells], is the formal basis of all life. It is the clay of the potter. . . . Beast and fowl, reptile and fish, mollusk, worm and polyp are all composed of structural units of the same character, namely, masses of protoplasm with a nucleus."[2]

What then determines the differences between different animals? What made one little speck of protoplasm grow into Einstein's dog and another, exactly the same, into Einstein himself? It's a mysterious something that has entered into this protoplasm. No eye can see it. No science has yet defined it. There's a different "something" for Newton's dog and a different something for Newton, such that though both use the same matter, they build it up in these widely different ways.

Let's follow a description of the process by a trained eyewitness. The observer is the great Thomas Huxley. He is watching, through a microscope, the development of one of the commonest animals out of a speck of protoplasm.

> Strange possibilities . . . lie dormant in that semi-fluid globule. Let a moderate supply of warmth reach its watery cradle and the plastic matter undergoes changes so rapid and yet so steady and purpose-like in their succession that one can only compare them to those operated by a skilled modeler upon a formless lump of clay. As with an invisible trowel, the mass is divided and subdivided into smaller and smaller portions, until it is

reduced to an aggregation of granules not too large to build withal the finest fabrics of the nascent organism. And, then, it is as if a delicate finger traced out the line to be occupied by the spinal column, and molded the contour of the body; pinching up the head at one end, the tail at the other, and fashioning flank and limb into due proportions in so artistic a way, that, after watching the process hour by hour, one is almost involuntarily possessed by the notion that some more subtle aid to vision than an achromatic would show the hidden artist, with our plan before us, striving with skillful manipulation to perfect our work.[3]

Notice that, in all that "skillful manipulation," the artist is not working at random but according to law. We have, as Huxley suggests, "our plan before us."

And while Huxley may have established this idea back in the mid-nineteenth century, much of twentieth-century biology continued to work at it. The National Institutes of Health and National Science Foundation in the United States provided millions of dollars in grant money to fund research addressing this and related issues. One outcome was the discovery of neuropeptides, chemicals produced in the brain and other organs of the body that change the way cells operate, a process beautifully illustrated in the film *What the Bleep Do We Know!?*

In the twenty-first century, continued exploration of this process has led to a whole new field: epigenetics. Following the work of Bruce Lipton and others,[4] biologists are discovering how it is that each individual cell may be affected by the changing chemicals and energy in their environment. The film *The Living Matrix* illustrates some of how this works.

UNITY OF TYPE

The scientific law by which this takes place is the law of conformity to type. It's part of the ordinary law of inheritance. Darwin called it the law of unity of type and defines it: "By Unity of Type is meant that fundamental agreement in structure which we see in organic beings of the same class, and which is quite independent of their habits of life."[5] According to this law, every living thing that comes into the world must stamp the image of itself on its offspring; the dog, according to its type, produces a dog; the bird, a bird.

MORPHOGENETIC FIELDS

Since the 1920s, biologists have called the "artist" who operates on matter in this subtle way and carries out this law a morphogenetic field. There are a great many different kinds of fields, from the field around a magnet or power line to the field generated in a microwave oven. There are many kinds of morphogenetic fields as well. There's one kind for people, another for mammals, another for fishes, and so forth. According to evolutionary biologist Rupert Sheldrake,

> Since the 1920s many developmental biologists have proposed that biological organization depends on fields, variously called biological fields, or developmental fields, or positional fields, or morphogenetic fields.
>
> All cells come from other cells, and all cells inherit fields of organization. Genes are part of this organization. They play an essential role. But they do not explain the organization itself. Why not? . . . Just making the right proteins at the right times cannot explain the complex skeletons of such structures without many other forces coming into play, including the organizing activity of cell membranes and microtubules. . . . morphogenetic fields work by imposing patterns on otherwise random or indeterminate patterns of activity. For example, they cause microtubules to crystallize in one part of the cell rather than another, even though the subunits from which they are made are present throughout the cell.[6]

Sheldrake goes on to say that these fields affect not just the single organism but the species as well.

The fields organizing the activity of the nervous system are . . . inherited through morphic resonance, conveying a collective, instinctive memory. Each individual both draws upon and contributes to the collective memory of the species. . . . The habits of nature depend on non-local similarity reinforcement. Through morphic resonance, the patterns of activity in self-organizing systems are influenced by similar patterns in the past, giving each species and each kind of self-organizing system a collective memory.[7]

In the development of offspring, then, wheat life, as a morphogenetic field, penetrates the wheat germ and develops it into the wheat plant. Bird life, another morphogenetic field, penetrates the bird germ and builds it up into a bird, the image of itself. Reptile life, yet another such field, penetrates another germinal speck, assimilates surrounding matter, and fashions it into a reptile, an incarnation of itself.

SPIRITUAL MORPHOGENESIS

Now we are nearing the point where the spiritual analogy appears. It's a wonderful analogy—so wonderful that one almost hesitates to put it into words, yet we are listening to Nature's voice. These lower phenomena of life, Nature tells us, are only the early stages of the process, serving to illustrate the later stage.

There's another kind of life that science has not yet really noticed. It obeys the same laws and builds up an organism into its own form: the spiritual life (which we will now start calling the spiritual Life to distinguish it from biological life).

As the bird life builds up a bird in the image of itself in the embryo, so the spiritual Life builds up a spirit in the image of itself in the soul, the inward essence of each person. Just as the natural life as a field of consciousness guides the process and gathers the material for the formation of the bird, the spiritual Life, another field of consciousness, seizes upon the soul, assimilating surrounding elements in the process, and begins to fashion it. According to the great law of conformity to type, this fashioning takes a specific form—that of the field, which is the "artist" who fashions it. And all through our lives this wonderful, mystical, glorious, yet perfectly definite process goes on in the fundamental, unformed essence that we call the soul.

There is much mystery in biology. With all the data, theories, and experiments that have been collected, developed, and performed, we still know almost nothing about life at this point, and even less about development. The same mystery is in the spiritual Life. In fact, there's no more mystery in the processes of spirituality than there is in biology. As we've seen over and over again, the laws of the natural and spiritual are the same, as unerring, as simple.

So now we have a real justification for the processes of the individual's new birth. For confirmation, let's appeal to the record of these processes. In what terms do the sacred scriptures describe it?

The study of the Kabbalah explains some of the Passover prayers as encouraging this kind of new birth.

> The Seventh Day of Pesach, a commemoration of the parting of the Red Sea, is also the day when the souls of the Jewish People were "born"—or brought down from *Atzilut* ["His house" or unity with the divine]. True, they already had souls, but this event was the revelation of the higher level of the souls.
>
> How did this "birth" take place? As mentioned above, all souls have their source in *Atzilut* where there is a complete unity among them and with G-d. . . . The energy must come from a higher level than *Atzilut* in order to "shake up" *Atzilut* and release the souls. This energy is the light from the first letter "*hei*" in G-d's name and serves as a catalyst for the "birth."[8]

In the New Testament, we find the apostle's reiteration that the Christian was a new creature, a new person, a babe, and that this new person was "begotten of God," God's workmanship, as well as this accurate expression of the law of conformity to type: "put on the new humanity, which is renewed in knowledge after the image of the Christ that created it," and "we are changed into the same image from glory to glory."[9]

The Hindu texts are equally clear.

> By detaching oneself from the body consciousness, by controlling the mind, by becoming wary of the play of . . . the senses, by constantly fixing the mind on the Higher Self, by performing the daily duties with a sense of detachment, one can achieve true liberation and the Highest Goal.[10]

If this, then that; if we stop identifying with the body, "fixing the mind on the Higher (in Christian terms, Christ) Self," we are transformed. We are filled with spiritual Life and experience a new state of being called liberation.

Across the traditions, it's the same. They did not mean to be scientific, only to be accurate, and their fearless accuracy has made them scientific. There was no other way of expressing this truth. It was a biological question.

Naturalists might just as well seek to incorporate geology with botany—the living with the dead—as try to explain spiritual Life in terms of mind alone. When will it be seen that the characteristic of spirituality is this Life? That a true theology must begin with a form of biology? Why do people try to treat the source of life as inorganic?

If this analogy is capable of being worked out, we should expect answers to at least three questions.

1. What corresponds to the protoplasm in the spiritual realm?
2. What is the field of Life, the hidden artist who fashions it?
3. What do we know of the process and the plan?

THE PROTOPLASM OF SPIRIT

Matter, like energy, is un-creatable and indestructible. Nature and humanity can only form and transform, so when a new organism or species is made, no new "clay" is made. Natural life merely enters into already existing matter, assimilates more of the same sort, and rebuilds it.

Spiritual Life works in the same way. We must have a peculiar kind of protoplasm, a basis for the organism, and that must already exist.

We've said so far that the mineral realm supplies the material for the vegetable kingdom. The vegetable supplies the material for the animal. Next in turn, the animal furnishes material for the mental realm, and lastly the mental for the spiritual. The new creature, the spiritual organism, is therefore fashioned out of the mental substance of the natural person.

But it's not enough to find an adequate supply of material; it must be of the right kind. There are two properties that allow lifeless protoplasm to become living tissue: the capacity for life and plasticity—the ability to shift from one shape or form into another.

Consider the capacity for life: not all kinds of matter have the power to be the vehicle of life—not even all kinds of matter can conduct electricity. We don't really know what there is in carbon, hydrogen, oxygen, and nitrogen such that when combined in a certain way they receive biological life. We only know that natural life is always associated with this particular combination of materials and almost never with any other.[11]

But we're not in the same darkness with regard to mental material. The mental protoplasm has something in addition to its instincts or habits. It has a capacity for more than itself; it longs and yearns, wastes and pines, waving its tentacles piteously in the empty air, feeling after the source of its life. This hunger for divinity is universal among peoples: in every land and in every age, there have been altars to the known or unknown god.

The other quality we must look for is plasticity, the ability to shift and change form. This is a marked characteristic of all forms of life, but it increases steadily as we rise in the scale of evolution. The inorganic realm is rigid: a crystal of silica dissolved and redissolved a thousand times will never assume any other form. Next the plant, though plastic

in its elements, is still relatively unchanging, if only in its life imprisonment in a single spot of earth. The animal in all parts is mobile,
sensitive, and free. The highest animal, humans, are the most mobile, the
freest from instinctive routine, the most impressionable, the most open
for change. And within mind and soul, this mobility and adaptability is
found in its most developed form.

When we regard the mind's susceptibility to impressions, its
lightning-like response to even the most subtle influences, its power of
instant adjustment, the delicacy and variety of its moods, or its vast
powers of growth, we're forced to recognize in the mind the greatest
capacity for change. This marvelous plasticity of mind contains at once
the possibility and the prophecy of its transformation.

The soul is a product of mentality that integrates our emotional and
intellectual experience. It is, as the Jungian psychoanalyst Thomas Moore
tells us, "midway between understanding and unconsciousness . . . its
instrument is neither the mind nor the body but imagination."[12] The
soul, he says, "is not a thing, but a quality or a dimension of experiencing
life and ourselves. It has to do with depth, value, relatedness, heart, and
personal substance."[13]

Neither matter nor energy, the soul is an abstraction that somehow
exists outside the physical but within the human experience. Moore
tells us that "the soul is partly in time and partly in eternity. We might
remember the part that resides in eternity when we feel despair over
the part that is in life."[14]

The soul constantly develops through our thought and action
and so, in a word, is made to be "converted" from one state to
another. The soul, then, is a form of protoplasm waiting for renewal
and transformation.

It's still spiritually lifeless, though. Like the minerals around the
roots in the soil or the proteins ingested by a pregnant woman, it's simply the material from which the new organism will emerge. However
active someone's intellectual or moral life may be, the soul of the
natural person is dead to the spiritual realm. It has not yet been "born
of the spirit."

LIFE, THE SPIRITUAL ARTIST

In every organism, we have these three things: formative matter (protoplasm), formed matter (cells), and the forming principle (life). In the human soul, we have the unformed essence (mental capacity), the renewed essence (the spiritual person), and the transforming principle (spiritual Life). The natural person, having mental capacity, is its basis. The spiritual person, having been reborn into a new organism, is its product, but the transforming principle itself is something different.

No one has ever seen this transforming principle. Like electricity and gravity, it can't be analyzed, weighed, or observed apart from its effects. But that's just what we expect. This invisibility is the same property that we found in the natural life-giving principle. We saw no life in the first embryos. It's invisible in the adult forms as well. So we can hardly wonder if we can't see it in the spiritual person—in fact, we shouldn't expect to see it! Even more than before, we would expect not to see it, for we're no longer dealing with coarse matter; we're moving now among ethereal and spiritual forms that our laboratory equipment can't yet measure.

Not seeing the transforming principle, some people have denied its existence, and for these people, it's hopeless to point out that one of the most recognizable characteristics of the natural life principle is its immeasurability. We don't pretend that science can define life. There is no scientific definition of natural life, much less of this spiritual Life. But there are converging lines of reasoning.

According to the law of biogenesis, life can only come from life. According to the law of conformity to type, when we see bird characteristics appear in an organism, we can assume that the bird life—which is to say, the morphogenetic field of that particular species—has been at work there.

So when we behold conformity to type in a spiritual person, doesn't it suggest that the field of that particular species has been at work here as well? If every effect demands a cause, what other cause is there for the spiritual person? The transforming Life that awakens any soul and molds it to conform with the type we see in White Buffalo Woman or Mother Mary, in Jesus the Nazarene or Gautama Buddha, in Elijah or Moses—to name a few beloved examples—must be the same Life that empowered those awakened and empowering souls.

THE PROCESS

Just as it's impossible to describe the details by which an ovule becomes a living being, it's impossible to describe any details of the great miracle by which soul protoplasm is conformed to the divine image. We're dealing with its general direction and results, so it's a question of morphology rather than of physiology.

CHOICE AND THE IDEAL

Describing the details is impossible, in part, because a new element comes in at this point, which leads us to leave zoology and physiology behind. This new element is the conscious power of choice. The animal follows its type involuntarily and compulsorily, and doesn't even know it's following it. We could also have been made to conform to the spiritual type with no more knowledge or power of choice than animals or machines, but then we could not have been human. It's simply not possible, given the kind of life that humanity is, not to choose. Our type requires that we choose, both as natural organisms with mental capacities and as souls with the capacity to become spiritual organisms.

Being aware and having this power of choice, the mind must have adequate knowledge of what's possible in order to choose. This means we need an example, some revelation of the type we're being called to take on.

To truly inform our choice, however, the example must be an ideal of the type. For all true human growth and achievement, an ideal is acknowledged to be indispensable. And all people whose lives are based on principle have set themselves a more or less perfect ideal. It's what first deflects the will from animal tendencies and turns the wayward life toward mental clarity and the divine.

Philosophy has failed to present people with their ideal. Economy and government also have failed. But spirituality has succeeded where others failed. Believers and unbelievers have been compelled to acknowledge that spirituality in all its forms holds up the missing type—the ideal—to the world. Whether it be the household gods of the ancients or the totem of the tribe, whether in the form of Mary, Tara, White Buffalo Woman, Krishna, Elijah, David, or Jesus the Nazarene—the ideal of the type is always offered to those who seek.

People everywhere are therefore quite clear about the ideal, and this recognition of the ideal is the first step in the direction of conformity to the type. But it's just the first step. There's no vital connection between seeing the ideal and being conformed to it. For example, thousands admire the Christ and never become Christians, and millions who call themselves Christians have not yet been conformed to the type. The same can be said of any other spiritual path.

AN EXPERIENCE, NOT AN ACTION

How to ensure that willing people shall attain the type is the great problem of spirituality. For millennia, people have strived to find ways and means to conform themselves to this type. Impressive motives have been pictured, the proper circumstances arranged, and the direction of effort defined, and people have toiled, struggled, and agonized to conform themselves to the image of divinity. And too often their efforts have failed.

So the great question still remains: How is the spiritual person to be molded in conformity with the type? The mere knowledge of the ideal is no more than a motive. How is the process to be practically accomplished? Who is to do it? Where, when, how?

From the standpoint of biology, this problem vanishes in a moment. It's probably the very simplicity of the law that has made people stumble, for nothing is so invisible to most people as transparency. The law here is the same biological law that exists in the natural world.

Can the protoplasm conform itself to its type? Can the embryo fashion itself? Is conformity to type produced by the matter or by the life, by the protoplasm or by the type?

We need only reflect on the automatic processes of our natural bodies to discover the universal law of life. What does anyone consciously do to manage breathing? What part do we take in circulating the blood, in keeping up the rhythm of our hearts? What control do we have over our growth? Who, by thinking, can make themselves taller? What part do we voluntarily take in digestion, in secretion, in the reflex actions? Aren't we, after all, virtually automatons? Every organ of our body is given to us, every function arranged for us; brain and nerve, thought and sensation, will and conscience, provided for us, ready-made. And yet how many of us take up our soul and wish to organize that by ourselves? Preposterous!

A living system is defined by its organization and activity. Is organization the cause of life or the effect of it? If we look at the development of the unformed embryo into the highly complex adult, it's clearly the effect of it. The individual's conformity to type, therefore, is secured by the morphogenetic field of the type.

The spiritual type is embodied in the ideal. Therefore, divinity incarnate, by whatever name, transforms the soul: Christ, the incarnation of Jehovah, makes the Christian; Krishna, the embodiment of limitlessness, liberates the yogi; Buddha, the awakened one, frees all who enter the state of Pure Awareness and nonattachment.

This is a humbling conclusion. And, therefore, people will resent it. Moreover, they'll still try to earn the ideal life, still try to improve their character or their morality, rather than try to become receptive to divinity and so become the character and live by the morals they cherish.

This doctrine of human inability, as the Christian church calls it, has always been objectionable to people who do not know themselves. Scientists and religionists alike have tended to reject its harsh presentation.

But to the biologist dealing in theory and law, it cannot die. It stands on the solid ground of Nature. It has a reason in the laws of life that must bring it back to life. Bird life makes the bird. Christ life makes the Christian; the limitless life of Krishna removes the limits of the natural life, the awakened Buddha releases the bonds of suffering. No one, by thinking, can grow an inch taller.

SUPPORT IN THE SCRIPTURES

We've already seen how the Passover prayers of the Jewish people commemorate this process: "the Jewish People were 'born'" at Mount Sinai.[15] They became spiritually alive, ready to receive and understand the law.

Here are the relevant statements in the New Testament. Observe the passive voice in the following:

- the new man which *is renewed* in knowledge after the image of the creator;[16]
- *begotten* of God;[17]
- we *are changed* into the same image;[18]
- predestinate *to be* conformed to the image of the Son;[19]
- except a man *be born again* he cannot see the kingdom of God;[20]
- except a man *be born of water* and of the spirit he cannot enter the kingdom of God.[21]

And there is one outstanding verse that makes it clear: "Work out your own salvation with fear and trembling ... for it is God which worketh in you both to will and to do."[22]

In the Bhagavad Gita, Krishna shares some of the same assertions: "Out of mere compassion for them, I, dwelling within their Self, destroy the darkness born of ignorance by the luminous lamp of knowledge."[23] And

Neither by the Vedas, nor by austerity, nor by gift, nor by sacrifice, can I be seen in this Form. . . . He who does all actions for Me, who looks upon Me as the Supreme, who is devoted to Me, who is free from attachment, who bears enmity towards no creature, he comes to Me.[24]

And in the Qur'an we read,

Believers are they whose hearts tremble with awe whenever God is mentioned, and whose faith is strengthened whenever His messages are conveyed unto them, and whose trust is placed in their Sustainer.[25]

Our Role in the Process

Are individual humans, then, totally powerless in determining their development? Are we mere clay in the hands of the potter, a machine, a tool, an automaton? Yes and no. If we were a tool, we would not be human. In maintaining this natural life, Nature has a share and humanity has a share, but by far the larger part is done for us—the breathing, the secreting, the circulating of the blood, the building up of the organism. And although ours is a minor part, it's no less essential to the well-being of the whole—and to its ongoing existence.

Now, whether there's an exact analogy between the voluntary and involuntary functions in the body and the corresponding processes in the soul, we don't know enough to say. But what we do know at least indicates that each person has a part to play. As we choose to live in and nourish the body, we can choose life and daily nourish our soul. As we choose to avoid objects and situations that might harm the physical body, we can avoid the animal tendencies of the natural life. We can choose to abide continuously as a living branch in the spiritual vine, and its true vine life will flow into our soul, assimilating, renewing, conforming us to type, till divinity, the promise of our own scientifically discovered law, is formed in us.

The Aim of Evolution

We've been dealing with spirituality at its most mystical point, and yet it's impossible not to notice once more its absolute naturalness. The pursuit of the type is just what all Nature is engaged in. Plant and insect, fish and reptile, bird and mammal—these all, in their own spheres, are striving after their type. To prevent the type's extinction, to ennoble it, to people earth and sea and sky with it—this is the meaning of the struggle for life. And this is our life—to pursue the type, to populate the world with it.

The British poet laureate Alfred Lord Tennyson, who studied all the sciences and knew Darwin's work before it was published, saw that Nature aimed to maintain each species, but he also saw that each species or type must pass away for another.

> So careful of the type she seems,
> So careless of the single life.
>
> "So careful of the type?" but no.
> from scarped cliff and quarried stone
> she cries, "A thousand types are gone:
> I care for nothing, all shall go."[26]

Each species, each genus, has gone through stages of development. And along the way, many have been allowed to pass away. Each form has contributed to the emergence of another form, more sophisticated, more effective in the constantly changing environment.

So our spirituality is not a mistake. This is what life is for! We're not "impractical," as people pronounce us, when we worship or celebrate the power of divinity. To follow the spiritual path is not to be, in the old phrase, "righteous overmuch." People are not rhapsodizing over nothing when they preach; nor are people wasting their lives who seem to waste themselves in extending the kingdom of heaven to include our earthly experience.

In the Hindu *Yoga Sutras of Patanjali*, we read,

> The transfer of the consciousness from a lower vehicle into a higher is part of the great creative and evolutionary process.

The practices and methods are not the true cause of the transfer of consciousness but they serve to remove obstacles, just as the husbandman prepares his ground for sowing.[27]

The spiritual person is acting in strict accordance with Nature's processes. This means that the spiritual experiences that many people call supernatural are, in fact, supremely natural.

This realization transforms the popular idea of salvation. It's not merely a final safety or forgiveness of sin or evading some curse. It's not, vaguely, "to get to heaven." No—it's to become the next form of life, to be freed in the image of the divine. It's for the limited elements of the earth to become the supreme beauty, at one with the source of life.

Our progress toward divinity is guaranteed by the law of conformity to type. And more than all that, it's the fulfillment of the most sublime of all prophecies: the type to which we are conformed is destined for unity as well as beauty: "all shall be one."

Until now, evolution had no future. It was a pillar with marvelous carvings, growing richer and finer toward the top but without a capstone. It was a pyramid, the vast base buried in the inorganic, towering higher and higher, tier above tier, life above life, mind above mind, ever more perfect in its workmanship, more noble in its symmetry, and yet incomplete. The most curious eye, following it upward, saw nothing. The cloud fell and covered it. Just what people wanted to see was hidden. The work of the ages had no apex.

But the work begun in the natural is necessarily finished by the supernatural—that which extends beyond and above the natural. And as the veil is lifted by spirituality, it strikes people dumb with wonder. For the goal of evolution is divinity incarnate: embodiment of the source of life.

Could science, in its most brilliant anticipations for the future of humanity, ever have forecast a development like this? Yet now that the revelation is considered, the scientist surely recognizes this as the missing point in evolution, the climax that all of Nature aims for.

The natural life is a topless pillar; the human species is potentially the peak of an unfinished pyramid. One by one, in sight of eternity, all human ideals fall short, and one by one, all human hopes dissolve, to be replaced by divine knowing. This is the essence of the Buddhist path, the Kabbalist's study, the shamanic fulfillment, the Christian communion.

"A thousand types are gone: I care for nothing, all shall go," was Tennyson's observation of Nature. All shall go? No. One type remains: the spiritual person. The soul, reborn, lifts the human to a new organism, a new species, transcending Nature but conforming to the One Law. What's been called the kingdom of God is the realm of the spirit, and it is at hand.

Essential Points

- Compare the plant and the animal in the earliest stages and there is still no measurable difference. Oak and palm, worm and human—all start in life as virtually the same.
- All natural life starts as a clear, jelly-like substance resembling albumen or egg white. It's made of complex molecules of carbon, hydrogen, oxygen, and nitrogen. Its name is protoplasm.
- In the development of offspring, the bird life, a form of morphogenetic field, seizes upon the bird germ in the protoplasm and builds it up into a bird, the image of itself.
- As the bird life builds up a bird in the image of itself in the embryo, so the spiritual Life builds up a spirit in the image of itself in the protoplasm of the soul, which is the inward essence of each person.
- It's impossible to describe any details of the great miracle by which this soul protoplasm is conformed to the divine image.
- Given the kind of life that humanity is, we are required to choose, to exercise the power of choice, both as natural organisms with mental capacities and as souls with the capacity to become spiritual organisms.
- In maintaining our natural life, by far the larger part is done for us—the breathing, the secreting, the circulating of the blood, the building up of the organism. And although our choosing is a minor part, it's no less essential to the well-being of the whole and its ongoing existence.

- We can choose to abide continuously as a living branch in the spiritual vine, and, in so doing, its true vine life will flow into our soul, assimilating, renewing, conforming us to type, till divinity, pledged by our own law, is formed in us.
- The goal of evolution is a new organism, a new species, transcending Nature but still conforming to the One Law.

Exercise

One fun way to get an understanding of what Drummond addresses in the early part of this essay is to take a few grains of brown rice, barley, oats, and some beans, lentils, and other seeds from the bulk-food bins at a grocery store and sprout them. About half a cup altogether is plenty. (You can cook what you don't sprout by simmering, in a two-to-one ratio of water to grains or beans, for about forty-five minutes—all but the biggest beans will cook in that time—or add them to soup.) Mix the seeds and grains, put them in a flat dish covered with water for a few hours, and then spread them out on a wet paper towel (newspaper works, but not as well) for a few days, keeping the paper moist the whole time. Observe how the grains and beans change from seed to seedling. Observe the differences and similarities between them. Try to tell the difference between the different varieties at different stages of the process. Write your observations in your Science and Spirituality notebook. (You can eat the sprouts when you're done; just add them to a salad, a stir-fry, or an omelet.)

VI

GROWTH

Two roads diverged in the woods and I—
I took the one less traveled by,
And that has made all the difference
Robert Frost, twentieth-century poet

Consider the lilies of the field, how they grow.
They neither toil nor do they spin.
The Sermon on the Mount

NATURAL GROWTH

In the verse from the New Testament quoted above, people are not being told to consider the lilies simply to admire their beauty, nor to dream over their delicate strength and grace. The point they are to consider is how the lilies grew—how the flower woke into loveliness without anxiety or care; how, without weaving, their leaves were woven; how, without toiling, these complex tissues spun themselves into beauty; and how, without any effort or friction, they slowly came out of the earth into glory.

The message is that, through natural processes, life will unfold for us, without our anxiety, just as the flower unfolds. So, the Nazarene says, you careworn, anxious people, you, too, need take no thought for your life.

What you shall eat or what you shall drink or what you shall put on. For if Nature clothes the grass of the field so beautifully, which is here today and tomorrow is burned or plowed under, wouldn't you, as human beings, be clothed by so much more, O ye of little faith?[1]

This nature lesson was a great novelty in its day, but now most people who even have "a little faith" have learned this secret of a composed life. Our past failures have taught most of us the folly of worrying, and we've given up the idea that, by thinking, we can add an inch to our height, much less manage the experience of others around us.

SPIRITUAL ANXIETY

But as soon as our life settles down to the calm trust that thinking in this new way provides, a new and greater anxiety begins. This time it's not for the body that we stress but for the soul. How are we to become better people? How are we to experience a deeper peace? Is there some thought by which we can add inches to our spiritual stature and reach the fullness of our humanity? And because we can't see how to do this, the old anxiety comes back again; our inner life is once more an agony of conflict and remorse.

All we've done at this point is transferred our anxious thoughts from the body to the soul. As a result, our efforts at spiritual growth seem only a succession of failures, and instead of rising into the beauty of holiness, our life seems a daily heartbreak and humiliation. Such is the nature of the natural mind—never to be at rest, always to be in anxiety.

AN ORGANIC PROCESS

Now, the reason for this falling back into anxiety is very plain: we've forgotten the parable of the lily. We've forgotten that exertion and efforts to grow are wholly wrong in principle, however well intentioned they may be. We need to remember that there's only one principle of growth, applying to both the natural and the spiritual, the animal and the plant, the body and the soul. One Law applies every-where and *all* growth is an organic process. We develop and grow simply because we exist—and all that's needed for our growth comes to us from our environment.

So the principle of growing in both beauty and grace is once more this: "Consider the lilies, how they grow." And there are two things about the lilies' growth, two characteristics of all growth, to consider: automatic spontaneity and mystery.

SPONTANEITY

We may seek along three lines for evidence of the automatic spontaneity of growth: science, experience, and the revelation of sacred scriptures.

The first is science, and the argument here could not be summed up better than in the phrases that follow the words from the New Testament quoted earlier. The lilies grow of themselves; they toil not, neither do they spin. They grow automatically, spontaneously, without trying, without laboring, without fretting, without thinking.

Applied everywhere, to plant, to animal, to the body, or to the soul, this law holds. For example, a child grows without trying. We would never think of telling a child to grow. One or two simple conditions are fulfilled, and the growth goes on. The child (or the parent) fulfills the conditions by habit; the result follows by nature. Both processes go steadily on from year to year, apart from the child's thoughts and actions and all but in spite of them.

A doctor has no prescription for growth. The physician can tell me how growth may be stunted or impaired, but the process itself is recognized in science as beyond control—one of the few and therefore very significant things Nature keeps in her own hands. Even modern procedures to stimulate the pituitary gland are performed with the expectation that both patient and doctor must wait and hope and trust the process over time.

Likewise, no minister or priest, no physician of souls has any prescription for spiritual growth. It's the question most often asked and most often answered wrongly. The clergy may prescribe more earnestness, more prayer, more self-denial, or more spiritual work. These are prescriptions for something, but not for growth. They may encourage growth, just as weeding around a plant encourages its growth; but the soul grows as the lily grows, without trying, without fretting, without ever thinking.

Manuals of devotion, with their complicated rules for getting on in the spiritual life, would do well to return to the simplicity of Nature. And those earnest souls who are attempting to achieve sanctification by struggle instead of by faith might be spared much frustration by learning the botany of the Sermon on the Mount we've been studying here. There can be no other principle of growth than this, and to try to make anything grow is as absurd as trying to help the tide come in or the sun rise.

Another argument for the spontaneity of growth is universal experience. A child not only grows without trying but cannot grow *by* trying. No one has ever added an inch to their height by thinking about it; nor has anyone ever achieved the stature of divinity by merely working at it. The divinity of Jesus the Christ, Gautama the Buddha, White Buffalo Woman, or Krishna the embodiment of Om was not reached by effort, and whoever thinks to approach its mystical height by anxious endeavor is really receding from it. The spiritual Life unfolded in these beings from a divine seed, planted centrally in their nature, which grew as naturally as a flower from a bud.

In fact, in the Hindu and Buddhist traditions, as well as in the ancient Egyptian understanding, the development of the spiritual being is symbolized by the lotus blossom or peony. The lotus, growing out of the mud and mire of the lake or pond, emerges as a small bud and blossoms into the beautiful flower that pleases the eye and attracts beautiful insects. In the same way, the blossom of our soul grows out of the muck and mire of our daily life to please the world. The peony, a plant that is reborn again and again, disappearing completely for most of the year, blossoms forth with thousands of petals on each bloom, and so represents the richness of the spiritual life emerging out of almost nothing.

Morality versus Spirituality

It's not possible to fake this process by putting on the appearance; moralistic behavior is not the same as blossoming spirituality. One can always tell an artificial flower. The human form may be copied in wax, yet somehow we can always detect the difference. And this is precisely the difference between the growth of spiritual principle in someone and the moralist's copy of it.

One is natural, the other mechanical. One is organic growth, the other crystalline accretion. The first grows vitally from within; the last adds new particles from the outside. And this, according to biology, is the fundamental distinction between the living and the not living, between an organism and a crystal. The living organism grows by extension; the dead crystal increases by accretion.

The whole difference between the spiritual person and the moralist lies here. The spiritual person works from the inner reality, the moralist from the outer appearance. The one is an organism, at the center of which is a living essence. The other is a crystal, perhaps very beautiful, but only a crystal—it lacks the vital principle of Life.

This difference is why that evolved state of fulfillment that's been called salvation or enlightenment is never directly connected with morality—a fact that's sometimes very difficult to see. It's not that fulfillment doesn't include morality but that the moralist can never achieve it. The experience of fulfillment is perfection—in mind, character, and life, which includes behaviors we call moral.

Striving for morality only develops the character in one or two directions, at most. It may perfect a single virtue here and there, but it can't perfect all, so it always fails to give that rounded harmony, that perfect tune to the whole orchestra, which is the most obvious characteristic of the spiritual person. True morality is a result of spiritual transformation, so the moralist may go a considerable distance toward this perfection but can never reach it.

It requires something with enormous power of movement, of growth, to overcome the obstacles to attaining the desired end state, and only spiritual Life can do that. This is why someone who has Life is nearer the desired state we call fulfillment, perfection, or salvation than one who has developed morality alone. The latter can never reach perfection; the former must. Life must develop the soul according to its type; it must unfold into the spiritual being it is destined to become.

A New Life-Form

This is not to say that spiritual perfection is the norm in the natural world. Nowhere is it said that the human character will develop in all its fullness in this life, so to sneer at the spiritually minded person's imperfections is poor judgment.

Consider, a blade of grass or grain is a small thing. At first it grows very near the earth, often dirty, crushed, and downtrodden. But it's a living thing and growing in ways that may not always be visible. That great dead stone beside the small blade of living green is more imposing, but it will never be anything other than a stone. This small blade, however, will eventually be an imposing cornstalk or beautiful stem of barley or wheat, and may become thousands more if the seeds it produces are planted and nurtured.

Seeing now that growth of all kinds can only be synonymous with a living, automatic process, we begin to understand why spiritual growth is always described in the language of physiology in the sacred scriptures.

And there's another way to help us understand the process of becoming a spiritual being: in sacred writing. Here the reborn soul is understood to be a new creature. The spiritual person, like the poet or engineer, is born, not made. Spiritual Life brings forth a new being. And this being, rooted and built up in divinity and dwelling there, not toiling or spinning, brings forth fruit. But the fruits of the spiritual person's character are not things that have been manufactured; they are living things—things that have grown from the secret germ; they are fruits of the living spirit, emerging without effort in the process of simply being.

MYSTERY

The other great characteristic of growth is mystery. This quality of growth is probably why so few people ever fathom its real character.

A lily grows mysteriously, pushing up its solid weight of stem and leaf against the force of gravity. Shaped into beauty by the secret and invisible fingers of its morphogenetic field, the flower develops we know not how. But we don't wonder at it. Every day the thing is done; it's Nature at work. We accept that.

But when the soul rises slowly above the world, pushing up its delicate virtues against the force of selfishness, shaping itself mysteriously into the image of divinity, people often deny that the power is beyond the individual. They say that a strong will, a high ideal, the reward of virtue account for it. Spiritual character, we assume, is merely the product of anxious work, self-command, and self-denial. They allow a miracle to the lily but none to the human being. The lily may miraculously grow and blossom, but the human must fret and toil and spin.

Now grant for a moment that by hard work and self-restraint a person may attain a very high character. We're not denying that this can be done. But we are denying that this is true growth or development, or that this process is spirituality.

And why do we deny it? We do so for the simple reason that it's not a mystery. The fact that you can account for it proves that it's not true growth. True growth, as we have seen, is mysterious; the peculiarity of it is that you can't account for it. If you can explain it, if you can account for it—by philosophical principles, by the doctrine of influence, by strength of will or a favorable environment—it's not truly growth.

The test of all spirituality is that you can't tell where it came from or where it's going. Remember that the word *spirit* has the same root as the word for *breath* or *wind*: "The wind blows wherever it pleases. You hear its sound, but you cannot tell where it comes from or where it is going. So it is with everyone born of the Spirit."[2] Another process may appear successful; it may be a perfectly honest, remarkable, and praise-worthy imitation, but it is not the real thing. It's been manufactured; its fruits are wax; the flowers are artificial—you can tell where it came from and where it's going.

Distinguishing the Spiritual Person

The distinctions resulting from these two approaches to achieving this fulfillment are plainly visible. The author James B. Mozley has drawn the two characters for us in graphic terms.

> Take an ordinary person of the world—what he thinks and what he does, our whole standard of duty, is taken from the society in which he lives. It is a borrowed standard: he is as good as other people are; he does, in the way of duty, what is generally considered proper and becoming among those with whom his lot is thrown. He reflects established opinion on such points. He follows its lead. His aims and objects in life again are taken from the world around him, and from its dictation. What it considers honorable, worth having, advantageous and good, he thinks so too and pursues it. His motives all come from a visible quarter. It would be absurd to say that there is any mystery in such a character as this, because it is formed from a known external influence—the influence of social opinion and the voice of the world. "Whence such a character cometh" we see; we venture to say that the source and origin of it is open and palpable, and we know it just as we know the physical causes of many common facts.[3]

This is a familiar character. We've seen representatives in the works of Charles Dickens, Jane Austen, Mark Twain, and Tom Clancy. The high-school principal usually fits this mode in most stories and movies about the challenges that teens face—like *Back to the Future*, the 2010 version of *Star Trek*, the Harry Potter films, or *Ferris Bueller's Day Off*. Mozley goes on to describe the other.

> There is a certain character and disposition of mind of which it is true to say that "thou canst not tell whence it cometh or whither it goeth."... There are those who stand out from

among the crowd, which reflects merely the atmosphere of feeling and standard of society around it, with an impress upon them which bespeaks a heavenly birth. . . . Now, when we see one of those characters, it is a question which we ask ourselves, "How has the man become possessed of it? Has he caught it from society around him?" That cannot be, because it is wholly different from that of the world around him. Has he caught it from the inoculation of crowds and masses, as the mere religious zealot catches our character? That cannot be either, for the type is altogether different from that which masses of people, under enthusiastic impulses, exhibit. There is nothing gregarious in this character; it is the individual's own; it is not borrowed, it is not a reflection of any fashion or tone of the world outside; it rises up from some fount within, and it is a creation of which the text says, We "know not whence it cometh."[4]

Here we have the familiar hero: Obi-Wan Kenobi, Superman, or Spider-Man at his best, David Carradine's role in the series *Kung Fu*, Captain Picard in *Star Trek: The Next Generation*, or Dumbledore in the Harry Potter series.

We've all met these two characters. One is eminently respectable, upright, virtuous, a trifle cold perhaps, and generally, when critically examined, showing signs of manufacture. The other, with divinity's breath still upon them, is an inspiration; not more virtuous but differently virtuous; not more humble but differently humble; wearing the meek and quiet spirit artlessly, in the old phrase "to the manner born." The otherworldliness of such a character is what strikes us; we're not prepared for what they will do or say or become next, for they move from a far-off center, and in spite of their transparency and sweetness, that presence always fills us with awe.

The teachers at Hogwarts in the Harry Potter stories illustrate both characters beautifully. In fact, much of British fiction is designed to contrast these two. From Jane Austen's *Pride and Prejudice* and *Sense and*

Sensibility to Charles Dickens's *The Pickwick Papers* and *Oliver Twist* and Agatha Christie's Miss Marple series, we are presented again and again with the one and then the other, and the issues that arise from confusing one with the other. Films such as *Mona Lisa Smile* with Julia Roberts or *Trouble with the Curve* with Clint Eastwood do so as well.

We never feel the discord of our own life, never hear the roar of the machinery by which we try to manufacture our own good points, until we've encountered this distinction and stood in the stillness of such a presence. Then we see the difference between growth and work. We have considered the lilies and how they grow.

NEITHER WORK NOR WORRY

We're not trying to once more strike the timeworn balance between faith and works. What's usually called works, as we have seen, is the result of Life transforming us and changing our surroundings, rather than any effort or thought on our part. Instead, we're considering how lilies grow, specifically to discover the mind-set the spiritual person must maintain regarding spiritual growth. And as we've seen, that mind-set is to be free from care.

This is not a plea for inactivity but for tranquility of the spiritual mind. The Nazarene's protest is not against work but against toiling effort and anxious thought.

Therefore, if we ask, "Is the spiritual person wrong in their cease - less and agonizing efforts to grow?" the answer is, "Yes, they are wrong." When children eat a meal or refuse indigestible things, there's no thought as to how it will help their growth. When they run a race, they're not saying to themselves, "This will help me get taller." It may or it may not be true that these things will help a child's growth, but it's irrelevant to their—and our—experience.

This is the point we're really dealing with. Our anxiety is altogether irrelevant and superfluous. Nature is far more bountiful than we think. When she gives us energy, she asks for none of it back. She doesn't ask us to save some for her to help us with later; she will attend to that.

"Give your work and your anxiety to others," the natural life says. "Trust me to add the inches to your height."

If Life is adding to our spiritual stature, growing the spiritual blossom within us, it's a mistake to keep twitching at the petals with our coarse fingers. As children learn in the vegetable garden, we can't keep pulling things up to see how they're growing. We must learn to let the spiritual artist—the morphogenetic field of the organism we're becoming—alone and let it do its work.

Yet somehow we're determined to supplement that free grace. We're determined to control the process and contribute to it. If spiritual Life is working on our soul, let us be still and know that it is working. And if we want work to focus on, we will find it in keeping still.

THE ONLY WORK

Letting divinity do its work, however, does not mean that there is no work to do for those of us who would grow into our fulfillment. There is strenuous work—work so great that the worker deserves to be relieved of all that is superfluous during the task. If the amount of energy lost in trying to grow our inner spirit were spent instead fulfilling the conditions of growth, we would have many more inches added to our spiritual height.

Let's observe for a moment what these conditions are and how they're related. For its growth, the lily plant needs warmth, light, air, and moisture. Does it go in search of its conditions? No; the conditions come to the plant. It simply stands still with its leaves spread out in unconscious prayer while Nature bathes it in sunshine, pours the nourishing air over and over it, and revives it graciously with nightly dew.

A spiritual person, therefore, need not go in search of these conditions or their spiritual equivalents. The spiritual Life, which has been called Grace, is as free as the air,[5] and in fact, in the Eastern traditions, is said to be part of the air—the *qi*, the *prana*, which we're calling Life— is considered to be the quantum-level essence of the air. We have no more need to manufacture these conditions than we have to manufacture our own soul. We are surrounded by them, bathed in them. We live and move and have our being in them. As the Hebrew texts tell us, the source of life is like the sun and the dew to spiritual people. Why would we go in search of them?

Clearly such a search is not our work. In the realm of spirit, we manufacture nothing; we earn nothing; we need be anxious for nothing; our one duty is to be in the best conditions for our fulfillment and satisfaction, to abide in them, to allow grace to play over us, to be still therein, and to know that it is divinity. The voice of Life simply says, "Be still."

The conflict begins and prevails the moment any of us forgets this. We struggle to grow ourselves instead of struggling to get back into position to receive. We make the church and temple into a workshop when they are meant to be beautiful gardens. And even in what the Nazarene called our "closet," that quiet sanctuary where we would ideally know only blessed stillness, the roar and tumult of our mental machinery—or the distracting chatter of our "monkey mind"—is too often heard.

True, a person will often have to wrestle with divinity, but not for growth. A spiritual life is a composed and peaceful life. The gospel, which means "good news," of all traditions is peace. Yet people desiring to be spiritual are often the most anxious people in the world. Too often for them, life is perpetually self-condemning because they are not growing as fast as they think they should.

And the effect is not only the loss of tranquility to the individual; sadly, it also means that energies meant to be spent on the work of spirit in the world are consumed in the soul's own fever of anxiety. So long as the soul's activities are focused on growth—individually or as a community—there's nothing to spare for the world.

To understand this more fully, consider this: a soldier's time is not spent earning the money to buy his armor, finding food and supplies, or seeking shelter. Governments provide these necessities so that soldiers may be free to complete their task. In the same way, for the ranks of spiritual people, all is provided. We are freed from seeking, trying, earning, and so on, so we can do the work of the spiritual realm.

Similarly, much work is done aboard a ship sailing across the Atlantic, but none of it is spent on making the ship go. The sailor's only work is to simply harness the vessel to the wind. Then, with sail and rudder in position, the miracle is wrought.

In the same way, everywhere, Life creates and humanity utilizes. All the work of the world—natural or spiritual—is merely to take advantage of energies already there. Such is the deeper lesson to be learned from considering the lily. Nature gives the wind, the water, and the heat. Humanity adjusts to the way of the wind, places the water wheel in the way of the river, and puts a piston in the way of the steam.

The work of a spiritual life, therefore, is simply this: to abide in awareness of the presence of the source of life, to be in position. That is all. Humanity has but to maintain the most receptive attitude and all is done. When we simply hold ourselves in position, all the energies of omnipotence flow through our lives. The one Law ensures it.

Essential Points

- The soul grows as the lily grows, without trying, without fretting, without ever thinking.
- Clergy and manuals of devotion, with complicated rules for living a spiritual life, would do well sometimes to return to this simplicity of nature.
- Growth is mysterious and spontaneous. If you can explain it, if you can account for it by philosophical principles, by the doctrine of influence, by strength of will, or by a favorable environment, it's not growth.
- We've seen two characters: moralistic and spiritual. One is respectable, upright, virtuous, a trifle cold perhaps, and yet, when critically examined, shows signs of manufacture. The other is an inspiration; not more virtuous but differently virtuous; not more humble but differently humble; wearing the meek and quiet spirit artlessly, as to the manner born.
- The mind-set of the spiritual person who can maintain that spiritual growth must be free from care. This is not a plea for inactivity but for the tranquility of the spiritual mind.

- All the work of the world—natural or spiritual—is merely to take advantage of energies already there.
- Humanity has to only maintain the most receptive attitude. To abide in awareness of the presence of the source of life, to be in position, that is all.

Exercises

1. Go to a park or playground and watch some children play. Observe how they use every part of their body as they move from one object to another—not intentionally working out but simply enjoying whatever has attracted their attention. Now imagine that you were to do the same thing. Simply move your body in all sorts of ways as you move from one interest to another. Write in your Science and Spirituality notebook what that might look like. Imagine what it might feel like. How long would it take for you to work all your muscles, to get your cardio workout? Now think about your mental life. What would you study, explore, and create if you could simply follow wherever your interests led? Write your thoughts in your notebook. Now make a list of all the reasons you may think why you can't do what you've described—physically and mentally—as the most fitting way for you to develop and maintain your body and mind. After making this list, take the time to reevaluate your activities. Is there a better way for you to do them? If so, then describe it in your notebook and begin it today.

2. If you're not already meditating, contemplating, or praying on a regu-lar basis, here's a way to start being still. Find a comfortable place to sit, where you can relax your body but won't go to sleep (a recliner pushed back may be too comfortable). It may help if you have some soft music, without words or any tune you can recognize, playing in the background, or a recording of someone playing bells or gongs. If you do, set it to a volume where you can just hear it if you pay attention. Sit comfortably with your back in a relatively straight line, from the hips to the head. If you're not sitting in the classic lotus position,[6] uncross your knees, ankles, and hands so you don't block

any circulation. Now find a point of light or color about five feet away and at about the height of your knees (a forty-five-degree angle, so your eyelids can relax partly closed), and gently allow your eyes to focus on it or simply close your eyes. Relax the body. Think of a word or sound that connects you with your Sustaining Source. Traditional words are Om, Peace, Love, One, and the various names of God, but you can use whatever feels calming and sustaining. Breathe in one long, slow, comfortable, deep breath and exhale, repeating that sound or word to yourself as you do so. Breathe another long, slow, deep, comfortable breath and, again, repeat the sound or word to yourself on the exhale. One more time. Now simply relax and breathe, repeating the sound or word with each exhale. If the mind wanders, simply bring it back to the breathing. If the eyes drift, bring them back to focus. Do so until you feel as if you're done. It doesn't really matter how long you do this, but it's best to do it at least once every day. Write a description of your experience in your notebook each time, until this practice (or something like it) is part of your daily routine.

VII

LOVE: THE GREATEST THING
IN THE WORLD

Love puts up with things and is kind; Love never envies;
Love doesn't show off, is not puffed up, never behaves inappropriately,
never seeks what belongs to her, is not easily provoked, thinks no evil;
Love doesn't rejoice in iniquity, but rejoices in the truth;
Love bears all things, believes all things, hopes all things, endures all things.
Love never fails.

The Christian apostle Paul

THE SUPREME GOOD

Everyone in all of human history has asked the question: What is the supreme good? You have life before you. You can live it only once. What is the noblest desire, the supreme gift to aim for?

In the churches, synagogues, mosques, and temples, we've been told that the greatest thing in spiritual life is faith. Faith has been the keynote for centuries of popular religion, and we've learned to consider it the greatest thing in the world.

Well, we are wrong. If we believe that, we may miss the mark. In his New Testament letter to the Corinthians, the apostle Paul says, "If I have all faith, so that I can remove mountains, and have not love, I am nothing." And then, "Now abide faith, hope, love," and without a moment's hesitation, he declares, "The greatest of these is love."[1]

This is not prejudice, either. A writer is likely to recommend to others his own strong point, but love was not Paul's strong point. We can detect a beautiful tenderness growing and ripening as Paul gets old, but the hand that wrote "The greatest of these is love" is that of a persecutor of Christians; it's stained with blood.

Nor is this letter to the Corinthians peculiar in singling out love as the greatest good. Elsewhere in the Christian literature, Peter's letter reads, "Above all, love each other deeply."[2] And John's gospel goes further: "God is love." Then there's the profound remark that Paul makes much later in his career: "Love is the fulfilling of the law."[3] This was a response to the Hebrew tradition in which people were working their passage to Heaven by keeping the Ten Commandments and the 110 other commandments they had manufactured out of them. Jesus the Nazarene saw the Israelites' distress and said, "I will show you a more simple way. If you do one thing, you will do these hundred and ten things, without ever thinking about them. If you love, you will unconsciously fulfill the whole law."[4] And you can readily see for yourself how that must be so.

The spiritual masterpieces of many traditions are agreed about this point.

Consider the Hebrew commandments as listed in the Book of Exodus. They're all based on one foundation: "Love the Lord your God with all your heart and all your mind and all your soul, and love your neighbor as yourself."

If someone loves God, that person doesn't need to be told that love is the fulfilling of that law; it's an experience. The second says, "Thou shalt have no other gods before Me." This is actually a promise in the Hebrew language. If we love anyone with all our heart and soul, there could never by anyone else before them in our minds. This principle applies similarly with the other statements that follow. We shall "take not His name in vain." Would we ever dream of taking His name in vain if we loved Him? "Remember the Sabbath day to keep it holy." Wouldn't anyone be too glad to have one day in seven to dedicate exclusively to the object of their affection?

Clearly, Love would fulfill all these laws regarding God. Likewise, if any of us truly loved humanity, no reminder would be needed to honor our father and mother. We could not do anything else. It would be pre-posterous to tell us not to kill. And how could anyone steal from their beloved? It's superfluous to beg a lover of humanity not to bear false witness against any neighbor. It would be the last thing thought of. And to covet what the neighbors have would be impossible; we would rather that those we love possess it than ourselves.

In this way, we can see that "love is the fulfilling of the law." It's the rule that fulfills all rules, the one commandment for keeping all the old commandments, the fulfillment of all the promises, the fundamental secret of the spiritual life.

Love is the essence of the Sufi tradition as well. As the great thirteenth-century poet Rumi tells us again and again, in hundreds of poems and lectures,

> Love calls—everywhere and always:
> We're sky bound.
> Are you coming?
> Wherever you are, and whatever you do, be in love.
> And still, after all this time, the Sun has never said to the Earth,
> "You owe me."
> Look what happens with love like that.
> It lights up the sky.[5]

In the Hindu tradition, the path of bhakti yoga, or devotion, is the one path anyone may take. Of the eight traditional yogas, this is the one of the heart, the one that all may follow, the one that leads to the final union (which is what yoga, the root of the word "yoke," means) with the divine. It is what Krishna, as the embodiment of the divine, tells the prince Arjuna to base his life on.

> Neither by the study of the Vedas and sacrifices, nor by gifts, nor by rituals, nor by severe austerities.... But by single-minded devotion can I, of this form, be known and seen in reality and also entered into, O Arjuna! He who does all

actions for Me, who looks upon Me as the Supreme, who is
devoted to Me, who is free from attachment, who bears
enmity towards no creature, he comes to Me.[6]

And among the indigenous people of the earth, whose spiritual
life is based not on scripture but on tradition and revelation, we hear
many voices encouraging us to rethink, reimagine, rediscover life as a
path of the heart. Carlos Castaneda quotes his Yaqui teacher Don Juan
Matus, "A path without a heart is never enjoyable. On the other hand,
a path with heart is easy—it does not make a warrior work at liking
it; it makes for a joyful journey; as long as a man follows it, he is one
with it."[7]

And so we see that the path of love is the essence of all spiritual paths.

CONTRASTING QUALITIES

In the letter quoted at the beginning of this essay, the Christian apostle
Paul begins by contrasting love with other things that men in those days
thought much of. He says, "If I speak with the tongues of men and of
angels, and have not love, I am become as sounding brass, or a tinkling
cymbal."[8] And we all know why. We have all felt the brazenness of
words without emotion, the hollowness, the unaccountable lack of per-
suasiveness or even eloquence, in words behind which lies no love.
Emerson reminds us of it over and over in his essays.

The way to speak and write what shall not go out of fashion is
to write sincerely.... The writer who takes his subject from
his ear, rather than his heart, should know that he has lost as
much as he seems to have gained.[9]

Both Krishna, in the Bhagavad Gita quoted earlier, and the Sufi
teacher Rumi say as much as well.

Paul goes on to contrast love with all the other gifts of the spirit.
He contrasts it with prophecy. He contrasts it with mysteries. He contrasts it with faith. He contrasts it with acts of charity.[10]

Why is love greater than faith? Because the end is greater than the means. What's faith for? To connect the soul with divinity, to help us maintain the receptive attitude that allows us to receive the support and supply that is everywhere around us. And what is the object of connecting humanity with divinity? That the human may become the spiritual being that is the pinnacle of evolution. But in the Western world, we call that divinity God (or Allah in Arabic), and in the faith traditions, we are taught that God is love. Faith, then, is the means to connect with the highest goal, Love. Love, therefore, must be greater than faith.

And why is love greater than acts of charity? Because the whole is greater than the part. Charity, as we use the term today, is only a little bit of love, one of the innumerable avenues by which love may be expressed, and there may even be, and too often is, a great deal of charity without love. It's an easy thing to toss a coin to somebody in need; in fact, it's generally an easier thing to do than not. If we really loved him, we would either do more for him or less. This is made clear in the Jewish and Muslim traditions of giving alms as well.

Then Paul contrasts love with sacrifice and martyrdom. Not only the New Testament but also the Qur'an tells us that though you give your body to be burned and have not love, it profits nothing—nothing! The reflection of the love of God (by whatever name), impressed on your own character, is the greatest thing you can offer a stricken world.

The Language of Love

This kind of love is the universal language, and your character is your message. It may take you years to speak the language of another country, but from the day you arrive there, the language of love, understood by all, will be pouring forth its unconscious eloquence.

For example, when I traveled in the lakes region of Africa, I met men and women who remembered the only white man they'd ever seen before me: Dr. David Livingstone. And as I crossed his footsteps in that continent, men's faces lit up as they spoke of the kind doctor who passed there years ago. They could not understand his words, but they felt the love that beat in his heart.

Generations later, Albert Schweitzer did the same for the people there and became a legend. Years after that, the love that Jane Goodall and Dian Fossey held for the furry primates they studied—and the people who cared for them—was so powerfully felt, regardless of their lack of the local language, that Fossey's cabin is kept as a shrine and Goodall is still lovingly received and guided on her way to visit what the locals call "Jane's Peak."

You can take nothing greater with you; you need take nothing less. It's not worthwhile going anywhere if you take anything less with you. You may take every accomplishment you've ever achieved; you may be braced for every sacrifice; but if you do not have love, it will profit you, and the rest of humanity, nothing.

THE COMPONENTS OF LOVE

In the quotation from Paul's letter to the Corinthians that opens this essay, Paul gives us, in three very short verses, an amazing analysis of what this supreme thing is.

Love is a compound thing, he tells us, like light. As you've seen a beam of light pass through a crystal prism and come out on the other side broken up into its component colors—all the colors of the rainbow—so Paul passes love through the magnificent prism of his inspired intellect, and it comes out on the other side broken up into its elements. Notice also how, by a multitude of small things and ordinary virtues, the supreme good is made up.

Paul tells us that the spectrum of Love has nine components:

Patience—"Love waits patiently."
Kindness—"And is kind."
Generosity—"Love never envies."
Humility—"Love never flaunts itself, is not puffed up."
Courtesy—"Never behaves inappropriately."
Unselfishness—"Love doesn't even seek what belongs to her."
Even-temperedness—"Is not easily provoked."

Guilelessness—"Sees no evil."

Sincerity—"Never rejoices in wickedness but rejoices in the truth."

These make up the supreme gift, the fullness of the perfected person, the mature spiritual organism. They are the gift of spiritual Life, and all apply to our normal lives, to the known today and the near tomorrow, not just the unknown eternity. They are the inspiration of the secular life, the breathing of an eternal spirit (which is what the word "inspiration" means) through this temporal world; it's not a strange or added thing. The supreme thing we all seek is, therefore, not a thing at all but a way of being that adds luster to the many words and actions that make up every common day.

PATIENCE

Love is patient. This is the normal attitude of love; it's passive, waiting to begin; not in a hurry; calm. Love is ready to do its work when the summons come, but in the meantime appears as a meek and quiet spirit. It puts up with delays and misbehaviors, responding appropriately. For love is understanding and therefore waits. As loving spouses understand their partner's need for an extra few minutes or as the beloved pet waiting by the door—without comment, without resentment, just accepting—love waits. As the loving parent sends the beloved child off to school or a party, believing the child can do well and hoping for the best, love waits.

KINDNESS

Kindness is love in action. Have you ever noticed how much of the Prophet Mohammed's and White Buffalo Woman's and Jesus the Nazarene's time on earth was spent doing kind things? Read about their lives with that in mind and you'll soon find that a large part of their time was spent simply in making people happy, in doing good things for people. The same could be said of the Dalai Lama today.

There's only one thing greater than happiness in the world, and that is holiness. Our own happiness and the happiness of those around us has been put in our power—and we accomplish our own and theirs by being kind to them.

Given that, I wonder, why is it that we are not all kinder than we are? How much the world needs it! How easily it is done! How instantaneous! How infallibly it is remembered! How superabundantly it pays itself back, for there is no debtor in the world so honorable, so superbly honorable, as the power we call love. Love never fails. Love is success, love is happiness, love is life. "Love, I say," Robert Browning tells us, "is energy of Life."

> For life, with all it yields of joy and woe
> And hope and fear,
> Is just our chance o' the prize of learning love—
> How love might be, hath been indeed, and is.[11]

Where love is, the source of life is working. So love; simply love. Love without making distinctions, without calculating results or procrastinating; simply love. Lavish it upon the people you see as poor, where it's very easy; lavish it especially upon those you consider rich, who often need it most; lavish it most of all upon your colleagues, friends, and family, which is often very difficult, and are also perhaps the people we tend to do least of all for.

Please note, though, that there's a huge difference between trying to please and actually making life more enjoyable for others. Give joy. Take every chance to make life enjoyable for everyone around you, for that's the constant, anonymous triumph of a truly loving spirit. In all things, find ways for those around you to experience more joy; just do the small things (and great) that delight them. It does so much and costs so little and often can only be done in this moment, now. As the poet says,

> I shall pass through this world but once.
> Any good thing therefore that I can do,
> or any kindness that I can show

to any human being, let me do it now.
Let me not defer it or neglect it,
for I shall not pass this way again.[12]

And as you do so, remember that you need not change how you think or dress or speak or present yourself or play to please another; that's not loving yourself or them.

GENEROSITY

Whenever we start any new work, the most unworthy attitude that can cloud any soul waits for us if we aren't fortified with the grace of generosity. That attitude is envy. Envy is a feeling of ill will toward those who are doing the same kind of work as ourselves, a coveting and detracting attitude that's based on comparing ourselves to others. "Love never envies." Whenever you begin a good work, you'll soon find others doing the same kind of work, and probably doing it better. Don't compare yourself to them. Don't envy them. They're on their path and you're on yours. There's only one thing we ever need feel anything like envy toward: the loving, generous soul that envies not.

HUMILITY

And then, after having learned all that, we have to learn the next thing: humility. This is not the false humility of one who pretends not to have the skills, talents, and accomplishments that all can see. To be truly humble is to put a seal on our lips and forget what we've done in the world. After you've been kind, after your love has done its beautiful work in the world, go back into the shade again and say nothing about it. Love hides even from itself. Love gives up self-satisfaction in the realization of self-fulfillment.

COURTESY

The fifth ingredient is a somewhat strange one to find in this list of the greatest goods: courtesy. This is love in society, love showing up as etiquette. We state it as "Love never behaves inappropriately"; it's never rude. Courtesy is said to be love in little things. You can put the most uneducated person into the highest society, and if they have a reservoir of love in their heart, they will not behave improperly. They simply cannot do it.

Years ago, the great historian Thomas Carlyle said of the Scots farmer Robert Burns that there was no truer gentleman in Europe than the ploughman-poet. It was because he loved everything—the mouse and the daisy and all things great and small. So with this simple passport, he could mingle with any society and enter courts and palaces anywhere in the world from his little cottage on the banks of the river Ayr. Americans may think of Davy Crockett or Daniel Boone in the same way.

In more modern times, we can think of the poor son of a single mom in Arkansas, William Jefferson Clinton, who learned to work with the wealthy and powerful of the world and has become one of the world's great statesmen in the process. Or the daughter of a grocer who became the Prime Minister of Britain, Margaret Thatcher, learning appropriate etiquette as she went (as portrayed by Meryl Streep in the film *Iron Lady*). Both of them let a high ideal of service to their country pull them into more and more perfected behavior.

You know the meaning of the word "gentleman." It means a man who does things gently, with love. And that is the whole art and mystery of it. The gentleman cannot do an ungentle or ungentlemanly thing. By contrast, the ungentle soul, the inconsiderate, unsympathetic nature, can't do anything else. Love never behaves inappropriately.

UNSELFISHNESS

Paul tells us that "Love doesn't even seek what belongs to her"—*not even that which is already her own*. In most democracies, the citizens are devoted to their rights, and there come times when we may exercise the even higher right of giving up our rights—as when the citizens of the Allied countries gave up their rights to unlimited access to fuel and food to support the defeat of the totalitarian states of Germany, Italy, and Japan during World War II. Yet love strikes much deeper. It would have us not seek our rights at all. Love would have us ignore them and eliminate the personal element altogether from our expectations—not to seek things for ourselves at all—knowing that our true wealth and well-being come from spiritual Life rather than things.

Things cannot be great. This is the essence of the Buddha's first Noble Truth, which, translated literally, is not about suffering per se but rather says, "No thing ever fully satisfies." Recognizing that nothing, in any form—no person, place, object, or work—will satisfy the soul's longing is the first step to freedom from suffering.

The most obvious lesson in the teaching of most spiritual leaders is that there is no happiness in having and getting anything but only in giving—and still, half the world is moving the wrong direction in the pursuit of happiness. Most people think that achieving happiness consists of having and getting and being served by others. Instead, the great spiritual teachers tell us it consists of giving and of serving others. Those who would be happy need to remember that it is more blessed—it makes us more happy—to give than to receive.

The principle is easy to apply to things. After we've sought them, bought them, won them, and cared for them, we have taken the gloss off them already. There's little pain then, perhaps, in giving them up.

It's harder to apply the principle to the attention, time, income, respect, or appreciation we believe we deserve. Then we need to remember that "love doesn't even seek what belongs to her."

Giving up such things has been called, and can feel like, self-denial. But self-denial for its own sake is nothing; it is almost a mistake. Only a great purpose or a mightier love can justify the waste of not being loving toward ourselves. Ideally, we love others as we love ourselves—not instead of loving ourselves.

We need to remember that there is no hardship in loving; the yoke is easy. It's an easier way than any other, a happier way than any other.

EVEN TEMPER

The next ingredient is a remarkable one. "Love is not easily pro-voked." We're inclined to look at a harsh temper as a relatively harmless weakness. We speak of it as a mere failing of our nature, a family trait, not a thing to take into serious account in estimating someone's character. And yet here, right in the heart of this analysis of love, it finds a place.

You know people who are almost perfect and others who would be entirely perfect but for an easily ruffled, quick-tempered, or touchy disposition. This combination of ill temper with high moral character is one of the strangest and saddest problems of social ethics.

There's a well-known parable in the New Testament, usually referred to as the Prodigal Son. In this story, a younger son demands his birthright and leaves, while the Elder Brother stays home and continues to work with their father. Most people who teach this story have no doubt that the younger son, the Prodigal, has done the most damage. But are they right?

If we really think about it, no form of vice—not lying, not greed, not even giving in to addictions—does more harm than an evil temper. For embittering life, for breaking up communities, for destroying the most sacred relationships, for devastating homes, for taking the bloom off childhood—in short, for sheer misery-producing power, a bad temper stands alone.

With that in mind, look at the Elder Brother. He is moral, hardworking, patient, dutiful—let him get all credit for his virtues—but look at him sulking outside his father's door when his younger brother is being welcomed home. "He was angry," we read, "and would not go in." Look at the effect of this behavior on the father, on the servants, on the guests. Consider its effect upon his brother. Analyze, as a study in temper, the thundercloud that gathers upon the Elder Brother's brow. What is it made of? Jealousy, anger, pride, uncharity, cruelty, self-righteousness, touchiness, doggedness, sullenness—these are the components of this dark and loveless soul, the ingredients of all ill temper.

Temper is destructive in itself, but it's more than that; it's a symptom, a revelation of an unloving nature at the bottom. It tells of an ongoing disease within. It's the occasional bubble escaping to the surface that betrays some rottenness underneath. The most hidden aspects of the soul, shown involuntarily when off guard, are all instantaneously revealed in one flash of temper.

The great American neurosurgeon Benjamin Carson discovered this in the mid-twentieth century. As he was growing up, his violent explosions of temper nearly landed him in jail and his beloved mother in the grave. He tried and tried again to control it, until, in deepest anguish, he knew only one place to seek help: the words of the Bible. As illustrated in the beautiful film *Gifted Hands*, with Cuba Gooding Jr., Benjamin was transformed. The energy that had been discharged through his temper became a sort of genius, encouraging him to challenge the distress that brain injuries and other conditions can cause children and leading him to make history with his remarkably successful results.

Mohandas Gandhi became known as Mahatma, or "great soul," because he found, through the guidelines in the Bhagavad Gita and the Christian Bible, the means to transform the temper that had nearly destroyed his life and marriage. And with the energy that replaced it, he led his country through a peaceful revolution from its colonists in the first half of the twentieth century. Ben Kingsley illustrates some of this process in the film *Gandhi*.

These examples illustrate that it's not enough to control the temper. We must go to the source and allow our inner nature to be transformed. Then the angry tendencies die away. Willpower does not change us. Time does not transform us. Souls are made sweet not by taking the bitterness out but by putting something in. A great love, a new spirit interpenetrating ours sweetens, purifies, and transforms all. Only this can wipe out what's wrong. Only this can work the necessary chemical change to renovate, regenerate, and rehabilitate the soul.

GUILELESSNESS

It's a wonderful thing that, here and there in this too often hard and judging world, there are a few rare souls left who think no evil. This is the great unworldliness. Paul tells us that love "sees no evil," assumes no hidden motive, sees the bright side, and puts the best interpretation on every action. What a delightful state of mind to live in!

This was the charm that won the heart of India for Gandhi and Mother Teresa and that of South Africa for Nelson Mandela. Some say it was George Washington's great gift as well. They all saw first and foremost the best in the people around them and in the citizens of the countries they served.

The books and films *Pollyanna* and *Heidi* illustrated this quality in the early twentieth century, and the comic strip, musical, and film based on the character Little Orphan Annie did the same in the late twentieth century. Part of the attraction of Harry Potter and The Lord of the Rings series is the guilelessness of the main characters.

Guilelessness is the transformer for suspicious people. And the possession of it is the great secret of personal influence. If you think for a moment, you'll find that the people who have influenced you most are people who believe in you. In an atmosphere of suspicion, people shrivel up, but in the presence of those who trust and anticipate the best of them, people expand and find encouragement and educative fellowship. What an inspiration it is to meet someone with this trait even for a day!

To be trusted is to be saved. And if we aim to influence or elevate others, we shall soon see that their success is in direct proportion to their belief that we believe in them. When we show respect for another it's often the first step toward restoring the self-respect they may have lost; our ideal of what they are becomes for them the hope and pattern of what they may become.

SINCERITY

"Love never rejoices in wickedness but rejoices in the Truth." I've called this sincerity. For those who love will love Truth no less than other people. They will rejoice in the highest truth they can experience, not in what they've been taught to believe; not in this religion's doctrine or in that one's; not in this ism or in that ism, but in the Truth. They will accept only what is real; will strive to get at the story behind the facts; will search for Truth with a humble and unbiased mind, and cherish whatever is found.

But what Paul really meant, as we read in another translation, is that love "does not rejoice in unrighteous behavior, but rejoices with the truth,"[13] which is a quality that probably no one word—and certainly not sincerity—adequately defines. It includes, perhaps more accurately, the self-restraint that refuses to take advantage of others' faults, the charity that avoids exposing the weakness of others but understands and helps cover it, and the sincerity of purpose that aims to see things as they truly are. Anyone with this quality rejoices to find people better than their suspicion feared or others' gossip denounced. It's the quality that we ascribe to our best friends—those we can trust to be authentically loving toward us through thick and thin.

PUTTING LOVE TO WORK

So much for the analysis of love. Now the business of our lives is to bring these qualities into our behavior.

The supreme work in this world is to learn to love. Life is full of opportunities for learning love. Every man and woman, every day, has a thousand of these chances! The world is not a playground or battlefield; it's a schoolroom. Life is not a holiday or a battle; it's an education. And the one eternal lesson for all of us is how we can love better.

What makes someone a good ball player? Practice. What makes anyone a good artist, a good sculptor, a good musician? Practice. What makes someone a good linguist, a good nurse, a good programmer? Practice. What makes anyone a good person? Practice. Nothing else.

There's nothing capricious about a spiritual life. The soul doesn't develop in different ways, under different laws, from those of the body and mind. If we don't exercise the arm, we develop no biceps muscle, and if we don't exercise the soul, there is no muscle there, either—no strength of character, no moral fiber, no beauty or spiritual growth.

Love is not a thing of enthusiastic emotion. It's a rich, strong, vigorous expression of the whole character—the soul's divine nature in its fullest development. And this great character can only be built up by ceaseless practice.

What was Mohammed doing in the cave? Practicing. He developed the stillness of mind that allows the ever-calling voice of the divine to be heard. What was Jesus (who became the Christ) doing in the carpenter's shop? Practicing. We read in the New Testament that he learned obedience and increased in wisdom. What was Gautama (who became the Buddha) doing in his father's palace? Practicing. He developed physical and moral discipline and strength. And in the forest with the ascetics? Again, practicing. He was developing nonattachment and will.

So don't complain about your lot in life, about its never-ceasing cares, its petty environment, the things you put up with, the small-minded people you live and work with. Above all, do not resent the temptations that life offers. Don't be perplexed because temptation seems to thicken around you more and more, and neither effort nor agony nor even prayer stops it. That's the practice that your growth requires of you, and its work is making you patient and humble, generous and unselfish, kind and courteous—all the qualities you admire most. Don't begrudge the hand that is molding the still, shapeless protoplasm within you. Like the embryo in the womb, it's growing more beautiful even though you can't see it, and every touch of what we call temptation may add to its perfection.

Don't isolate yourself, either. It's best to keep in the midst of life. Live among people, among things, among troubles and difficulties and obstacles. Remember the words of the great transcendentalist Johann von Goethe: "Talent develops itself in solitude, character in the stormy stream of life." He's referring to the talent of faith, of meditation, of seeing the unseen, of speaking the word. Character grows in the stream of the world's life, because that's where people learn the art and science of love.

EXPERIENCING LOVE'S POWER

We've named a few of the elements of love, but these are only elements. Love itself can never be defined. Love, like light, is something more than the sum of its ingredients—a glowing, dazzling, vibrating radiance.

By synthesis of all the colors, we can make whiteness in the light, but we cannot manufacture light. By synthesis of all the virtues, people can make a virtuous character, but they cannot manufacture love.

We try to copy those who have it. We lay down rules about it. We watch. We pray. But these things alone will not bring love into our nature. Love is an effect. And only as we fulfill the right condition can the effect be produced.

So if love is an effect, what's the cause?

In every spiritual tradition, from the hunting-gathering tribes of the deep forest and high plains to the highest church in Rome or England, from the greatest mosque in Mecca to the Hindu temples of India and Southeast Asia and the Buddhist monasteries of Tibet and Nepal, one thing is clear: divinity, by whatever name, loves humanity. Whether the heart calls out to Tara or Kali, Mary or St. Teresa, David, Jesus, or Krishna, the one God Allah, or to the Great Spirit, White Buffalo Woman, the Mother, the Father, the Goddess, or even to the Horned God, there is an answering call, a loving Presence—the immanent aspect of the divine.

The nineteenth-century physician H. Emilie Cady defined in *Lessons in Truth* the nature of what she called God as both immanent and transcendent. She said that the transcendent aspect of the divine is what the Hindus and Buddhists call Brahman, the "ground of being." It's the infinite Power through which all matter and energy emerge. The immanent aspect of the divine is just as real and very personal: a loving Presence called, in Hebrew, Emanuel.[14]

In the New Testament, Jesus called this loving Presence "the Father" or, even more tenderly, *abba*, which means "daddy." In the Hebrew Bible, the prophets proclaim over and over the great love that the Lord has for his people. In the Bhagavad Gita, the embodiment of all creative and destructive power everywhere shows up in the heartbroken prince Arjuna's chariot as Krishna, showing his love for all who are devoted to the power and wisdom he embodies.

How, then, are we to have this transcendent living whole conveyed into our souls? How can we experience this immanent presence?

If you turn to John's first letter in the New Testament, you will find these words: "We love, because He first loved us." Consider the word *because*; the love we receive is the cause, and our loving is the effect.

Because we are loved, we love the divinity that sustains us, and we love all humanity. We can't help it—and the promise of the Torah is fulfilled. As we realize this love, our heart is slowly changed. Contemplate the love of the Mother, Mohammed, Krishna, Tara, White Buffalo Woman, or Christ, and you will love. Stand before the mirror of divine love and you will be changed into the same image of tenderness. This is the practice of Tibetan lamas; they focus on the image of the Buddha or Tara, allowing the being represented in the image to merge with their own being so they may have the qualities the image represents.

There is no other way. You cannot love simply because you decided to. You can only look at the lovely object, fall in love with it, and grow into its likeness. Love begets love.

Rumi, the Sufi poet, is perhaps the most famous proclaimer of the intoxicating effect of realizing divine love.

> Is it really so that the one I love is everywhere?
> If in thirst you drink water from a cup, you see God in it.
> Those who are not in love with God will see only their own
>   faces in it.[15]

It's a process of induction. Put a piece of iron in the presence of a magnetized body, and that piece of iron becomes magnetized. It's charged in the mere presence of the original field, and as long as you leave the two side by side, they are both magnets.

Similarly, remain side by side with the source of life who is always loving us, and you, too, will become a powerful, permanently attractive force. Like Moses, David, Jesus, the blessed Mohammed, and the Buddha of old, or Nelson Mandela, Pope John Paul II, Mother Teresa, or Princess Diana in recent years, you'll draw all people to you and you'll be drawn to all. That's the inevitable effect of love. *Anyone* who fulfills that cause must have that effect produced within.

Edward Irving went to see a dying boy once, and when he entered the room, he just put his hand on the sufferer's head, and said, "My boy, God loves you," and went away. Immediately the boy started from his bed and called out to the people in the house, "God loves me! God loves me!" It changed that boy. The sense that God loved him overpowered him, melted him down, and began the creating of a new heart in him.

And that is how awareness of the abiding love that is available to us all melts down the unloving heart and begets the new organism, the spiritual being who is patient, humble, gentle, and unselfish. And there is no other way to get it.

Try to give up the idea that the spiritual life comes to us by chance, by mystery, or by effort. It comes to us by natural law and by supernatural law, for all law is universal. There is no mystery about it: We love others; we love everybody, even our enemies, because we realize that the source of life first loved us.

UNLIMITED AND UNFAILING

What is Paul's final reason for singling out love as the supreme possession? It's a remarkable reason: it lasts. "Love never fails," he tells us.

Can you think of any single thing that will last forever? Not money, fortune, or fame, certainly. They are what the Hindus and Buddhists call *maya*, which means "changeable"; they change and pass away. Paul brushed aside even the great things that philosophers and leaders of his time thought had some worth. He had no charge against these things in themselves; all he said about them was that they would not last. They were great things but not supreme things; there are things beyond them. Throughout the Hebrew Bible and the New Testament, we read, "it came to pass." The gospel of John says of this world, not that it is wrong but simply that it "passes away." There's a great deal in the world that is delightful and beautiful; there's a great deal in it that is great and engrossing, but none of it will last forever.

All that is in the world, all the things people lust after, and all the pride of a good living exist for only a little while. This is the essence of the Buddha's first noble truth: "No thing ever fully satisfies." It means that people who focus on having the things of this world must be dissatisfied, too often suffering over loss and degradation.

Love not the world, therefore. Nothing that it contains is worth the life and attention of an immortal soul. The immortal soul must give itself to something that is immortal. As the great New Thought teacher Emma Curtis Hopkins says in her first lesson,

> God doesn't work in the lie that you speak when you say you seek a job; God works in Truth. And the Truth is that you seek unlimited resources. You are a limitless being with limitless powers and nothing less than the infinite will ever fully satisfy you.[16]

LOVE AS LIFE'S PURPOSE

To love abundantly is to live abundantly, and to love forever is to live forever. Hence, eternal life is inextricably bound up with love.

We want to live forever for the same reason that we want to live tomorrow. Why do you want to live tomorrow? For most of us, we want to see someone tomorrow who loves us and we want to be with them and love them back.

There's no other reason why we should live on forever than that we experience the fulfillment that comes with being loving and beloved. People commit suicide when they think there's no one to love them. So long as they have friends who love them and whom they love, they will live, because to live is to love. If it's only the love of a dog, it will keep a person living; but let that go and there's no contact with life, no reason to live. The energy of life has failed.

No worse fate can befall anyone in this world than to live and grow old alone, unloving and unloved. This is the point of Charles Dickens's *A Christmas Carol* and the plight of Darth Vader in *Star Wars* and Q in *Star Trek: The Next Generation*.

Eternal life is also called knowing, or union with, divinity. It's what Jesus the Nazarene called "the kingdom at hand."

From the Toltec teacher Don Miguel Ruiz, we have the following:

Imagine that you have the ability to see the world with different eyes, whenever you choose. . . . Close your eyes now, and then open them and look outside.

What you will see is love coming out of the trees, love coming out of the sky, love coming out of the light. You will perceive love from everything around you. This is the state of bliss . . . Heaven on Earth.[17]

By whatever name we use—Mother, Lord, Allah, Father, Goddess, Krishna, Christ, Great Spirit—the immanent Presence is the very essence of love. So that love must be eternal. The Presence is the source of life; then love is life. Love never fails, and life never fails as long as there is love. That's the philosophy Paul is showing us; that's the reason why, in the nature of things, Love must be the supreme thing, because it's going to last; because, in truth, love is eternal Life.

And that eternal Life is something we're living now, not something we get when we die. Moreover, we'll have a poor chance of experiencing it when we die unless we are living it now.

To be lost, then, or fallen, is to live loveless and unloved; to be saved, free, and fulfilled is to love. And whoever dwells in love dwells in the divine Presence, for the source of Life, both natural and spiritual, is eternal Love: expressing though the one law, one consistent set of principles and processes, for all and everywhere.

Essential Points

- "Love is the fulfilling of the law." It's the rule that fulfills all rules, the one commandment for keeping all the old commandments, the fundamental secret of the spiritual life.
- Patience, kindness, generosity, humility, courtesy, unselfishness, good temper, guilelessness, sincerity—these make up the supreme gift, the fullness of the perfect person, the mature spiritual organism.

- The supreme work in this world is to learn to love. Life is full of opportunities for learning Love—the world is a schoolroom, and the one eternal lesson for all of us is how we can love better.
- Don't be perplexed because temptation seems to thicken around you and neither effort nor agony, nor even prayer, stops it. That's the practice that your path appoints you; making you patient and humble, generous and unselfish, kind and courteous—all the things you want to be.
- Try to give up the idea that the spiritual life comes to us by chance, by mystery, or by effort. It comes to us by natural law and by supernatural law, for all law is universal.
- All the things in the world exist for only a little while. This is the essence of the Buddha's first noble truth: "No thing ever fully satisfies." It means that people who focus on having the things of this world must be dissatisfied, too often suffering.
- Love is life. Love never fails, and life never fails as long as there is love.
- To be lost or fallen is to live loveless and unloved, and to be saved, free, and fulfilled is to love, for the source of Life, both natural and spiritual, is Love: expressing through the one Law, one consistent set of principles and processes, for all and everywhere.

Exercises

In your Science and Spirituality notebook, make a table that lists the nine components of love on one edge, and twenty-eight days on the other (see opposite page):

1. Pick one quality at a time, and for twenty-eight days, mark every day that you use that quality. This is how Benjamin Franklin developed the virtues he wanted to embody. (He did it for thirty days.)
2. Choose an ideal, a "model of the type," you'd like to emulate. Find some object, picture, or set of words that helps you focus on that being's qualities. Dedicate twenty-nine pages in your Science and Spirituality notebook for this exercise and put the picture or words on the first page. Each day for the next twenty-eight days, write on

PATIENCE	KINDNESS	GENEROSITY	HUMILITY	COURTESY	UNSELFISHNESS	GOOD TEMPER	GUILELESSNESS	SINCERITY
1.								
2.								
3.								
4.								
5.								
6.								
7.								
8.								
...								

a page in your notebook a description of the qualities you're ready to experience, and then close your eyes and imagine that you are merging with your ideal—your body and that body are now one body; your mind and that mind are now one mind. Some days this will be easy; others it will be harder. Just go through the process. When you've completed the imagining, write on that page a description of what worked in this experience. If you miss doing this exercise for more than a day, start over. You're rewiring the neurons in your brain to focus on these qualities instead of whatever your norm was before, and it takes that many days to do so. As you follow through on this exercise, however, you'll find that you've begun to grow a new self, from the inside out—and the world around you will reflect it.

NOTES

INTRODUCTION

1. *Science, Philosophy and Religion: A Symposium* (New York: Conference on Science, Philosophy and Religion in Their Relation to the Democratic Way of Life, Inc., 1941).
2. Taken from the essay "Growth" in the first section of this volume.
3. For more details about Drummond and his life, see Cuthbert Lennox, *The Practical Life Work of Henry Drummond* (New York: James Pott, 1901). Also available in digital format: http://archive.org/stream/practicallifewor00lenn#page /116/mode/2up.

FOREWORD

1. Taken from an address at Princeton Theological Seminary, May 19, 1939. It was published in *Out of My Later Years* (New York: Philosophical Library, 1950).
2. Walter Bagehot, *Physics and Politics; or, Thoughts on the Application of the Principles of "Natural Selection" and "Inheritance" to Political Society* (London: Henry S. King, 1872).
3. Karl Marx and Friedrich Engels were the authors of *Das Kapital*, the basis for Marxist-Leninist Communism.
4. Spencer is best known for coining the concept of "survival of the fittest" in *Principles of Biology* (1864).

5. E. O. Wilson, *Sociobiology: The New Synthesis* (Boston: Harvard University Press, 1975).

6. Albert Einstein, from *Science, Philosophy and Religion: A Symposium* (New York: Conference on Science, Philosophy and Religion in Their Relation to the Democratic Way of Life, Inc., 1941).

7. Sir Francis Bacon, "Meditationes Sacræ," 10:100. Available online at Google Books.

8. Einstein, from *Science, Philosophy and Religion.*

THE ROLE OF LAW IN SCIENCE (INTRODUCTION: PART I)

1. Thomas Aquinas, *Summa Theologica*, 1:20.

2. Thomas H. Huxley, "Mister Darwin's Critics," *Darwiniana* (New York: Appleton, 1887), 148. [Note: this is the accurate reference, not the one in Drummond's original.]

3. Ralph Waldo Emerson, *Nature*, chapter IV.

4. Augustin Pyrame de Candolle (February 4, 1778–September 9, 1841) was a Swiss botanist who documented hundreds of plant families and created a new natural plant classification system.

MANY FIELDS, ONE LAW (INTRODUCTION, PART II)

1. George Douglas Campbell (The Duke of Argyll), "The Unity of Nature," *Littell's Living Age*, no. 1895, October 9, 1880, 70.

2. Many of these experiments have been documented by the Institute of Noetic Sciences and some are illustrated in the film *Something Unknown Is Doing We Don't Know What* (Beyond Words Publishing, 2009).

3. Sir Arthur Eddington, comment on the uncertainty principle in quantum physics, 1927.

4. Balfour Stewart, *The Unseen Universe* (London: Macmillan, 1875), 235.

5. Ibid., 286.

6. A. S. Eddington, "Science and the Unseen World," Swarthmore Lecture 1929 (New York: Macmillan, 1929), 36.

7. Sir Arthur Eddington, *The Nature of the Physical World* (Cambridge, UK: Cambridge University Press, 1928), 276–81.

8. Many texts explore this idea. Fred Alan Wolf's *Taking the Quantum Leap* (New York: HarperCollins, 1988) and his animated graphics in *What the Bleep!? Down the Rabbit Hole* (20th Century Fox, 2006) are perhaps the most accessible.

9. Emma Curtis Hopkins, *Scientific Christian Mental Practice*, lesson 2 (various editions).

10. Thomas Carlyle, *Sartor Resartus*—a satirical novel published as a series, released by Frazier Magazine, London, in 1833-34, and then as a book in 1837 in Boston by Ralph Waldo Emerson. Available on Project Gutenberg, http://www .gutenberg.org/files/1051/1051-h/1051-h.htm.

11. Emanuel Swedenborg, *An Hieroglyphic Key to Natural and Spiritual Mysteries, by Way of Representations and Correspondences*, original ed. (London: Swedenborg Association, 1845), viii.

12. Ralph Waldo Emerson, *Nature*, chapter IV.

13. James Hinton, *Philosophy and Religion* (London: K. Paul Trench, 1885), 40.

BIOGENESIS

1. H. Charlton Bastian, *The Beginnings of Life*, vol. 2 (London: Macmillan, 1872), 633.

2. Balfour Stewart and Peter Guthrie Tait, *The Unseen Universe*, 6th ed. (London: Macmillan, 1875), 229.

3. J. Hutchison Stirling, *As Regards Protoplasm* (New York: Van Nostrand, University Series, 1879), 42. Available online at Google Books.

4. Steen Rasmussen, Mark A. Bedau, Liaohai Chen, David Deamer, David C. Krakauer, Norman H. Packard, and Peter F. Stadler, ed., *Protocells: Bridging Nonliving and Living Matter* (Cambridge, MA: MIT Press, 2009).

5. Shvetashvatara Upanishad 1:5–6.

6. Qur'an, 24:42.

7. Hazrat Inayat Khan, The Sufi Order, http://www.sufisage.org/sufisagequotesfa .html.

8. A. Hultkrantz, "The Shaman and the Medicine-Man," *Social Science Medicine* (1985) 20(5): 511–515.

9. R. Goodman, *Lakota Star Knowledge: Studies in Lakota Stellar Theology*, 2nd ed. (Rosebud, SD: Sinte Gleska University, 1992), 40. Quoted in Robert Waxman, "Theism and Shamanism," http://www.robertwaxman.com.

10. While there are many introductions to the Kabbalah, one of the simplest and most complete is Will Parfitt's *The Elements of the Qabalah* (London: Element Books, 1991; New York: Barnes & Noble, 1999).

11. John 3:5.

12. Romans 8:6.

13. Revelation 3:1 (WEB).

14. 1 Timothy 5:6 (WEB). (Commentary explains that the pleasure referred to is "to live in luxury, voluptuously; to indulge freely in eating and drinking; to yield to the indulgence of the appetites. It does not indicate grossly criminal pleasures, but the kind of pleasure connected with luxurious living, and with pampering the appetites.)

15. Ephesians 2:1, 5.

16. 1 Corinthians 2:14 (WEB).

17. Herbert Spencer, *First Principles*, 2nd ed., (New York: Appleton, 1864) 17. Sixth edition available online at Google Books.

18. Robert H. Super, ed., *The Complete Prose Works of Matthew Arnold* in Eleven Volumes (Ann Arbor: University of Michigan Press, 1960–1977), 176.

19. 1 John 3:2.

20. 2 Corinthians 7:5 (Aramaic Bible in Plain English).

21. John 14:20.

22. John 14:21–23.

23. John 15:4.

24. Galatians 2:20 (New Living Translation).

25. John 14:10 (American King James Version).

26. Exodus 3:1–15.

27. Acts 9:5.

28. Sahih Bukhari, vol 4, book 55, number, 605, 1/2–3.

29. Christopher Isherwood and Pravananda, the Bhagavad-Gita (Hollywood: Vedanta Press, 1969) 7.8.

ENVIRONMENT

1. Bruce Lipton, *The Biology of Belief: Unleashing the Power of Consciousness, Matter, and Miracles* (Carlsbad, CA: Hay House, 2008).

2. Described in Karl Semper's *The Natural Conditions of Existence as They Affect Animal Life*; originally published in Sir Edward Horne's *Lectures in Comparative Anatomy*, vol. 1 (1814): 217; cited in an article in *Nature*, March 17, 1881, by Sir Norman Lockyer.

3. Ibid.

4. Alfred Russel Wallace, *Tropical Nature and Other Essays* (London: Clay and Sons, 1878).

5. Jo S. Hermansen, Stein A. Sæther, Tore O. Elgvin, Thomas Borge, Elin Hjelle, Glenn-Peter Sætre, "Hybrid Speciation in Sparrows I: Phenotypic Intermediacy, Genetic Admixture and Barriers to Gene Flow," *Molecular Ecology* 20, no. 18 (September 2011), 3812–3822.

6. Bhagavad Gita, 10:9.

7. John 15:5 (Aramaic Bible in Plain English).

8. Psalms 62:5.

9. Syrah 39:49.

10. Herbert Spencer, *The Principles of Biology* (New York: Appleton, 1871) 57. Available online at Google Books.

11. John 15:4 (WEB).

12. 2 Corinthians 12:10.

13. Khurram Murad, *Way to the Qur'an*, SunniPath Online Library, http://www.sunnipath.com/library/Books/.

14. Surah 57:16.

15. Psalms 121:1–2.

16. Jeremiah 30:15 (God's Word Translation).

17. Bhagavad Gita 15:12–15.

18. Chandogya Upanishad.

19. This is thoroughly studied in what's called "the closed system problem" in general systems theory. So far there has been no system discovered that doesn't receive inputs of matter, energy, and information—as well as outputs of the same. Even the universe, once thought to be self-contained, seems to receive inputs through what some people call "white holes."

20. Ecclesiastes 1:18.

21. Matthew 11:29.

22. Matthew 19:17; Mark 10:18; Luke 18:19.

23. Psalms 142:4–5.

24. Jonathan Star and Shahram Shiva, *A Garden Beyond Paradise: The Mystical Poetry of Rumi* (New York: Bantam, 1992) Ode 442.

25. Idris Shah, *The Teachings of Rumi* (London: Octagon Press, 1994) Masnawi III, 1420-24.

26. Psalms 42:1.

27. Psalms 46:1.

28. Matthew 11:28.

29. Colossians 2:10, American King James Version.

30. Bhagavad Gita 9:29.

31. Bhagavad Gita 10:9.

32. Stan Rosenthal (translator), *Tao Te Ching: A Translation* (Cardiff, UK, 1984), online at http://www.integralbook.com.

33. This is a quote from Balfour Stewart, *The Unseen Universe*, 6th ed. (London: Macmillan, 1878), 100. In addition, however, it is the whole exploration of what's now called "dark matter." Current assessments of the volume of the universe and the quantity of measurable matter and energy have required scientists

to postulate that there is some substance that cannot be measured present everywhere throughout the universe.

Conformity to Type

1. Lionel S. Beale, *Bioplasm: An Introduction to the Study of Physiology and Medicine* (London: J. & A. Churchill, 1872), 17–18.
2. Thomas Huxley, *Lay Sermons*, 6th ed., 127, 129.
3. Ibid., 261.
4. See Bruce Lipton's *Biology of Belief* (New York: Hay House, 2008), and Richard C. Francis, *Epigenetics: How Environment Shapes Our Genes* (New York: W. W. Norton, 2012), among others.
5. Charles Darwin, *The Origin of Species* (London: Gramercy, 1995), 166.
6. Rupert Sheldrake, 2005, www.sheldrake.org.
7. Ibid.
8. Adapted from Likutei Torah, "*Hayam Ra'ah Vyanos*," 16, http://www.kabalahonline.org.
9. 2 Corinthians 5:17; 1 John 5:18; 1 Peter 1:3; Colossians 3:9, 10.
10. Bhagavad Gita, 9.
11. The deep-sea sulfur-based organisms being the only known exception at this point.
12. Thomas Moore, *Care of the Soul* (New York: Harper, 1994), xiii.
13. Ibid., 5.
14. Ibid., 96.
15. Will Parfitt, *The Elements of the Qabalah* (London: Element Books, 1991; New York: Barnes & Noble, 1999).
16. Colossians 3:10.
17. This is from the Nicene (and Apostle's) creed, which is the statement defining a Christian. It draws on John 5:18.
18. 2 Corinthians 3:18.
19. Romans 8:29.
20. John 3:3.
21. John 3:5.
22. Philippians 2:12.
23. Bhagavad Gita 10–11.
24. Bhagavad Gita 7:54–55.
25. Surah 8:2.
26. Alfred Lord Tennyson, "In Memoriam A. H. H," available online at Poetry Foundation, http://www.poetryfoundation.org/poem/174603.

27. Archie J. Bahm, *Yoga Sutras of Patanjali* (Fremont, CA: Jain Publishing, 1993), "Illumination" Pada IV: 2–3.

GROWTH

1. Matthew 5.
2. John 3:8 (New International Version).
3. James B. Mozley, *Sermons Preached before the University of Oxford, and on Various Occasions* (Oxford: 1876), reprinted by Kessinger Press, 2010, 234–241.
4. Ibid.
5. There is a doctrinal argument based on the notion that "there is no free Grace." But so many passages in the Christian Bible and other spiritual traditions contradict this, that we must accept that Grace is given freely "where it listeth."
6. What's called the Lotus position was developed so that someone meditating without a chair or anything else supporting the body would be in the most stable position possible when no longer paying attention to the body. If you can do it without cutting off the circulation to the feet or ankles, feel free to use it.

LOVE: THE GREATEST THING IN THE WORLD

1. 1 Corinthians 13.
2. 1 Peter 4:8 (New International Version).
3. Romans 13:10.
4. This is a paraphrasing and synthesis of several of the quotations in the New Testament gospels.
5. Coleman Barks, trans., *The Essential Rumi* (New York: Harper, 1995).
6. Bhagavad Gita 12:52–54.
7. Carlos Castaneda, *The Teachings of Don Juan: A Yaqui Way of Knowledge* (New York: Ballantine, 1968).
8. 1 Corinthians 13:12.
9. Ralph Waldo Emerson, "Spiritual Laws," in *Natural Abundance: Ralph Waldo Emerson's Guide to Prosperity*, ed. Ruth L. Miller (New York: Beyond Words/Atria, 2011), 140.
10. In many translations of the New Testament, the word "charity" is used in place of the word "love." This is because the Latin word is *caritas*, which clearly looks most like charity but means something more like "heart-centered" or "heartfelt." In modern terms, then, love is much closer to his intent.

11. Robert Browning, "A Death in the Desert," available online at Poetry Foundation, http://www.poetryfoundation.org/poem/173008.
12. Apparently written by Joseph A. Torrey, a nineteenth-century British clergyman, and on the tomb of Edward Courtenay, Earl of Devonshire. See "The Literary Querist," in *The Book Buyer: A Summary of American and Foreign Literature*, XI, no. 1 (New York: Charles Scribner's Sons, 1894). Available online at Google Books.
13. 1 Corinthians 13:6 (New American Standard Bible).
14. H. Emilie Cady, *Lessons in Truth* (Lee's Summit, MO: Unity Press), various editions.
15. Coleman Barks, trans., *The Essential Rumi* (New York: Harper, 1995).
16. Emma Curtis Hopkins, *Scientific Christian Mental Practice*, lesson 1 (various editions). Also quoted in *Unveiling Your Hidden Power: Emma Curtis Hopkins' Metaphysics for the 21st Century* by Ruth L. Miller (Portland, OR: Wise Woman Press, 2006), 6.
17. Don Miguel Ruiz, *The Four Agreements: A Toltec Wisdom Book* (San Rafael, CA: Amber-Allen, 1984), 126.

Original Text
Abridged

Natural Law in the
Spiritual World
Published in 1883

The Greatest Thing
in the World*
Published in 1889

* Based on notes from a series of talks presented to students at the University of Edinburgh and to a graduating class of missionaries from the Moody Free Baptist seminary in Glascow. Drummond prepared this first of his "little books" as a sort of "Christmas Card" for publication in December 1889 (New York: James Pott, 1901). Available online at http://archive.org/stream/practicallifewor00lenn#page/116/mode /2up.

PREFACE

N o class of works is received with more suspicion, I had almost said derision, than those which deal with Science and Religion. Science is tired of reconciliations between two things which never should have been contrasted; Religion is offended by the patronage of an ally which it professes not to need; and the critics have rightly discovered that, in most cases where Science is either pitted against Religion or fused with it, there is some fatal misconception to begin with as to the scope and province of either. But although no initial protest, probably, will save this work from the unhappy reputation of its class, the thoughtful mind will perceive that the fact of its subject-matter being Law—a property peculiar neither to Science nor to Religion—at once places it on a somewhat different footing.

The real problem I have set myself may be stated in a sentence. Is there not reason to believe that many of the Laws of the Spiritual World, hitherto regarded as occupying an entirely separate province, are simply the Laws of the Natural World? Can we identify the Natural Laws, or any one of them, in the Spiritual sphere? That vague lines everywhere run through the Spiritual World is already beginning to be recognized. Is it possible to link them with those great lines running through the visible universe which we call the Natural Laws, or are they fundamentally distinct? In a word, Is the Supernatural natural or unnatural?

❢ ❢ ❢

It has been my privilege for some years to address regularly two very different audiences on two very different themes. On week days I've lectured to a class of students on the Natural Sciences, and on Sundays to an audience consisting for the most part of working men on subjects of a moral and religious character. I cannot say that this collocation ever appeared as a difficulty to myself, but to certain of my friends it was more than a problem. It was solved to me, however, at first, by what then seemed the necessities of the case—I must keep the two departments entirely by themselves. They lay at opposite poles of thought; and for a time I succeeded in keeping the Science and the Religion shut off from one another in two separate compartments of my mind. But gradually the wall of partition showed symptoms of giving way. The two fountains of knowledge also slowly began to overflow, and finally their waters met and mingled. The great change was in the compartment which held the Religion. . . . The subject-matter Religion had taken on the method of expression of Science, and I discovered myself enunciating Spiritual Law in the exact terms of Biology and Physics.

Now this was not simply a scientific coloring given to Religion, the mere freshening of the theological air with natural facts and illustrations. It was an entire re-casting of truth. And when I came seriously to consider what it involved, I saw, or seemed to see, that it meant essentially the introduction of Natural Law into the Spiritual World.

❢ ❢ ❢

To the objection that even a basis in Law is no warrant for so great a trespass as the intrusion into another field of thought of the principles of Natural Science. I would reply that in this I find that I am following a lead which in other departments has not only been allowed but has achieved results as rich as they were unexpected. What is the Physical Politic of Walter Bagehot but the extension of Natural Law to the Political World? What is the Biological Sociology of Herbert Spencer but the application of Natural Law to the Social World? Will it be charged that the splendid achievements of such thinkers are hybrids between things which Nature has meant to remain apart? Nature usually solves such problems for herself. Inappropriate hybridism is checked by the Law of Sterility. Judged by this great Law, these modern developments of our knowledge stand uncondemned. Within their own sphere the results of Mr. Herbert Spencer are far from sterile—the application of Biology to Political Economy is already revolutionizing the Science. If the introduction of Natural Law into the Social sphere is no violent contradiction, but a genuine and permanent contribution, shall its further extension to the Spiritual sphere be counted an extravagance? Does the principle of Continuity demand its application in every direction?

*   *   *

When I began to follow out these lines, I had no idea where they would lead me. I was prepared, nevertheless, at least for the time, to be loyal to the method throughout, and share with Nature whatever consequences might ensue. But in almost every case, after stating what appeared to be the truth in words gathered directly from the lips of Nature, I was sooner or later startled by a certain similarity in the general idea to something I had heard before, and this often developed, and when I was least expecting it, into recognition of some familiar article of faith. I was not watching for this result. I did not begin by tabulating the doctrines, as I did the Laws of Nature, and then proceed with the attempt to pair them. The majority of them seemed at first too far removed from the natural world even to suggest this. Still less did I begin with doctrines and work downwards to find their relations in the natural sphere. It was the opposite process entirely. I ran up the Natural Law as far as it would go, and the appropriate doctrine seldom even loomed in sight till I had reached the top. Then it burst into view in a single moment.

I can scarcely now say whether in those moments I was more overcome with thankfulness that Nature was so like Revelation, or more filled with wonder that Revelation was so like Nature. Nature, it is true, is a part of Revelation—a much greater part doubtless than is yet believed—and one could have anticipated nothing but harmony here. But that a derived Theology, in spite of the venerable verbiage which has gathered round it, should be at bottom and in all cardinal respects so faithful a transcript of "the truth as it is in Nature" came as a surprise, and to me at least as a rebuke.

❦ ❦ ❦

It is recognized by all that the younger and abler minds of this age find the most serious difficulty in accepting or retaining the ordinary forms of belief. Especially is this true of those whose culture is scientified. And the reason is palpable. No man can study modern Science without a change coming over his view of truth. What impresses him about Nature is its solidity. He is standing there upon actual things, among fixed laws. And the integrity of the scientific method so seizes him that all other forms of truth begin to appear comparatively unstable. He did not know before that any form of truth could so hold him; and the immediate effect is to lessen his interest in all that stands on other bases. This he feels in spite of himself; he struggles against it in vain; and he finds perhaps to his alarm that he is drifting fast into what looks at first like pure Positivism. This is an inevitable result of the scientific training. It is quite erroneous to suppose that science ever overthrows Faith, if by that is implied that any natural truth can oppose successfully any single spiritual truth. Science cannot overthrow Faith; but it shakes it. Its own doctrines, grounded in Nature, are so certain, that the truths of Religion, resting for most men on Authority, are felt to be strangely insecure. The difficulty, therefore, which men of Science feel about Religion is real and inevitable, and in so far as Doubt is a tribute to the inviolability of Nature it is entitled to respect.

None but those who have passed through it can appreciate the radical nature of the change wrought by Science in the whole mental attitude of its disciples. What they really cry out for in Religion is a new standpoint—a standpoint like their own. The one hope, therefore, for Science is more Science. Again, to quote Bacon—we shall hear enough from the moderns by-and-by—

> This I dare affirm in knowledge of Nature, that a little natural philosophy, and the first entrance into it, doth dispose the opinion to atheism; but, on the other side, much natural philosophy, and wading deep into it, will bring about men's minds to religion.[2]

٤ ٤ ٤

Men must oppose with every energy they possess what seems to them to oppose the eternal course of things. And the first step in their deliverance must not be to "reconcile" Nature and Religion, but to exhibit Nature in Religion. Even to convince them that there is no controversy between Religion and Science is insufficient. A mere flag of truce, in the nature of the case, is here impossible; at least, it is only possible so long as neither party is sincere. No man who knows the splendor of scientific achievement or cares for it, no man who feels the solidity of its method or works with it, can remain neutral with regard to Religion. He must either extend his method into it, or, if that is impossible, oppose it to the knife. On the other hand, no one who knows the content of Christianity, or feels the universal need of a Religion, can stand idly by while the intellect of his age is slowly divorcing itself from it. What is required, therefore, to draw Science and Religion together again—for they began the centuries hand in hand—is the disclosure of the naturalness of the supernatural. Then, and not till then, will men see how true it is, that to be loyal to all of Nature, they must be loyal to the part defined as Spiritual. . . . And even as the contribution of Science to Religion is the vindication of the naturalness of the Supernatural, so the gift of Religion to Science is the demonstration of the supernaturalness of the Natural. Thus, as the Supernatural becomes slowly Natural, will also the Natural become slowly Supernatural.

I

INTRODUCTION—
PART I: A NEW SCIENCE

*By Science I understand all knowledge which rests upon evidence and
reasoning of a like character to that which claims his assent to ordinary
scientific propositions; and if any one is able to make good the
assertion that his theology rests upon valid evidence and sound
reasoning, then it appears to me that such theology must
take its place as a part of science.*
Huxley, "Science and Culture"

Natural Law is a new word. It is the last and the most magnificent
discovery of science. No more telling proof is open to the modern world of the greatness of the idea than the greatness of the attempts
which have always been made to justify it. In the earlier centuries,
before the birth of science, Phenomena were studied alone. The world
then was a chaos, a collection of single, isolated, and independent facts.
Deeper thinkers saw, indeed, that relations must subsist between these
facts, but the Reign of Law was never more to the ancients than a far-
off vision. Their philosophies, conspicuously those of the Stoics and
Pythagoreans, heroically sought to marshal the discrete materials of the
universe into thinkable form, but from these artificial and fantastic systems nothing remains to us now but an ancient testimony to the
grandeur of that harmony which they failed to reach.

With Copernicus, Galileo, and Kepler, the first regular lines of the
universe began to be discerned. When Nature yielded to Newton her
great secret, Gravitation was felt to be not greater as a fact in itself than as
a revelation that Law was fact. And thenceforth the search for individual

Phenomena gave way before the larger study of their relations. The pursuit of Law became the passion of science.

What that discovery of Law has done for Nature, it is impossible to estimate. As a mere spectacle the universe to-day discloses a beauty so transcendent that he who disciplines himself by scientific work finds it an overwhelming reward simply to behold it. In these Laws one stands face to face with truth, solid and unchangeable. Each single Law is an instrument of scientific research, simple in its adjustments, universal in its applications, infallible in its results. And despite the limitations of its sphere on every side Law is still the largest, richest, and surest source of human knowledge.

It is not necessary for the present to more than lightly touch on definitions of Natural Law. The Duke of Argyll[3] indicates five senses in which the word is used, but we may content ourselves here by taking it in its most simple and obvious significance. The fundamental conception of Law is an ascertained working sequence or constant order among the Phenomena of Nature. This impression of Law as order it is important to receive in its simplicity, for the idea is often corrupted by having attached to it erroneous views of cause and effect. In its true sense Natural Law predicates nothing of causes. The Laws of Nature are simply statements of the orderly condition of things in Nature, what is found in Nature by a sufficient number of competent observers. What these Laws are in themselves is not agreed. That they have any absolute existence even is far from certain. They are relative to man in his many limitations, and represent for him the constant expression of what he may always expect to find in the world around him. But that they have any causal connection with the things around him is not to be conceived. The Natural Laws originate nothing, sustain nothing; they are merely responsible for uniformity in sustaining what has been originated and what is being sustained. They are modes of operation, therefore, not operators; processes, not powers. The Law of Gravitation, for instance, speaks to science only of process. It has no light to offer as to itself. Newton did not discover Gravity—that is not discovered yet. He discovered its Law, which is Gravitation, but tells us nothing of its origin, of its nature, or of its cause.

The Natural Laws then are great lines running not only through the world, but, as we now know, through the universe, reducing it like parallels of latitude to intelligent order.

❧ ❧ ❧

Since Plato enunciated his doctrine of the Cave or of the twice-divided line; since Christ spake in parables; since Plotinus wrote of the world as an imaged image; since the mysticism of Swedenborg; since Bacon and Pascal; since "Sartor Resartus" and "In Memoriam," it has been all but a commonplace with thinkers that "the invisible things of God from the creation of the world are clearly seen, being understood by the things that are made." Milton's question—

What if earth
Be but the shadow of heaven, and things therein
Each to other like more than on earth is thought?

is now superfluous. "In our doctrine of representations and correspondences," says Swedenborg, "we shall treat of both these symbolical and typical resemblances, and of the astonishing things that occur, I will not say in the living body only, but throughout Nature, and which correspond so entirely to supreme and spiritual things, that one would swear that the physical world was purely symbolical of the spiritual world."[4] And Carlyle: "All visible things are emblems. What thou seest is not there on its own account; strictly speaking is not there at all. Matter exists only spiritually, and to represent some idea and body it forth."[5]

But the analogies of Law are a totally different thing from the analogies of Phenomena and have a very different value. To say generally, with Pascal, that "La nature est une image de la grace," is merely to be poetical. The function of Hervey's "Meditations in a Flower Garden," or Flavel's "Husbandry Spiritualized," is mainly homiletical. That such works have an interest is not to be denied. The place of parable in teaching, and especially after the sanction of the greatest of

Teachers, must always be recognized. The very necessities of language indeed demand this method of presenting truth. The temporal is the husk and framework of the eternal, and thoughts can be uttered only through things.[6]

But analogies between Phenomena bear the same relation to analogies of Law that Phenomena themselves bear to Law. The light of Law on truth, as we have seen, is an immense advance upon the light of Phenomena. The discovery of Law is simply the discovery of Science. And if the analogies of Natural Law can be extended to the Spiritual World, that whole region at once falls within the domain of science and secures a basis as well as an illumination in the constitution and course of Nature.

❝ ❝ ❝

The position we have been led to take up is not that the Spiritual Laws are analogous to the Natural Laws, but that *they are the same Laws*. It is not a question of analogy but of *Identity*. The Natural Laws are not the shadows or images of the Spiritual in the same sense as autumn is emblematical of Decay, or the falling leaf of Death. The Natural Laws, as the Law of Continuity might well warn us, do not stop with the visible and then give place to a new set of Laws bearing a strong similitude to them. The Laws of the invisible are the same Laws, projections of the natural not supernatural. Analogous Phenomena are not the fruit of parallel Laws, but of the same Laws—Laws which at one end, as it were, may be dealing with Matter, at the other end with Spirit.

❝ ❝ ❝

What if Religion be yet brought within the sphere of Law? Law is the revelation of time. One by one slowly through the centuries the Sciences have crystallized into geometrical form, each form not only perfect in itself, but perfect in its relation to all other forms. Many forms had to be perfected before the form of the Spiritual. The Inorganic has to be worked out before the Organic, the Natural before the Spiritual. Theology at present has merely an ancient and provisional philosophic form. By-and-by it will be seen whether it be not susceptible of another. For Theology must pass through the necessary stages of progress, like any other science. The method of science-making is now fully established. In almost all cases the natural history and development are the same. Take, for example, the case of Geology. A century ago there was none. Science went out to look for it, and brought back a Geology which, if Nature were a harmony, had falsehood written almost on its face. It was the Geology of Catastrophism, a Geology so out of line with Nature as revealed by the other sciences, that on *à priori* grounds a thoughtful mind might have been justified in dismissing it as a final form of any science. And its fallacy was soon and thoroughly exposed. The advent of modified uniformitarian principles all but banished the word catastrophe from science, and marked the birth of Geology as we know it now. Geology, that is to say, had fallen at last into the great scheme of Law.

● ● ●

The Botany of Linnæus, a purely artificial system, was a splendid contribution to human knowledge, and did more in its day to enlarge the view of the vegetable kingdom than all that had gone before. But all artificial systems must pass away. None knew better than the great Swedish naturalist himself that his system, being artificial, was but provisional. Nature must be read in its own light. And as the botanical field became more luminous, the system of Jussieu and De Candolle slowly emerged as a native growth, unfolded itself as naturally as the petals of one of its own flowers, and forcing itself upon men's intelligence as the very voice of Nature, banished the Linnæan system for ever. It were unjust to say that the present Theology is as artificial as the system of Linnæus; in many particulars it wants but a fresh expression to make it in the most modern sense scientific. But if it has a basis in the constitution and course of Nature, that basis has never been adequately shown.

It has depended on Authority rather than on Law; and a new basis must be sought and found if it is to be presented to those with whom Law alone is Authority.

It is not of course to be inferred that the scientific method will ever abolish the radical distinctions of the Spiritual World. True science proposes to itself no such general leveling in any department. Within the unity of the whole there must always be room for the characteristic differences of the parts, and those tendencies of thought at the present time which ignore such distinctions, in their zeal for simplicity really create confusion.

❦ ❦ ❦

The perfection of unity is attained where there is infinite variety of phenomena, infinite complexity of relation, but great simplicity of Law. Science will be complete when all known phenomena can be arranged in one vast circle in which a few well known Laws shall form the radii—these radii at once separating and uniting, separating into particular groups, yet uniting all to a common center. To show that the radii for some of the most characteristic phenomena of the Spiritual World are already drawn within that circle by science is the main object of the papers which follow.

II

INTRODUCTION—
PART II: ONE LAW

---

*Matter is (though it may seem paradoxical to say so) the less
important half of the material of the physical universe.*[19]

The Law of Continuity furnishes an *à priori* argument for the position we are attempting to establish . . . It is altogether unlikely that
man spiritual should be violently separated in all the conditions of
growth, development, and life, from man physical. It is indeed difficult
to conceive that one set of principles should guide the natural life, and
these at a certain period—the very point where they are needed—
suddenly give place to another set of principles altogether new and
unrelated. Nature has never taught us to expect such a catastrophe. She
has nowhere prepared us for it. And Man cannot in the nature of things,
in the nature of thought, in the nature of language, be separated into
two such incoherent halves.

The spiritual man, it is true, is to be studied in a different department of science from the natural man. But the harmony established by
science is not a harmony within specific departments. It is the universe
that is the harmony, the universe of which these are but parts. And the
harmonies of the parts depend for all their weight and interest on
the harmony of the whole. While, therefore, there are many harmonies,
there is but one harmony. The breaking up of the phenomena of the
universe into carefully guarded groups, and the allocation of certain
prominent Laws to each, it must never be forgotten, and however much
Nature lends herself to it, are artificial. We find an evolution in Botany,

157

another in Geology, and another in Astronomy, and the effect is to lead one insensibly to look upon these as three distinct evolutions. But these sciences, of course, are mere departments created by ourselves to facilitate knowledge—reductions of Nature to the scale of our own intelligence. And we must beware of breaking up Nature except for this purpose. Science has so dissected everything, that it becomes a mental difficulty to put the puzzle together again; and we must keep ourselves in practice by constantly thinking of Nature as a whole, if science is not to be spoiled by its own refinements. Evolution being found in so many different sciences, the likelihood is that it is a universal principle. And there is no presumption whatever against this Law and many others being excluded from the domain of the spiritual life. On the other hand, there are very convincing reasons why the Natural Laws should be continuous through the Spiritual Sphere—not changed in any way to meet the new circumstances, but continuous as they stand.

❧ ❧ ❧

Probably the most satisfactory way to secure for oneself a just appreciation of the Principle of Continuity is to try to conceive the universe without it. The opposite of a continuous universe would be a discontinuous universe, an incoherent and irrelevant universe—as irrelevant in all its ways of doing things as an irrelevant person. In effect, to withdraw Continuity from the universe would be the same as to withdraw reason from an individual. The universe would run deranged; the world would be a mad world.

There used to be a children's book which bore the fascinating title of *The Chance World*. It described a world in which everything happened by chance. The sun might rise or it might not; or it might appear at any hour, or the moon might come up instead. When children were born they might have one head or a dozen heads, and those heads might not be on their shoulders—there might be no shoulders—but arranged about the limbs. If one jumped up in the air it was impossible to predict whether he would ever come down again. That he came down yesterday was no guarantee that he would do it next time. For every day antecedent and consequent varied, and gravitation and everything else changed from hour to hour. Today a child's body might be so light that it was impossible for it to descend from its chair to the floor; but to-morrow, in attempting the experiment again, the impetus might drive it through a three-story house and dash it to pieces somewhere near the center of the earth. In this chance world cause and effect were abolished. Law was annihilated. And the result to the inhabitants of such a world could only be that reason would be impossible. It would be a lunatic world with a population of lunatics.

Now this is no more than a real picture of what the world would be without Law, or the universe without Continuity. And hence we come in sight of the necessity of some principle of Law according to which Laws shall be, and be "continuous" throughout the system.

$$\text{\textbf{(((}}$$

The most striking examples of the continuousness of Law are perhaps those furnished by Astronomy, especially in connection with the more recent applications of spectrum analysis. But even in the case of the simpler Laws the demonstration is complete. There is no reason apart from Continuity to expect that gravitation for instance should prevail outside our world. But wherever matter has been detected throughout the entire universe, whether in the form of star or planet, comet or meteorite, it is found to obey that Law. "If there were no other indica-tion of unity than this, it would be almost enough. For the unity which is implied in the mechanism of the heavens is indeed a unity which is all-embracing and complete. The structure of our own bodies, with all that depends upon it, is a structure governed by, and therefore adapted to, the same force of gravitation which has determined the form and the movements of myriads of worlds. Every part of the human organism is fitted to conditions which would all be destroyed in a moment if the forces of gravitation were to change or fail."[24]

❛ ❛ ❛

It may seem an obvious objection that many of the Natural Laws have no connection whatever with the Spiritual World, and as a matter of fact are not continued through it. Gravitation for instance—what direct application has that in the Spiritual World? The reply is threefold. First, there is no proof that it does not hold there. If the spirit be in any sense material it certainly must hold. In the second place, gravitation may hold for the Spiritual Sphere although it cannot be directly proved. The spirit may be armed with powers which enable it to rise superior to gravity. During the action of these powers gravity need be no more suspended than in the case of a plant which rises in the air during the process of growth. It does this in virtue of a higher Law and in apparent defiance of the lower. Thirdly, if the spiritual be not material it still cannot be said that gravitation ceases at that point to be continuous. It is not gravitation that ceases—it is matter.

This point, however, will require development for another reason. In the case of the plant just referred to, there is a principle of growth or vitality at work superseding the attraction of gravity. Why is there no trace of that Law in the Inorganic world? Is not this another instance of the discontinuousness of Law? If the Law of vitality has so little connection with the Inorganic kingdom—less even than gravitation with the Spiritual, what becomes of Continuity? Is it not evident that each kingdom of Nature has its own set of Laws which continue possibly untouched for the specific kingdom but never extend beyond it?

It is quite true that when we pass from the Inorganic to the Organic, we come upon a new set of Laws. But the reason why the lower set do not seem to act in the higher sphere is not that they are annihilated, but that they are overruled. And the reason why the higher Laws are not found operating in the lower is not because they are not continuous downward, but because there is nothing for them there to act upon. It is not Law that fails, but opportunity. The biological Laws are continuous for life. Wherever there is life, that is to say, they will be found acting, just as gravitation acts wherever there is matter.

We have purposely, in the last paragraph, indulged in a fallacy. We have said that the biological Laws would certainly be continuous in the lower or mineral sphere were there anything there for them to act upon. Now Laws do not act upon anything. It has been stated already, although apparently it cannot be too abundantly emphasized, that Laws are only modes of operation, not themselves operators. The accurate statement, therefore, would be that the biological Laws would be continuous in the lower sphere were there anything there for them, not to act upon, but to keep in order. If there is no acting going on, if there is nothing being kept in order, the responsibility does not lie with Continuity. The Law will always be at its post, not only when its services are required, but wherever they are possible.

$$\textbf{\textit{❢ ❢ ❢}}$$

The *life* with which it deals in the Natural World does not enter at all into the Spiritual World, and therefore, it might be argued, the Law of Biogenesis cannot be capable of extension into it. The Law of Continuity seems to be snapped at the point where the natural passes into the spiritual. The vital principle of the body is a different thing from the vital principle of the spiritual life. Biogenesis deals with βιος, with the natural life, with cells and germs, and as there are no exactly similar cells and germs in the Spiritual World, the Law cannot therefore apply. All which is as true as if one were to say that the fifth proposition of the First Book of Euclid applies when the figures are drawn with chalk upon a blackboard, but fails with regard to structures of wood or stone.

The proposition is continuous for the whole world, and, doubtless, likewise for the sun and moon and stars. The same universality may be predicated likewise for the Law of life. Wherever there is life we may expect to find it arranged, ordered, governed according to the same Law. At the beginning of the natural life we find the Law that natural life can only come from pre-existing natural life; and at the beginning of the spiritual life we find that the spiritual life can only come from preëxisting spiritual life. But there are not two Laws; there is one—

Biogenesis. At one end the Law is dealing with matter, at the other with spirit. The qualitative terms natural and spiritual make no difference. Biogenesis is the Law for all life and for all kinds of life, and the particular substance with which it is associated is as indifferent to Biogenesis as it is to Gravitation. Gravitation will act whether the substance be suns and stars, or grains of sand, or raindrops. Biogenesis, in like manner, will act wherever there is life. The conclusion finally is, that from the nature of Law in general, and from the scope of the Principle of Continuity in particular, the Laws of the natural life must be those of the spiritual life.

This does not exclude, observe, the possibility of there being new Laws in addition within the Spiritual Sphere; nor does it even include the supposition that the old Laws will be the conspicuous Laws of the Spiritual World, both which points will be dealt with presently. It simply asserts that whatever else may be found, these must be found there; that they must be there though they may not be seen there; and that they must project beyond there if there be anything beyond there. If the Law of Continuity is true, the only way to escape the conclusion that the Laws of the natural life are the Laws, or at least are Laws, of the spiritual life, is to say that there is no spiritual life. It is really easier to give up the phenomena than to give up the Law.

❢ ❢ ❢

The argument might then be advanced that since, in Nature generally, we come upon new Laws as we pass from lower to higher kingdoms, the old still remaining in force, the newer Laws which one would expect to meet in the Spiritual World would so transcend and overwhelm the older as to make the analogy or identity, even if traced, of no practical use. The new Laws would represent operations and energies so different, and so much more elevated, that they would afford the true keys to the Spiritual World. As Gravitation is practically lost sight of when we pass into the domain of life, so Biogenesis would be lost sight of as we enter the Spiritual Sphere.

❢ ❢ ❢

What we lose sight of, to a certain extent, is the natural βιος. In the Spiritual World that is not the conspicuous thing, and it is obscure there just as gravity becomes obscure in the Organic, because something higher, more potent, more characteristic of the higher plane, comes in. That there are higher energies, so to speak, in the Spiritual World is, of course, to be affirmed alike on the ground of analogy and of experience; but it does not follow that these necessitate other Laws. A Law has nothing to do with potency. We may lose sight of a substance, or of an energy, but it is an abuse of language to talk of losing sight of Laws.

❢ ❢ ❢

With regard to the supposed new Laws of the Spiritual World—those Laws, that is, which are found for the first time in the Spiritual World, and have no analogies lower down—there is this to be said, that there is one strong reason against exaggerating either their number or importance—their importance at least for our immediate needs. The connection between language and the Law of Continuity has been referred to incidentally already. It is clear that we can only express the Spiritual Laws in language borrowed from the visible universe. Being dependent for our vocabulary on images, if an altogether new and foreign set of Laws existed in the Spiritual World, they could never take shape as definite ideas from mere want of words. The hypothetical new Laws which may remain to be discovered in the domain of Natural or Mental Science may afford some index of these hypothetical higher Laws, but this would of course mean that the latter were no longer foreign but in analogy, or, likelier still, identical. If, on the other hand, the Natural Laws of the future have nothing to say of these higher Laws, what can be said of them? Where is the language to come from in which to frame them? If their disclosure could be of any practical use to us, we may be sure the clue to them, the revelation of them, in some way would have been put into Nature.

❦ ❦ ❦

The Natural Laws as at present known, whatever additions may yet be made to them, give a fair rendering of the facts of Nature. And their analogies or their projections in the Spiritual sphere may also be said to offer a fair account of that sphere, or of one or two conspicuous departments of it. The time has come for that account to be given. The greatest among the theological Laws are the Laws of Nature in disguise. It will be the splendid task of the theology of the future to take off the mask and disclose to a waning skepticism the naturalness of the supernatural.

❦ ❦ ❦

There is nothing so especially exalted therefore in the Natural Laws in themselves as to make one anxious to find them blood relations of the Spiritual. It is not only because these Laws are on the ground, more accessible therefore to us who are but groundlings; not only, as the "Unseen Universe" points out in another connection, "because they are at the bottom of the list—are in fact the simplest and lowest—that they are capable of being most readily grasped by the finite intelligences of the universe."[26] But their true significance lies in the fact that they are on the list at all, and especially in that the list is the same list. Their dignity is not as Natural Laws, but as Spiritual Laws, Laws which, as already said, at one end are dealing with Matter, and at the other with Spirit. "The physical properties of matter form the alphabet which is put into our hands by God, the study of which, if properly conducted, will enable us more perfectly to read that great book which we call the 'Universe.'"[27] But, over and above this, the Natural Laws will enable us to read that great duplicate which we call the "Unseen Universe," and to think and live in fuller harmony with it. After all, the true greatness of Law lies in its vision of the Unseen. Law in the visible is the Invisible in the visible. And to speak of Laws as Natural is to define them in their application to a part of the universe, the sense-part, whereas a wider survey would lead us to regard all Law as essentially

Spiritual. To magnify the Laws of Nature, as Laws of this small world of ours, is to take a provincial view of the universe. Law is great not because the phenomenal world is great, but because these vanishing lines are the avenues into the eternal Order.

❧ ❧ ❧

The lines of the Spiritual existed first, and it was . . . the Natural World would become an incarnation, a visible representation, a working model of the spiritual. The whole function of the material world lies here. The world is only a thing that . . . teaches, yet not even a thing—a show that shows, a teaching shadow. However useless the demonstration otherwise, philosophy does well in proving that matter is a non-entity. We work with it as the mathematician with an x. The reality is alone the Spiritual. "It is very well for physicists to speak of 'matter,' but for men generally to call this 'a material world' is an absurdity. Should we call it an x-world it would mean as much, viz., that we do not know what it is."[31]

III

BIOGENESIS

I am thus of opinion that a standing miracle exists,
and that it has ever existed—a direct and continued influence
exerted by the supernatural on the natural.
Paradoxical Philosophy

"Omne vivum ex vivo."
Harvey

For two hundred years the scientific world has been rent with discussions upon the Origin of Life. Two great schools defended exactly opposite views—one that matter can spontaneously generate life, the other that life can only come from pre-existing life. The doctrine of Spontaneous Generation, as the first is called, was held most publically by Dr. Bastian, after a series of elaborate experiments on the Beginnings of Life. Stated in his own words, his conclusion is this: "Both observation and experiment unmistakably testify to the fact that living matter is constantly being formed *de novo*, in obedience to the same laws and tendencies which determine all the more simple chemical combinations."[33] Life, that is to say, is not the Gift of Life. It is capable of springing into being of itself. It can be Spontaneously Generated.

This announcement called into the field a phalanx of observers, and the highest authorities in biological science engaged themselves afresh upon the problem. The experiments necessary to test the matter can be followed or repeated by any one possessing the slightest manipulative skill. Glass vessels are three-parts filled with infusions of hay or any organic matter. They are boiled to kill all germs of life, and hermetically sealed to exclude the outer air. The air inside, having been exposed to the boiling temperature for many hours, is supposed to be likewise dead; so that any life which may subsequently appear in the closed flasks must have sprung into being of itself. In Bastian's experiments, after every expedient to secure sterility, life did appear inside in myriad quantity. Therefore, he argued, it was spontaneously generated.

But the phalanx of observers found two errors in this calculation. Professor Tyndall repeated the same experiment. . . . After every care he conceived there might still be undestroyed germs in the air inside the flasks. If the air were absolutely germless and pure, would the myriad life appear? He manipulated his experimental vessels in an atmosphere which under the high test of optical purity—the most delicate known test—was absolutely germless. Here not a vestige of life appeared. He varied the experiment in every direction, but matter in the germless air never yielded life.

The other error was detected by Mr. Dallinger. He found among the lower forms of life the most surprising and indestructible vitality. Many animals could survive much higher temperatures than Dr. Bastian had applied to annihilate them. Some germs almost refused to be annihilated—they were all but fire-proof!

These experiments have practically closed the question. A decided and authoritative conclusion has now taken its place in science. So far as science can settle anything, this question is settled. The attempt to get the living out of the dead has failed. Spontaneous Generation has had to be given up. And it is now recognized on every hand that Life can only come from the touch of Life.

For much more than two hundred years a similar discussion has dragged its length through the religious world. Two great schools here also have defended exactly opposite views—one that the Spiritual Life in man can only come from pre-existing Life, the other that it can Spontaneously Generate itself. . . . One small school, in the face of derision and opposition, has persistently maintained the doctrine of Biogenesis. Another, larger and with greater pretension to philosophic form, has defended Spontaneous Generation. The weakness of the former school consists—though this has been much exaggerated—in its more or less general adherence to the extreme view that religion has nothing to do with the natural life; the weakness of the latter lay in yielding to the more fatal extreme that it had nothing to do with anything else. That man, being a worshiping animal by nature, ought to maintain certain relations to the Supreme Being, was indeed to some extent conceded by the naturalistic school, but religion itself was looked upon as a thing to be spontaneously generated by the evolution of character in the laboratory of common life.

The difference between the two positions is radical. Translating from the language of Science into that of Religion, the spiritual theory of Spontaneous Generation is simply that a man can become gradually better and better until in course of the process he reaches that quantity of religious nature known as Spiritual Life. This Life is not something added *ab extra* to natural man; it is the normal and appropriate development of the natural man. Biogenesis opposes to this the whole doctrine of Regeneration. The Spiritual Life is the gift of the Living Spirit. The spiritual man is no mere development of the natural man. He is a New Creation born from Above. As well expect a hay infusion to become gradually more and more living until in course of the process it reached Vitality, as expect a man by becoming better and better to attain the Eternal Life.

The advocates of Biogenesis in Religion have founded their argument hitherto all but exclusively on Scripture. The relation of the doctrine to the constitution and course of Nature was not disclosed. Its importance, therefore, was solely as a dogma; and being directly concerned with the Supernatural, it was valid for those alone who chose to accept the Supernatural. . . . They have nothing more to oppose to the rationalistic view than the *ipse dixit* of Revelation. The argument from experience, in the nature of the case, is seldom easy to apply, and Christianity has always found at this point a genuine difficulty in meeting the challenge of Natural Religions. The direct authority of Nature, using Nature in its limited sense, was not here to be sought for. On such a question its voice was necessarily silent, and all that the apologist could look for lower down was a distant echo of analogy. All that is really possible, indeed, is an analogy; and if that can now be found in Biogenesis, Christianity in its most central position secures at length a support and basis in the Laws of Nature.

Up to the present time the analogy required has not been forth-coming. There was no known parallel in Nature for the spiritual phenomena in question. But now the case is altered. With the elevation of Biogenesis to the rank of a scientific fact, all problems concerning the Origin of Life are placed on a different footing. And it remains to be seen whether Religion cannot at once re-affirm and re-shape its argument in the light of this modern truth.

If the doctrine of the Spontaneous Generation of Spiritual Life can be met on scientific grounds, it will mean the removal of the most serious enemy Christianity has to deal with, and especially within its own borders, at the present day. The religion of Jesus has probably always suf-fered more from those who have misunderstood than from those who have opposed it. Of the multitudes who confess Christianity at this hour how many have clear in their minds the cardinal distinction established by its Founder between "born of the flesh" and "born of the Spirit"? By how many teachers of Christianity even is not this fundamental postulate persistently ignored? A thousand modern pulpits every seventh day are preaching the doctrine of Spontaneous Generation. The finest and best of recent poetry is colored with this same error. Spontaneous Generation is the leading theology of the modern religious or irreligious novel; and much of the most serious and cultured writing of the day devotes itself to earnest preaching of this impossible gospel. The current conception of the Christian religion in short—the conception which is held not only popularly but by men of culture—is founded upon a view of its origin which, if it were true, would render the whole scheme abortive.

Let us first place vividly in our imagination the picture of the two great Kingdoms of Nature, the inorganic and organic, as these now stand in the light of the Law of Biogenesis. What essentially is involved in saying that there is no Spontaneous Generation of Life? It is meant that the passage from the mineral world to the plant or animal world is hermetically sealed on the mineral side. This inorganic world is staked off from the living world by barriers which have never yet been crossed from within. No change of substance, no modification of environment, no chemistry, no electricity, nor any form of energy, nor any evolution can endow any single atom of the mineral world with the attribute of Life. Only by the bending down into this dead world of some living form can these dead atoms be gifted with the properties of vitality, without this preliminary contact with Life they remain fixed in the inorganic sphere for ever. It is a very mysterious Law which guards in this way the portals of the living world. And if there is one thing in Nature more worth pondering for its strangeness it is the spectacle of this vast helpless world of the dead cut off from the living by the Law of Biogenesis and denied for ever the possibility of resurrection within itself. So very strange a thing, indeed, is this broad line in Nature, that Science has long and urgently sought to obliterate it. Biogenesis stands in the way of some forms of Evolution with such stern persistency that the assaults upon this Law for number and thoroughness have been unparalleled. But, as we have seen, it has stood the test. Nature, to the modern eye, stands broken in two. The physical Laws may explain the inorganic world; the biological Laws may account for the development of the organic. But of the point where they meet, of that strange borderland between the dead and the living, Science is silent. It is as if God had placed everything in earth and heaven in the hands of Nature, but reserved a point at the genesis of Life for His direct appearing.

The power of the analogy, for which we are laying the foundations, to seize and impress the mind, will largely depend on the vividness with which one realizes the gulf which Nature places between the living and the dead.[36] But those who, in contemplating Nature, have found their attention arrested by this extraordinary dividing-line severing the visible universe eternally into two; those who in watching the progress of science have seen barrier after barrier disappear—barrier between plant and plant, between animal and animal, and even between animal and plant—but this gulf yawn more hopelessly wide with every advance of knowledge, will be prepared to attach a significance to the Law of Biogenesis and its analogies more profound perhaps than to any other fact or law in Nature. If, as Pascal says, Nature is an image of grace; if the things that are seen are in any sense the images of the unseen, there must lie in this great gulf fixed, this most unique and startling of all natural phenomena, a meaning of peculiar moment.

Where now in the Spiritual spheres shall we meet a companion phenomena to this? What in the Unseen shall be likened to this deep dividing-line, or where in human experience is another barrier which never can be crossed?

There is such a barrier. In the dim but not inadequate vision of the Spiritual World presented in the Word of God, the first thing that strikes the eye is a great gulf fixed. The passage from the Natural World to the Spiritual World is hermetically sealed on the natural side. The door from the inorganic to the organic is shut, no mineral can open it; so the door from the natural to the spiritual is shut, and no man can open it. This world of natural men is staked off from the Spiritual World by barriers which have never yet been crossed from within. No organic change, no modification of environment, no mental energy, no moral effort, no evolution of character, no progress of civilization can endow any single human soul with the attribute of Spiritual Life. The Spiritual World is guarded from the world next in order beneath it by a law of Biogenesis—*except a man be born again ... except a man be born of water and of the Spirit, he cannot enter the Kingdom of God.*

❛ ❛ ❛

It is not said, in this enunciation of the law, that if the condition be not fulfilled the natural man *will not* enter the Kingdom of God. The word is *cannot*. For the exclusion of the spiritually inorganic from the Kingdom of the spiritually organic is not arbitrary. Nor is the natural man refused admission on unexplained grounds. His admission is a scientific impossibility. Except a mineral be born "from above"—from the Kingdom just *above* it—it cannot enter the Kingdom just above it. And except a man be born "from above," by the same law, he cannot enter the Kingdom just above us. There being no passage from one Kingdom to another, whether from inorganic to organic, or from organic to spiritual, the intervention of Life is a scientific necessity if a stone or a plant or an animal or a man is to pass from a lower to a higher sphere. The plant stretches down to the dead world beneath it, touches its minerals and gases with its mystery of Life, and brings them up ennobled and transformed to the living sphere. The breath of God, blowing where it listeth, touches with its mystery of Life the dead souls of men, bears them across the bridgeless gulf between the natural and the spiritual, between the spiritually inorganic and the spiritually organic, endows them with its own high qualities, and develops within them these new and secret faculties, by which those who are born again are said to *see the Kingdom of God.*

What is the evidence for this great gulf fixed at the portals of the Spiritual World? Does Science close this gate, or Reason, or Experience, or Revelation? We reply, all four. The initial statement, it is not to be denied, reaches us from Revelation. But is not this evidence here in court? Or shall it be said that any argument deduced from this is a transparent circle—that after all we simply come back to the unsubstantiality of the *ipse dixit*? Not altogether, for the analogy lends an altogether new authority to the *ipse dixit.* How substantial that argument really is, is seldom realized. We yield the point here much too easily. The right of the Spiritual World to speak of its own phenomena is as secure as the right of the Natural World to speak of itself. What is Science but what the Natural World has said to natural men? What is Revelation but what the Spiritual World has said to Spiritual men? Let us at least ask what Revelation has announced with reference to this Spiritual Law of Biogenesis; afterward we shall inquire whether Science, while indorsing the verdict, may not also have some further vindication of its title to be heard.

The words of Scripture which preface this inquiry contain an explicit and original statement of the Law of Biogenesis for the Spiritual Life. "He that hath the Son hath Life, and he that hath not the Son of God hath not Life." Life, that is to say, depends upon contact with Life. It cannot spring up of itself. It cannot develop out of anything that is not Life. There is no Spontaneous Generation in religion any more than in Nature. Christ is the source of Life in the Spiritual World; and he that hath the Son hath Life, and he that hath not the Son, whatever else he may have, hath not Life. Here, in short, is the categorical denial of Abiogenesis and the establishment in this high field of the classical formula *Omne vivum ex vivo*—no Life without antecedent Life. In this mystical theory of the Origin of Life the whole of the New Testament writers are agreed. And, as we have already seen, Christ Himself founds Christianity upon Biogenesis stated in its most literal form. "Except a man be born of water and of the Spirit he cannot enter into the Kingdom of God. That which is born of the flesh is flesh; and that which is born of the Spirit is Spirit. Marvel not that I said unto you, ye must be born again."[37] Why did He add *Marvel not*? Did He seek to allay the fear in the bewildered ruler's mind that there was more in this novel doctrine than a simple analogy from the first to the second birth?

The attitude of the natural man, again, with reference to the Spiritual, is a subject on which the New Testament is equally pronounced. Not only in his relation to the spiritual man, but to the whole Spiritual World, the natural man is regarded as *dead*. He is as a crystal to an organism. The natural world is to the Spiritual as the inorganic to the organic. "To be carnally minded is *Death*."[38] "Thou hast a name to live, but art *Dead*."[39] "She that liveth in pleasure is *Dead* while she liveth."[40] "To you he Hath given Life which were *Dead* in trespasses and sins."[41]

It is clear that a remarkable harmony exists here between the Organic World as arranged by Science and the Spiritual World as arranged by Scripture. We find one great Law guarding the thresholds of both worlds, securing that entrance from a lower sphere shall only take place by a direct regenerating act, and that emanating from the world next in order above. There are not two laws of Biogenesis, one for the natural, the other for the Spiritual; one law is for both. Wherever there is Life, Life of any kind, this same law holds. The analogy, therefore, is only among the phenomena; between laws there is no analogy—there is Continuity. In either case, the first step in peopling these worlds with the appropriate living forms is virtually miracle. Nor in one case is there less of mystery in the act than in the other. The second birth is scarcely less perplexing to the theologian than the first to the embryologist.

A moment's reflection ought now to make it clear why in the Spiritual World there had to be added to this mystery the further mystery of its proclamation through the medium of Revelation. This is the point at which the scientific man is apt to part company with the theologian. He insists on having all things materialized before his eyes in Nature. If Nature cannot discuss this with him, there is nothing to discuss. But Nature can discuss this with him—only she cannot open the discussion or supply all the material to begin with. If Science averred that she could do this, the theologian this time must part company with such Science. For any Science which makes such a demand is false to the doctrines of Biogenesis. What is this but the demand that a lower world, hermetically sealed against all communication with a world above it, should have a mature and intelligent acquaintance with its phenomena and laws? Can the mineral discourse to me of animal Life? Can it tell me what lies beyond the narrow boundary of its inert being? Knowing nothing of other than the chemical and physical laws, what is its criticism worth of the principles of Biology? And even when some visitor from the upper world, for example some root from a living tree, penetrating its dark recess, honors it with a touch, will it presume to define the form and purpose of its patron, or until the bioplasm has done its gracious work can it even know that it is being touched? The barrier which separates Kingdoms from one another restricts mind not less than matter. Any information of the Kingdoms above it that could come to the mineral world could only come by a communication from above. An analogy from the lower world might make such communication intelligible as well as credible, but the information in the first instance must be vouchsafed as a *revelation*. Similarly if those in the Organic Kingdom are to know anything of the Spiritual World, that knowledge must at least begin as Revelation. Men who reject this source of information, by the Law of Biogenesis, can have no other. It is no spell of ignorance arbitrarily laid upon certain members of the Organic Kingdom that prevents them reading the secrets of the Spiritual World. It is a scientific necessity. No exposition of the case could be more truly scientific than this: "The natural man receiveth not the things of the Spirit of God; for they are foolishness unto him: *neither can we know them*, because they are spiritually discerned."[42] The verb here, it will be again observed, is potential. This is not a dogma of theology, but a necessity of Science. And Science, for the most part, has consistently accepted the situation. It has always proclaimed its ignorance of the Spiritual World. When Mr. Herbert Spencer affirms, "Regarding Science as a gradually increasing sphere we may say that every addition to its surface does but bring it into wider contact with surrounding nescience,"[43] from his standpoint he is quite correct. The endeavors of well-meaning persons to show that the Agnostic's position, when he asserts his ignorance of the Spiritual World, is only a pretence; the attempts to prove that he really knows a great deal about it if he would only admit it, are quite misplaced. He really does not know. The verdict that the natural man receiveth not the things of the Spirit of God, that they are foolishness unto him, that *neither can* he know them, is final as a statement of scientific truth—a statement on which the entire Agnostic literature is simply one long commentary.

We are now in a better position to follow out the more practical bearings of Biogenesis. There is an immense region surrounding Regeneration, a dark and perplexing region where men would be thankful for any light. It may well be that Biogenesis in its many ramifications may yet reach down to some of the deeper mysteries of the Spiritual Life. But meantime there is much to define even on the surface. And for the present we shall content ourselves by turning its light upon one or two points of current interest.

It must long ago have appeared how decisive is the answer of Science to the practical question with which we set out as to the possibility of a Spontaneous Development of Spiritual Life in the individual soul. The inquiry into the Origin of Life is the fundamental question alike of Biology and Christianity. We can afford to enlarge upon it, therefore, even at the risk of repetition. When men are offering us a Christianity without a living Spirit, and a personal religion without *conversion*, no emphasis or reiteration can be extreme. Besides, the clearness as well as the definiteness of the Testimony of Nature to any Spiritual truth is of immense importance. Regeneration has not merely been an outstanding difficulty, but an overwhelming obscurity. Even to earnest minds the difficulty of grasping the truth at all has always proved extreme. Philosophically one scarcely sees either the necessity or the possibility of being born again. Why a virtuous man should not simply grow better and better until in his own right he enters the Kingdom of God is what thousands honestly and seriously fail to understand. Now Philosophy cannot help us here. Her arguments are, if anything, against us. But Science answers to the appeal at once. If it be simply pointed out that this is the same absurdity as to ask why a stone should not grow more and more living till it enters the Organic World, the point is clear in an instant.

What now, let us ask specifically, distinguishes a Christian man from a non-Christian man? Is it that he has certain mental charac - teristics not possessed by the other? Is it that certain faculties have been trained in him, that morality assumes special and higher manifestations, and character a nobler form? Is the Christian merely an ordinary man who happens from birth to have been surrounded with a peculiar set of ideas? Is his religion merely that peculiar quality of the moral life defined by Mr. Matthew Arnold as "morality touched by emotion"? And does the possession of a high ideal, benevolent sympathies, a reverent spirit, and a favorable environment account for what men call his Spiritual Life?

The distinction between them is the same as that between the Organic and the Inorganic, the living and the dead. What is the difference between a crystal and an organism, a stone and a plant? They have much in common. Both are made of the same atoms. Both display the same properties of matter. Both are subject to the Physical Laws. Both may be very beautiful. But besides possessing all that the crystal has, the plant possesses something more—a mysterious something called Life. This Life is not something which existed in the crystal only in a less developed form. There is nothing at all like it in the crystal. There is nothing like the first beginning of it in the crystal, not a trace or symptom of it. This plant is tenanted by something new, an original and unique possession added over and above all the properties common to both. When from vegetable Life we rise to animal Life, here again we find something original and unique—unique at least as compared with the mineral. From animal Life we ascend again to Spiritual Life. And here also is something new, something still more unique. He who lives the Spiritual Life has a distinct kind of Life added to all the other phases of Life which he manifests—a kind of Life infinitely more distinct than is the active Life of a plant from the inertia of a stone. The Spiritual man is more distinct in point of fact than is the plant from the stone. This is the one possible comparison in Nature, for it is the widest distinction in Nature; but compared with the difference between the Natural and the Spiritual the gulf which divides the organic from the inorganic is a hair's-breadth. The natural man belongs essentially to this present order of things. He is endowed simply with a high quality of the natural animal Life. But it is Life of so poor a quality that it is not Life at all. He that hath not the Son *hath not Life*; but he that hath the Son hath Life—a new and distinct and supernatural endowment. He is not of this world. He is of the timeless state, of Eternity. *It doth not yet appear what he shall be.*

The difference between the Spiritual man and the Natural man is not a difference of development, but of generation. It is a distinction of quality not of quantity. A man cannot rise by any natural development from "morality touched by emotion," to "morality touched by Life." Were we to construct a scientific classification, Science would compel us to arrange all natural men, moral or immoral, educated or vulgar, as one family. One might be high in the family group, another low; yet, practically, they are marked by the same set of characteristics—they eat, sleep, work, think, live, die. But the Spiritual man is removed from this family so utterly by the possession of an additional characteristic that a biologist, fully informed of the whole circumstances, would not hesitate a moment to classify him elsewhere. And if he really entered into these circumstances it would not be in another family but in another King-dom. It is an old-fashioned theology which divides the world in this way—which speaks of men as Living and Dead, Lost and Saved—a stern theology all but fallen into disuse. This difference between the Living and the Dead in souls is so unproved by casual observation, so impalpable in itself, so startling as a doctrine, that schools of culture have ridiculed or denied the grim distinction. Nevertheless the grim distinction must be retained. It is a scientific distinction. "He that hath not the Son hath not Life."

Now it is this great Law which finally distinguishes Christianity from all other religions. It places the religion of Christ upon a footing altogether unique. There is no analogy between the Christian religion and, say, Buddhism or the Mohammedan religion. There is no true sense in which a man can say, He that hath Buddha hath Life. Buddha has nothing to do with Life. He may have something to do with morality. He may stimulate, impress, teach, guide, but there is no distinct new thing added to the souls of those who profess Buddhism. These religions *may* be developments of the natural, mental, or moral man. But Christi-anity professes to be more. It is the mental or moral man *plus* something else or some One else. It is the infusion into the Spiritual man of a New Life, of a quality unlike anything else in Nature. This constitutes the sep-arate Kingdom of Christ, and gives to Christianity alone of all the religions of mankind the strange mark of Divinity.

Shall we next inquire more precisely what is this something extra which constitutes Spiritual Life? What is this strange and new endow-ment in its nature and vital essence? And the answer is brief—it is Christ. He that hath *the Son* hath Life.

Are we forsaking the lines of Science in saying so? Yes and No. Sci-ence has drawn for us the distinction. It has no voice as to the nature of the distinction except this—that the new endowment is a something different from anything else with which it deals. It is not ordinary Vitality, it is not intellectual, it is not moral, but something beyond. And Revelation steps in and names what it is—it is Christ. Out of the multitude of sentences where this announcement is made, these few may be selected: "Know ye not your own selves how that *Jesus Christ is in you?*"[44] "Your bodies are the members of Christ."[45] "At that day ye shall know that I am in the Father, and ye in Me, and I in you."[46] "We will come unto him and make our abode with him."[47] "I am the Vine, ye are the branches."[48] "I am crucified with Christ, nevertheless I live, yet not I, but Christ liveth in me."[49]

Three things are clear from these statements: First, They are not mere figures of rhetoric. They are explicit declarations. If language means anything these words announce a literal fact. In some of Christ's own statements the literalism is if possible still more impressive. For instance, "Except ye eat the flesh of the Son of man and drink his blood, ye have no life in you. Whoso eateth My flesh and drinketh My blood hath eternal life; and I will raise him up at the last day. For My flesh is meat indeed, and My blood is drink indeed. He that eateth My flesh and drinketh My blood *dwelleth in Me and I in him.*"

In the second place, Spiritual Life is not something outside ourselves. The idea is not that Christ is in heaven and that we can stretch out some mysterious faculty and deal with Him there. This is the vague form in which many conceive the truth, but it is contrary to Christ's teaching and to the analogy of nature. Vegetable Life is not contained in a reservoir somewhere in the skies, and measured out spasmodically at certain seasons. The Life is *in* every plant and tree, inside its own substance and tissue, and continues there until it dies. This localization of Life in the individual is precisely the point where Vitality differs from the other forces of nature, such as magnetism and electricity. Vitality has much in common with such forces as magnetism and electricity, but there is one inviolable distinction between them—that Life is permanently fixed and rooted in the organism. The doctrines of conservation and transformation of energy, that is to say, do not hold for Vitality. The electrician can demagnetize a bar of iron, that is, he can transform its energy of magnetism into something else—heat, or motion, or light— and then re-form these back into magnetism. For magnetism has no root, no individuality, no fixed indwelling. But the biologist cannot devitalize a plant or an animal and revivify it again.[50] Life is not one of the homeless forces which promiscuously inhabit space, or which can be gathered like electricity from the clouds and dissipated back again into space. Life is definite and resident; and Spiritual Life is not a visit from a force, but a resident tenant in the soul.

This is, however, to formulate the statement of the third point, that Spiritual Life is not an ordinary form of energy or force. The analogy from Nature indorses this, but here Nature stops. It cannot say what Spiritual Life is. Indeed what natural Life is remains unknown, and the word Life still wanders through Science without a definition. Nature is silent, therefore, and must be as to Spiritual Life. But in the absence of natural light we fall back upon that complementary revelation which always shines, when truth is necessary and where Nature fails. We ask with Paul when this Life first visited him on the Damascus road, What is this? "Who art Thou, Lord?" And we hear, "I am Jesus."[51]

We must expect to find this denied. Besides a proof from Revelation, this is an argument from experience. And yet we shall still be told that this Spiritual Life is a force. But let it be remembered what this means in Science, it means the heresy of confounding Force with Vitality. We must also expect to be told that this Spiritual Life is simply a development of ordinary Life—just as Dr. Bastian tells us that natural Life is formed according to the same laws which determine the more simple chemical combinations. But remember what this means in Science. It is the heresy of Spontaneous Generation, a heresy so thoroughly discredited now that scarcely an authority in Europe will lend his name to it. Who art Thou, Lord? Unless we are to be allowed to hold Spontaneous Generation there is no alternative: Life can only come from Life: "I am Jesus."

A hundred other questions now rush into the mind about this Life: How does it come? Why does it come? How is it manifested? What faculty does it employ? Where does it reside? Is it communicable? What are its conditions? One or two of these questions may be vaguely answered, the rest bring us face to face with mystery. Let it not be thought that the scientific treatment of a Spiritual subject has reduced Spirituality to a problem of physics, or demonstrated God by the laws of biology. A Spirituality without mystery is an absurdity. Even Science has its mysteries, none more inscrutable than around this Science of Life. It taught us sooner or later to expect mystery, and now we enter its domain. Let it be carefully marked, however, that the cloud does not fall and cover us till we have ascertained the most momentous truth of Spirituality—that Christ is in the Christian.

Not that there is anything new in this. The Churches have always held that Christ was the source of Life. No spiritual man ever claims that his spirituality is his own. "I live," he will tell you; "nevertheless it is not I, but Christ liveth in me." Christ our Life has indeed been the only doctrine in the Christian Church from Paul to Augustine, from Calvin to Newman. Yet, when the Spiritual man is cross-examined upon this confession it is astonishing to find what uncertain hold it has upon his mind. Doctrinally he states it adequately and holds it unhesitatingly. But when pressed with the literal question he shrinks from the answer. We do not really believe that the Living Christ has touched us, that He makes His abode in us. Spiritual Life is not as real to us as natural Life. And we cover our retreat into unbelieving vagueness with a plea of reverence, justified, as we think, by the "Thus far and no farther" of ancient Scriptures. There is often a great deal of intellectual sin concealed under this old aphorism. When men do not really wish to go farther they find it an honorable convenience sometimes to sit down on the outermost edge of the Holy Ground on the pretext of taking off their shoes. Yet we must be certain that, making a virtue of reverence, we are not merely excusing ignorance; or, under the plea of mystery, evading a truth which has been stated in the New Testament a hundred times, in the most literal form, and with all but monotonous repetition. The greatest truths are always the most loosely held. And not the least of the advantages of taking up this question from the present standpoint is that we may see how a confused doctrine can really bear the luminous definition of Science and force itself upon us with all the weight of Natural Law.

What is mystery to many men, what feeds their worship, and at the same time spoils it, is that area round all great truth which is really capable of illumination, and into which every earnest mind is permitted and commanded to go with a light. We cry mystery long before the region of mystery comes. True mystery casts no shadows around. It is a sudden and awful gulf yawning across the field of knowledge; its form is irregular, but its lips are clean cut and sharp, and the mind can go to the very verge and look down the precipice into the dim abyss—

"Where writhing clouds unroll,
Striving to utter themselves in shapes."

We have gone with a light to the very verge of this truth. We have seen that the Spiritual Life is an endowment from the Spiritual World, and that the Living Spirit of Christ dwells in the Christian. But now the gulf yawns black before us. What more does Science know of life? Nothing. It knows nothing further about its origin in detail. It knows nothing about its ultimate nature. It cannot even define it. There is a helplessness in scientific books here, and a continual confession of it which to thoughtful minds is almost touching. Science, therefore, has not eliminated the true mysteries from our faith, but only the false. And it has done more. It has made true mystery scientific. Spirituality in having mystery is in analogy with all around it. Where there is exceptional mystery in the Spiritual world it will generally be found that there is a corresponding mystery in the natural world. And, as Origen centuries ago insisted, the difficulties of Religion are simply the difficulties of Nature.

One question more we may look at for a moment. What can be gathered on the surface as to the process of Regeneration in the individual soul? From the analogies of Biology we should expect three things: First, that the New Life should dawn suddenly; Second, that it should come "without observation"; Third, that it should develop gradually. On two of these points there can be little controversy. The gradualness of growth is a characteristic which strikes the simplest observer. Long before the word Evolution was coined Christ applied it in this very connection—"First the blade, then the ear, then the full corn in the ear." It is well known also to those who study the parables of Nature that there is an ascending scale of slowness as we rise in the scale of Life. Growth is most gradual in the highest forms. Man attains his maturity after a score of years; the monad completes its humble cycle in a day. What wonder if development be tardy in the Creature of Eternity? A Christian's sun has sometimes set, and a critical world has seen as yet no corn in the ear. As yet? "As yet," in this long Life, has not begun. Grant us the years proportionate to his place in the scale of Life. "The time of harvest is *not yet*."

Again, in addition to being slow, the phenomena of growth are secret. Life is invisible. When the New Life manifests itself it is a surprise. *Thou canst not tell whence it cometh or whither it goeth.* When the plant lives whence has the Life come? When it dies whither has it gone? . . . *Thou canst not tell—so is every one that is born of the Spirit. For the kingdom of God cometh without observation.*

Yet once more—and this is a point of strange and frivolous dispute—this Life comes suddenly. This is the only way in which Life can come. Life cannot come gradually—health can, structure can, but not Life. A new theology has laughed at the Doctrine of Conversion. Sudden Conversion especially has been ridiculed as untrue to philosophy and impossible to human nature. We may not be concerned in buttressing any theology because it is old. But we find that this old theology is scientific. There may be cases—they are probably in the majority—where the moment of contact with the Living Spirit though sudden has been obscure. But the real moment and the conscious moment are two different things. Science pronounces nothing as to the conscious moment. If it did it would probably say that that was seldom the real moment—just as in the natural Life the conscious moment is not the real moment. The moment of birth in the natural world is not a conscious moment—we do not know we are born till long afterward. Yet there are men to whom the Origin of the New Life in time has been no difficulty. To Paul, for instance, Christ seems to have come at a definite period of time, the exact moment and second of which could have been known. And this is certainly, in theory at least, the normal Origin of Life, according to the principles of Biology. The line between the living and the dead is a sharp line. When the dead atoms of Carbon, Hydrogen, Oxygen, Nitrogen, are seized upon by Life, the organism at first is very lowly. It possesses few functions. It has little beauty. Growth is the work of time. But Life is not. That comes in a moment. At one moment it was dead; the next it lived. This is conversion, the "passing," as the Bible calls it, "from Death unto Life." Those who have stood by another's side at the solemn hour of this dread possession have been conscious sometimes of an experience which words are not allowed to utter—a something like the sudden snapping of a chain, the waking from a dream.

IV

ENVIRONMENT

When I talked with an ardent missionary and pointed out to him
that his creed found no support in my experience, he replied:
"It is not so in your experience, but is so in the other world."
I answer: "Other world! There is no other world.
God is one and omnipresent; here or nowhere is the whole fact."
Emerson

"Ye are complete in Him."
Paul

Whatever amount of power an organism expends in any shape
is the correlate and equivalent of a power that was
taken into it from without.
Herbert Spencer

S tudents of Biography will observe that in all well-written Lives attention is concentrated for the first few chapters upon two points. We are first introduced to the family to which the subject of memoir belonged. The grandparents, or even the more remote ancestors, are briefly sketched and their chief characteristics brought prominently into view. Then the parents themselves are photographed in detail. Their appearance and physique, their character, their disposition, their mental qualities, are set before us in a critical analysis. And finally we are asked to observe how much the father and the mother respectively have transmitted of their peculiar nature to their offspring. How faithfully the ancestral lines have met in the latest product, how mysteriously the joint characteristics of body and mind have blended, and how unexpected yet how entirely natural a recombination is the result—these points are elaborated with cumulative effect until we realize at last how little we are dealing with an independent unit, how much with a survival and reorganization of what seemed buried in the grave.

In the second place, we are invited to consider more external influences—schools and schoolmasters, neighbors, home, pecuniary circumstances, scenery, and, by-and-by, the religious and political atmosphere of the time. These also we are assured have played their part in making the individual what he is. We can estimate these early influences in any particular case with but small imagination if we fail to see how powerfully they also have moulded mind and character, and in what subtle ways they have determined the course of the future life.

This twofold relation of the individual, first, to his parents, and second, to his circumstances, is not peculiar to human beings. These two factors are responsible for making all living organisms what they are. When a naturalist attempts to unfold the life-history of any animal, he proceeds precisely on these same lines. Biography is really a branch of Natural History; and the biographer who discusses his hero as the resultant of these two tendencies, follows the scientific method as rigidly as Mr. Darwin in studying "Animals and Plants under Domestication."

Mr. Darwin, following Weismann, long ago pointed out that there are two main factors in all Evolution—the nature of the organism and the nature of the conditions. We have chosen our illustration from the highest or human species in order to define the meaning of these factors in the clearest way; but it must be remembered that the development of man under these directive influences is essentially the same as that of any other organism in the hands of Nature. We are dealing therefore with universal Law. It will still further serve to complete the conception of the general principle if we now substitute for the casual phrases by which the factors have been described the more accurate terminology of Science. Thus what Biography describes as parental influences, Biology would speak of as Heredity; and all that is involved in the second factor— the action of external circumstances and surroundings—the naturalist would include under the single term Environment. These two, Heredity and Environment, are the master-influences of the organic world. These have made all of us what we are. These forces are still ceaselessly playing upon all our lives. And he who truly understands these influences; he who has decided how much to allow to each; he who can regulate new forces as they arise, or adjust them to the old, so directing them as at one moment to make them co-operate, at another to counteract one another, understands the rationale of personal development. To seize continuously the opportunity of more and more perfect adjustment to better and higher conditions, to balance some inward evil with some purer influence acting from without, in a word to make his Environment at the same time that it is making us—these are the secrets of a well-ordered and successful life.

In the spiritual world, also, the subtle influences which form and transform the soul are Heredity and Environment. And here especially where all is invisible, where much that we feel to be real is yet so ill-defined, it becomes of vital practical moment to clarify the atmosphere as far as possible with conceptions borrowed from the natural life. Few things are less understood than the conditions of the spiritual life. The distressing incompetence of which most of us are conscious in trying to work out our spiritual experience is due perhaps less to the diseased will which we commonly blame for it than to imperfect knowledge of the right conditions. It does not occur to us how natural the spiritual is. We still strive for some strange transcendent thing; we seek to promote life by methods as unnatural as they prove unsuccessful; and only the utter incomprehensibility of the whole region prevents us seeing fully—what we already half-suspect—how completely we are missing the road. Living in the spiritual world, nevertheless, is just as simple as living in the natural world; and it is the same kind of simplicity. It is the same kind of simplicity for it is the same kind of world—there are not two kinds of worlds. The conditions of life in the one are the conditions of life in the other. And till these conditions are sensibly grasped, as the conditions of all life, it is impossible that the personal effort after the highest life should be other than a blind struggle carried on in fruitless sorrow and humiliation.

Of these two universal factors, Heredity and Environment, it is unnecessary to balance the relative importance here. The main influence, unquestionably, must be assigned to the former. In practice, however, and for an obvious reason, we are chiefly concerned with the latter. What Heredity has to do for us is determined outside ourselves. No man can select his own parents. But every man to some extent can choose his own Environment. His relation to it, however largely determined by Heredity in the first instance, is always open to alteration. And so great is his control over Environment and so radical its influence over him, that we can so direct it as either to undo, modify, perpetuate or intensify the earlier hereditary influence within certain limits. But the aspects of Environment which we have now to consider do not involve us in questions of such complexity. In what high and mystical sense, also, Heredity applies to the spiritual organism we need not just now inquire. In the simpler relations of the more external factor we shall find a large and fruitful field for study.

The influence of Environment may be investigated in two main aspects. First, one might discuss the modern and very interesting question as to the power of Environment to induce what is known to recent science as Variation. A change in the surroundings of any animal, it is now well-known, can so react upon it as to cause it to change. By the attempt, conscious or unconscious, to adjust itself to the new conditions, a true physiological change is gradually wrought within the organism. Hunter, for example, in a classical experiment, so changed the Environment of a sea-gull by keeping it in captivity that it could only secure a grain diet. The effect was to modify the stomach of the bird, normally adapted to a fish diet, until in time it came to resemble in structure the gizzard of an ordinary grain-feeder such as the pigeon. Holmgrén again reversed this experiment by feeding pigeons for a lengthened period on a meat-diet, with the result that the gizzard became transformed into the carnivorous stomach. Mr. Alfred Russel Wallace mentions the case of a Brazilian parrot which changes its color from green to red or yellow when fed on the fat of certain fishes. Not only changes of food, however, but changes of climate and of temperature, changes in surrounding organisms, in the case of marine animals even changes of pressure, of ocean currents, of light, and of many other circumstances, are known to exert a powerful modifying influence upon living organisms. These relations are still being worked out in many directions, but the influence of Environment as a prime factor in Variation is now a recognized doctrine of science.[81]

Even the popular mind has been struck with the curious adaptation of nearly all animals to their *habitat*, for example in the matter of color. The sandy hue of the sole and flounder, the white of the polar bear with its suggestion of Arctic snows, the stripes of the Bengal tiger—as if the actual reeds of its native jungle had nature-printed themselves on its hide;—these, and a hundred others which will occur to every one, are marked instances of adaptation to Environment, induced by Natural Selection or otherwise, for the purpose, obviously in these cases at least, of protection.

To continue the investigation of the modifying action of Environment into the moral and spiritual spheres, would be to open a fascinating and suggestive inquiry. One might show how the moral man is acted upon and changed continuously by the influences, secret and open, of his surroundings, by the tone of society, by the company he keeps, by his occupation, by the books he reads, by Nature, by all, in short, that constitutes the habitual atmosphere of his thoughts and the little world of his daily choice. Or one might go deeper still and prove how the spiritual life also is modified from outside sources—its health or disease, its growth or decay, all its changes for better or for worse being determined by the varying and successive circumstances in which the religious habits are cultivated. But we must rather transfer our attention to a second aspect of Environment, not perhaps so fascinating but yet more important.

So much of the modern discussion of Environment revolves round the mere question of Variation that one is apt to overlook a previous question. Environment as a factor in life is not exhausted when we have realized its modifying influence. Its significance is scarcely touched. The great function of Environment is not to modify but to *sustain*. In sustaining life, it is true, it modifies. But the latter influence is incidental, the former essential. Our Environment is that in which we live and move and have our being. Without it we should neither live nor move nor have any being. In the organism lies the principle of life; in the Environment are the conditions of life. Without the fulfillment of these conditions, which are wholly supplied by Environment, there can be no life. An organism in itself is but a part; Nature is its complement. Alone, cut off from its surroundings, it is not. Alone, cut off from my surroundings, I am not—physically I am not. I am, only as I am sustained. I continue only as I receive. My Environment may modify me, but it has first to keep me. And all the time its secret transforming power is indirectly moulding body and mind it is directly active in the more open task of ministering to my myriad wants and from hour to hour sustaining life itself.

To understand the sustaining influence of Environment in the animal world, one has only to recall what the biologist terms the extrinsic or subsidiary conditions of vitality. Every living thing normally requires for its development an Environment containing air, light, heat, and water. In addition to these, if vitality is to be prolonged for any length of time, and if it is to be accompanied with growth and the expenditure of energy, there must be a constant supply of food. When we simply remember how indispensable food is to growth and work, and when we further bear in mind that the food-supply is solely contributed by the Environment, we shall realize at once the meaning and the truth of the proposition that without Environment there can be no life. Seventy per cent, at least, of the human body is made of pure water, the rest of gases and earth. These have all come from Environment. Through the secret pores of the skin two pounds of water are exhaled daily from every healthy adult. The supply is kept up by Environment. The Environment is really an unappropriated part of ourselves. Definite portions are continuously abstracted from it and added to the organism. And so long as the organism continues to grow, act, think, speak, work, or perform any other function demanding a supply of energy, there is a constant, simultaneous, and proportionate drain upon its surroundings.

This is a truth in the physical, and therefore in the spiritual, world of so great importance that we shall not mis-spend time if we follow it, for further confirmation, into another department of nature. Its significance in Biology is self-evident; let us appeal to Chemistry.

When a piece of coal is thrown on the fire, we say that it will radiate into the room a certain quantity of heat. This heat, in the popular conception, is supposed to reside in the coal and to be set free during the process of combustion. In reality, however, the heat energy is only in part contained in the coal. It is contained just as truly in the coal's Environment—that is to say, in the oxygen of the air. The atoms of carbon which compose the coal have a powerful affinity for the oxygen of the air. Whenever they are made to approach within a certain distance of one another, by the initial application of heat, they rush together with inconceivable velocity. The heat which appears at this moment, comes neither from the carbon alone, nor from the oxygen alone. These two substances are really inconsumable, and continue to exist, after they meet in a combined form, as carbonic acid gas. The heat is due to the energy developed by the chemical embrace, the precipitate rushing together of the molecules of carbon and the molecules of oxygen. It comes, therefore, partly from the coal and partly from the Environment. Coal alone never could produce heat, neither alone could Environment. The two are mutually dependent. And although in nearly all the arts we credit everything to the substance which we can weigh and handle, it is certain that in the most cases the larger debt is due to an invisible Environment.

This is one of those great commonplaces which slip out of general reckoning by reason of their very largeness and simplicity. How profound, nevertheless, are the issues which hang on this elementary truth, we shall discover immediately. Nothing in this age is more needed in every department of knowledge than the rejuvenescence of the commonplace.

In the spiritual world especially, he will be wise who courts acquaintance with the most ordinary and transparent facts of Nature; and in laying the foundations for a religious life he will make no unworthy beginning who carries with him an impressive sense of so obvious a truth as that without Environment there can be no life.

For what does this amount to in the spiritual world? Is it not merely the scientific re-statement of the reiterated aphorism of Christ, "Without Me ye can do nothing"? There is in the spiritual organism a principle of life; but that is not self-existent. It requires a second factor, a something in which to live and move and have its being, an Environment. Without this it cannot live or move or have any being. Without Environment the soul is as the carbon without the oxygen, as the fish without the water, as the animal frame without the extrinsic conditions of vitality.

And what is the spiritual Environment? It is God. Without this, therefore, there is no life, no thought, no energy, nothing—"without Me ye can do nothing."

The cardinal error in the religious life is to attempt to live without an Environment. Spiritual experience occupies itself, not too much, but too exclusively, with one factor—the soul. We delight in dissecting this much tortured faculty, from time to time, in search of a certain something which we call our faith—forgetting that faith is but an attitude, an empty hand for grasping an environing Presence. And when we feel the need of a power by which to overcome the world, how often do we not seek to generate it within ourselves by some forced process, some fresh girding of the will, some strained activity which only leaves the soul in further exhaustion? To examine ourselves is good; but useless unless we also examine Environment. To bewail our weakness is right, but not remedial. The cause must be investigated as well as the result. And yet, because we never see the other half of the problem, our fail -ures even fail to instruct us. After each new collapse we begin our life anew, but on the old conditions; and the attempt ends as usual in the repetition—in the circumstances the inevitable repetition—of the old disaster. Not that at times we do not obtain glimpses of the true state of the case. After seasons of much discouragement, with the sore sense upon us of our abject feebleness, we do confer with ourselves, insisting for the thousandth time, "My soul, wait thou only upon God." But, the lesson is soon forgotten. The strength supplied we speedily credit to our own achievement; and even the temporary success is mistaken for a symptom of improved inward vitality. Once more we become self-existent. Once more we go on living without an Environment. And once more, after days of wasting without repairing, of spending without replenishing, we begin to perish with hunger, only returning to God again, as a last resort, when we have reached starvation point.

Now why do we do this? Why do we seek to breathe without an atmosphere, to drink without a well? Why this unscientific attempt to sustain life for weeks at a time without an Environment? It is because we have never truly seen the necessity for an Environment. We have not been working with a principle. We are told to "wait only upon God," but we do not know why. It has never been as clear to us that without God the soul will die as that without food the body will perish. In short, we have never comprehended the doctrine of the Persistence of Force. Instead of being content to transform energy we have tried to create it.

The Law of Nature here is as clear as Science can make it. In the words of Mr. Herbert Spencer, "It is a corollary from that primordial truth which, as we have seen, underlies all other truths, that whatever amount of power an organism expends in any shape is the correlate and equivalent of a power that was taken into it from without,"[82] We are dealing here with a simple question of dynamics. Whatever energy the soul expends must first be "taken into it from without." We are not Creators, but creatures; God is our refuge *and strength*. Communion with God, therefore, is a scientific necessity; and nothing will more help the defeated spirit which is struggling in the wreck of its religious life than a common-sense hold of this plain biological principle that without Environment he can do nothing. What he wants is not an occasional view, but a principle—a basal principle like this, broad as the universe, solid as nature. In the natural world we act upon this law unconsciously. We absorb heat, breathe air, draw on Environment all but automatically for meat and drink, for the nourishment of the senses, for mental stimulus, for all that, penetrating us from without, can prolong, enrich, and elevate life. But in the spiritual world we have all this to learn. We are new creatures, and even the bare living has to be acquired.

Now the great point in learning to live is to live naturally. As closely as possible we must follow the broad, clear lines of the natural life. And there are three things especially which it is necessary for us to keep continually in view. The first is that the organism contains within itself only one-half of what is essential to life; the second is that the other half is contained in the Environment; the third, that the condition of receptivity is simple union between the organism and the Environment.

Translated into the language of religion these propositions yield, and place on a scientific basis, truths of immense practical interest. To say, first, that the organism contains within itself only one-half of what is essential to life, is to repeat the evangelical confession, so worn and yet so true to universal experience, of the utter helplessness of man. Who has not come to the conclusion that he is but a part, a fraction of some larger whole? Who does not miss at every turn of his life an absent God? That man is but a part, he knows, for there is room in him for more. That God is the other part, he feels, because at times He satisfies his need. Who does not tremble often under that sicklier symptom of his incompleteness, his want of spiritual energy, his helplessness with sin? But now he understands both—the void in his life, the powerlessness of his will. He understands that, like all other energy, spiritual power is contained in Environment. He finds here at last the true root of all human frailty, emptiness, nothingness, sin. This is why "without Me ye can do nothing." Powerlessness is the normal state not only of this but of every organism—of every organism apart from its Environment.

The entire dependence of the soul upon God is not an exceptional mystery, nor is man's helplessness an arbitrary and unprecedented phenomenon. It is the law of all Nature. The spiritual man is not taxed beyond the natural. He is not purposely handicapped by singular limitations or unusual incapacities. God has not designedly made the religious life as hard as possible. The arrangements for the spiritual life are the same as for the natural life. When in their hours of unbelief men challenge their Creator for placing the obstacle of human frailty in the way of their highest development, their protest is against the order of nature. They object to the sun for being the source of energy and not the engine, to the carbonic acid being in the air and not in the plant. They would equip each organism with a personal atmosphere, each brain with a private store of energy; they would grow corn in the interior of the body, and make bread by a special apparatus in the digestive organs. They must, in short, have the creature transformed into a Creator. The organism must either depend on his environment, or be self-sufficient. But who will not rather approve the arrangement by which man in his creatural life may have unbroken access to an Infinite Power? What soul will seek to remain self-luminous when it knows that "The Lord God is a *Sun*"? Who will not willingly exchange his shallow vessel for Christ's well of living water? Even if the organism, launched into being like a ship putting out to sea, possessed a full equipment, its little store must soon come to an end. But in contact with a large and bounteous Environment its supply is limitless. In every direction its resources are infinite.

There is a modern school which protests against the doctrine of man's inability as the heartless fiction of a past theology. While some forms of that dogma, to any one who knows man, are incapable of defence, there are others which, to any one who knows Nature, are incapable of denial. Those who oppose it, in their jealousy for humanity, credit the organism with the properties of Environment. All true theology, on the other hand, has remained loyal to at least the root-idea in this truth. The New Testament is nowhere more impressive than where it insists on the fact of man's dependence. In its view the first step in religion is for man to feel his helplessness. Christ's first beatitude is to the poor in spirit. The condition of entrance into the spiritual kingdom is to possess the child-spirit—that state of mind combining at once the profoundest helplessness with the most artless feeling of dependence. Substantially the same idea underlies the countless passages in which Christ affirms that He has not come to call the righteous, but sinners to repentance. And in that farewell discourse into which the Great Teacher poured the most burning convictions of His life, He gives to this doctrine an ever increasing emphasis. No words could be more solemn or arresting than the sentence in the last great allegory devoted to this theme, "As the branch cannot bear fruit of itself except it abide in the vine, no more can ye except ye abide in Me." The word here, it will be observed again, is *cannot*. It is the imperative of natural law. Fruit-bearing without Christ is not an improbability, but an impossibility. As well expect the natural fruit to flourish without air and heat, without soil and sunshine. How thoroughly also Paul grasped this truth is apparent from a hundred pregnant passages in which he echoes his Master's teaching. To us life was hid with Christ in God. And that we embraced this not as a theory but as an experimental truth we gather from our constant confession, "When I am weak, then am I strong."

This leads by a natural transition to the second of the three points we are seeking to illustrate. We have seen that the organism contains within itself only one half of what is essential to life. We have next to observe, as the complement of this, how the second half is contained in the Environment.

One result of the due apprehension of our personal helplessness will be that we shall no longer waste our time over the impossible task of manufacturing energy for ourselves. Our science will bring to an abrupt end the long series of severe experiments in which we have indulged in the hope of finding a perpetual motion. And having decided upon this once for all, our first step in seeking a more satisfactory state of things must be to find a new source of energy. Following Nature, only one course is open to us. We must refer to Environment. The natural life owes all to Environment, so must the spiritual. Now the Environment of the spiritual life is God. As Nature therefore forms the complement of the natural life, God is the complement of the spiritual.

The proof of this? That Nature is not more natural to my body than God is to my soul. Every animal and plant has its own Environment. And the further one inquires into the relations of the one to the other, the more one sees the marvelous intricacy and beauty of the adjustments. These wonderful adaptations of each organism to its surroundings—of the fish to the water, of the eagle to the air, of the insect to the forest bed; and of each part of every organism—the fish's swim-bladder, the eagle's eye, the insect's breathing tubes—which the old argument from design brought home to us with such enthusiasm, inspire us still with a sense of the boundless resources and skill of Nature in perfecting her arrangements for each single life. Down to the last detail the world is made for what is in it; and by whatever process things are as they are, all organisms find in surrounding Nature the ample complement of themselves. Man, too, finds in his Environment provision for all capacities, scope for the exercise of every faculty, room for the indulgence of each appetite, a just supply for every want. So the spiritual man at the apex of the pyramid of life finds in the vaster range of his Environment a provision, as much higher, it is true, as he is higher, but as delicately adjusted to his varying needs. And all this is supplied to him just as the lower organisms are ministered to by the lower environment, in the same simple ways, in the same constant sequence, as appropriately and as lavishly. We fail to praise the ceaseless ministry of the great inanimate world around us only because its kindness is unobtrusive. Nature is always noiseless. All her greatest gifts are given in secret. And we forget how truly every good and perfect gift comes from without, and from above, because no pause in her changeless beneficence teaches us the sad lesson of deprivation.

It is not a strange thing, then, for the soul to find its life in God. This is its native air. God as the Environment of the soul has been from the remotest age the doctrine of all the deepest thinkers in religion. How profoundly Hebrew poetry is saturated with this high thought will appear when we try to conceive of it with this left out. True poetry is only science in another form. And long before it was possible for religion to give scientific expression to its greatest truths, men of insight uttered themselves in psalms which could not have been truer to Nature had the most modern light controlled the inspiration. "As the hart panteth after the water-brooks, so panteth my soul after Thee, O God." What fine sense of the analogy of the natural and the spiritual does not underlie these words. As the hart after its Environment, so man after him; as the water-brooks are fitly designed to meet the natural wants, so fitly does God implement the spiritual need of man. It will be noticed that in the Hebrew poets the longing for God never strikes one as morbid, or unnatural to the men who uttered it. It is as natural to them to long for God as for the swallow to seek her nest. Throughout all their images no suspicion rises within us that they are exaggerating. We feel how truly they are reading themselves, their deepest selves. No false note occurs in all their aspiration. There is no weariness even in their ceaseless sighing, except the lover's weariness for the absent—if they would fly away, it is only to be at rest. Men who have no soul can only wonder at this. Men who have a soul, but with little faith, can only envy it. How joyous a thing it was to the Hebrews to seek their God! How artlessly they call upon Him to entertain them in His pavilion, to cover them with His feathers, to hide them in His secret place, to hold them in the hollow of His hand or stretch around them the everlasting arms! These men were true children of Nature. As the humming-bird among its own palm-trees, as the ephemera in the sunshine of a summer evening, so they lived their joyous lives. And even the full share of the sadder experiences of life which came to all of them but drove them the further into the Secret Place, and led them with more consecration to make, as they expressed it, "the Lord their portion." All that has been said since from Marcus Aurelius to Swedenborg, from Augustine to Schleiermacher of a beset-ting God as the final complement of humanity is but a repetition of the Hebrew poets' faith. And even the New Testament has nothing higher to offer man than this. The psalmist's "God is our refuge and strength" is only the earlier form, less defined, less practicable, but not less noble, of Christ's "Come unto Me, and I will give you rest."

There is a brief phrase of Paul's which defines the relation with almost scientific accuracy—"Ye are complete in Him." In this is summed up the whole of the Bible anthropology—the completeness of man in God, his incompleteness apart from God.

If it be asked, In what is man incomplete, or, In what does God complete us? the question is a wide one. But it may serve to show at least the direction in which the Divine Environment forms the complement of human life if we ask ourselves once more what it is in life that needs complementing. And to this question we receive the significant answer that it is in the higher departments alone, or mainly, that the incompleteness of our life appears. The lower departments of Nature are already complete enough. The world itself is about as good a world as might be. It has been long in the making, its furniture is all in, its laws are in perfect working order; and although wise men at various times have suggested improvements, there is on the whole a tolerably unanimous vote of confidence in things as they exist. The Divine Environment has little more to do for this planet so far as we can see, and so far as the existing generation is concerned. Then the lower organic life of the world is also so far complete. God, through Evolution or otherwise, may still have finishing touches to add here and there, but already it is "all very good." It is difficult to conceive anything better of its kind than a lily or a cedar, an ant or an ant-eater. These organisms, so far as we can judge, lack nothing. It might be said of them, "they are complete in Nature." Of man also, of man the animal, it may be affirmed that his Environment satisfies him. He has food and drink, and good food and good drink. And there is in him no purely animal want which is not really provided for, and that apparently in the happiest possible way.

But the moment we pass beyond the mere animal life we begin to come upon an incompleteness. The symptoms at first are slight, and betray themselves only by an unexplained restlessness or a dull sense of want. Then the feverishness increases, becomes more defined, and passes slowly into abiding pain. To some come darker moments when the unrest deepens into a mental agony of which all the other woes of earth are mockeries—moments when the forsaken soul can only cry in terror for the Living God. Up to a point the natural Environment supplies man's wants, beyond that it only derides us. How much in man lies beyond that point? Very much—almost all, all that makes man man.

The first suspicion of the terrible truth—so for the time let us call it—wakens with the dawn of the intellectual life. It is a solemn moment when the slow-moving mind reaches at length the verge of its mental horizon, and, looking over, sees nothing more. Its straining makes the abyss but more profound. Its cry comes back without an echo. Where is the Environment to complete this rational soul? Men either find one—One—or spend the rest of their days in trying to shut their eyes. The alternatives of the intellectual life are Christianity or Agnosticism. The Agnostic is right when he trumpets his incompleteness. He who is not complete in Him must be for ever incomplete. Still more grave becomes man's case when he begins further to explore his moral and social nature. The problems of the heart and conscience are infinitely more perplexing than those of the intellect. Has love no future? Has right no triumph? Is the unfinished self to remain unfinished? Again, the alternatives are two, Christianity or Pessimism. But when we ascend the further height of the religious nature, the crisis comes. There, without Environment, the darkness is unutterable. So maddening now becomes the mystery that men are compelled to construct an Environment for themselves. No Environment here is unthinkable. An altar of some sort men must have—God, or Nature, or Law. But the anguish of Atheism is only a negative proof of man's incompleteness. A witness more over-whelming is the prayer of the Christian. What a very strange thing, is it not, for man to pray? It is the symbol at once of his littleness and of his greatness. Here the sense of imperfection, controlled and silenced in the narrower reaches of his being, becomes audible. Now he must utter himself. The sense of need is so real, and the sense of Environment, that he calls out to it, addressing it articulately, and imploring it to satisfy his need. Surely there is nothing more touching in Nature than this? Man could never so expose himself, so break through all constraint, except from a dire necessity. It is the suddenness and unpremeditatedness of Prayer that gives it a unique value as an apologetic.

Man has three questions to put to his Environment, three symbols of his incompleteness. They come from three different centers of his being. The first is the question of the intellect, What is Truth? The natural Environment answers, "Increase of Knowledge increaseth Sorrow," and "much study is a Weariness." Christ replies, "Learn of Me, and ye shall find Rest." Contrast the world's word "Weariness" with Christ's word "Rest." No other teacher since the world began has ever associated "learn" with "Rest." Learn of me, says the philosopher, and you shall find Restlessness. Learn of Me, says Christ, and ye shall find Rest. Thought, which the godless man has cursed, that eternally starved yet ever living specter, finds at last its imperishable glory; Thought is complete in Him. The second question is sent up from the moral nature, Who will show us any good? And again we have a contrast: the world's verdict, "There is none that doeth good, no, not one;" and Christ's, "There is none good but God only." And finally, there is the lonely cry of the spirit, most pathetic and most deep of all, Where is he whom my soul seeketh? And the yearning is met as before, "I looked on my right hand, and beheld, but there was no man that would know me; refuge failed me; no man cared for my soul. I cried unto Thee, O Lord: I said, Thou are my refuge and my portion in the land of the living."[83]

Are these the directions in which men in these days are seeking to complete their lives? The completion of Life is just now a supreme question. It is important to observe how it is being answered. If we ask Science or Philosophy they will refer us to Evolution. The struggle for Life, they assure us, is steadily eliminating imperfect forms, and as the fittest continue to survive we shall have a gradual perfecting of being. That is to say, that completeness is to be sought for in the organism— we are to be complete in Nature and in ourselves. To Evolution, certainly, all men will look for a further perfecting of Life. But it must be an Evolution which includes all the factors. Civilization, it may be said, will deal with the second factor. It will improve the Environment step by step as it improves the organism, or the organism as it improves the Environment. This is well, and it will perfect Life up to a point. But beyond that it cannot carry us. As the possibilities of the natural Life become more defined, its impossibilities will become the more appalling. The most perfect civilization would leave the best part of us still incomplete. Men will have to give up the experiment of attempting to live in half an Environment. Half an Environment will give but half a Life. Half an Environment? He whose correspondences are with this world alone has only a thousandth part, a fraction, the mere rim and shade of an Environment, and only the fraction of a Life! How long will it take Science to believe its own creed, that the material universe we see around us is only a fragment of the universe we do not see? The very retention of the phrase "Material Universe," we are told, is the confession of our unbelief and ignorance; since "matter is the less important half of the material of the physical universe."[84]

The thing to be aimed at is not an organism self-contained and self-sufficient, however high in the scale of being, but an organism complete in the whole Environment. It is open to any man to aim at a self-sufficient Life, but he will find no encouragement in Nature. The Life of the body may complete itself in the physical world; that is its legitimate Environment. The Life of the senses, high and low, may perfect itself in Nature. Even the Life of thought may find a large complement in surrounding things. But the higher thought, and the conscience, and the religious Life, can only perfect themselves in God. To make the influence of Environment stop with the natural world is to doom the spiritual nature to death. For the soul, like the body, can never perfect itself in isolation. The law for both is to be complete in the appropriate Environment. And the perfection to be sought in the spiritual world is a perfection of relation, a perfect adjustment of that which is becoming perfect to that which is perfect.

The third problem, now simplified to a point, finally presents itself. Where do organism and Environment meet? How does that which is becoming perfect avail itself of its perfecting Environment? And the answer is, just as in Nature. The condition is simple receptivity. And yet this is perhaps the least simple of all conditions. It is so simple that we will not act upon it. But there is no other condition. Christ has condensed the whole truth into one memorable sentence, "As the branch cannot bear fruit of itself except it abide in the vine, no more can ye except ye abide in Me." And on the positive side, "He that abideth in Me, the same bringeth forth much fruit."

V

CONFORMITY TO TYPE

"So careful of the type?" but no.
From scarpèd cliff and quarried stone
She cries, "A thousand types are gone:
I care for nothing, all shall go."

"Thou makest thine appeal to me;
I bring to life, I bring to death:
The spirit does but mean thy breath:
I know no more." And he, shall he,

Man, her last work, who seem'd so fair,
Such splendid purpose in his eyes,
Who roll'd the psalm to wintry skies,
Who built him fanes of fruitless prayer,

Who trusted God was love indeed
And love Creation's final law—
Tho' Nature, red in tooth and claw
With ravine, shriek'd against his creed—

Who loved, who suffer'd countless ills,
Who battled for the True, the Just,
Be blown about the desert dust
Or seal'd within the iron hills?
    —In Memoriam

Until Christ be formed in you.
Paul

The one end to which, in all living beings,
the formative impulse is tending—the one scheme
which the Archæus of the old speculators strives to carry out,
seems to be to mould the offspring into the likeness of the parent.
It is the first great law of reproduction,
that the offspring tends to resemble its parent
or parents more closely than anything else.
Huxley

If a botanist be asked the difference between an oak, a palm-tree, and a lichen, he will declare that they are separated from one another by the broadest line known to classification. Without taking into account the outward differences of size and form, the variety of flower and fruit, the peculiarities of leaf and branch, we see even in their general architecture types of structure as distinct as Norman, Gothic and Egyptian. But if the first young germs of these three plants are placed before him and he is called upon to define the difference, he finds it impossible. He cannot even say which is which. Examined under the highest powers of the microscope they yield no clue. Analyzed by the chemist with all the appliances of his laboratory they keep their secret.

The same experiment can be tried with the embryos of animals. Take the ovule of the worm, the eagle, the elephant, and of man himself. Let the most skilled observer apply the most searching tests to distinguish one from the other and he will fail. But there is something more surprising still. Compare next the two sets of germs, the vegetable and the animal. And there is still no shade of difference. Oak and palm, worm and man all start in life together. No matter into what strangely different forms they may afterward develop, no matter whether they are to live on sea or land, creep or fly, swim or walk, think or vegetate, in the embryo as it first meets the eye of Science they are indistinguishable.

The apple which fell in Newton's garden, Newton's dog Diamond, and Newton himself, began life at the same point.[85]

If we analyze this material point at which all life starts, we shall find it to consist of a clear structureless jelly-like substance resembling albumen or white of egg. It is made of Carbon, Hydrogen, Oxygen and Nitrogen. Its name is protoplasm. And it is not only the structural unit with which all living bodies start in life, but with which they are subsequently built up. "Protoplasm," says Huxley, "simple or nucleated, is the formal basis of all life. It is the clay of the Potter." "Beast and fowl, reptile and fish, mollusk, worm and polype are all composed of structural units of the same character, namely, masses of protoplasm with a nucleus."[86]

What then determines the difference between different animals? What makes one little speck of protoplasm grow into Newton's dog Diamond, and another, exactly the same, into Newton himself? It is a mysterious something which has entered into this protoplasm. No eye can see it. No science can define it. There is a different something for Newton's dog and a different something for Newton; so that though both use the same matter they build it up in these widely different ways. Protoplasm being the clay, this something is the Potter. And as there is only one clay and yet all these curious forms are developed out of it, it follows necessarily that the difference lies in the potters. There must in short be as many potters as there are forms. There is the potter who segments the worm, and the potter who builds up the form of the dog, and the potter who moulds the man. To understand unmistakably that it is really the potter who does the work, let us follow for a moment a description of the process by a trained eye-witness. The observer is Mr. Huxley. Through the tube of his microscope he is watching the development, out of a speck of protoplasm, of one of the commonest animals: "Strange possibilities," he says, "lie dormant in that semi-fluid globule. Let a moderate supply of warmth reach its watery cradle and the plastic matter undergoes changes so rapid and yet so steady and purposelike in their succession that one can only compare them to those operated by a skilled modeler upon a formless lump of clay. As with an invisible trowel the mass is divided and subdivided into smaller and smaller portions, until it is reduced to an aggregation of granules not too large to build withal the finest fabrics of the nascent organism. And, then, it is as if a delicate finger traced out the line to be occupied by the spinal column, and moulded the contour of the body; pinching up the head at one end, the tail at the other, and fashioning flank and limb into due proportions in so artistic a way, that, after watching the process hour by hour, one is almost involuntarily possessed by the notion, that some more subtle aid to vision than an achromatic would show the hidden artist, with his plan before him, striving with skillful manipulation to perfect his work."[87]

Besides the fact, so luminously brought out here, that the artist is distinct from the "semi-fluid globule" of protoplasm in which he works, there is this other essential point to notice, that in all his "skillful manipulation" the artist is not working at random, but according to law. He has "his plan before him." In the zoological laboratory of Nature it is not as in a workshop where a skilled artisan can turn his hand to anything—where the same potter one day moulds a dog, the next a bird, and the next a man. In Nature one potter is set apart to make each. It is a more complete system of division of labor. One artist makes all the dogs, another makes all the birds, a third makes all the men. Moreover, each artist confines himself exclusively to working out his own plan. He appears to have his own plan somehow stamped upon himself, and his work is rigidly to reproduce himself.

The Scientific Law by which this takes place is the Law of Conformity to Type. It is contained, to a large extent, in the ordinary Law of Inheritance; or it may be considered as simply another way of stating what Darwin calls the Laws of Unity of Type. Darwin defines it thus: "By Unity of Type is meant that fundamental agreement in structure which we see in organic beings of the same class, and which is quite independent of their habits of life."[88] According to this law every living thing that comes into the world is compelled to stamp upon its offspring the image of itself. The dog, according to its type, produces a dog; the bird a bird.

The Artist who operates upon matter in this subtle way and carries out this law is Life. There are a great many different kinds of Life. If one might give the broader meaning to the words of the apostle: "All life is not the same life. There is one kind of life of men, another life of beasts, another of fishes, and another of birds." There is the Life, or the Artist, or the Potter who segments the worm, the potter who forms the dog, the potter who moulds the man.[89]

What goes on then in the animal kingdom is this—the Bird-Life seizes upon the bird-germ and builds it up into a bird, the image of itself. The Reptile Life seizes upon another germinal speck, assimilates surrounding matter, and fashions it into a reptile. The Reptile-Life thus simply makes an incarnation of itself. The visible bird is simply an incarnation of the invisible Bird-Life.

Now we are nearing the point where the spiritual analogy appears. It is a very wonderful analogy, so wonderful that one almost hesitates to put it into words. Yet Nature is reverent; and it is her voice to which we listen. These lower phenomena of life, she says, are but an allegory. There is another kind of Life of which Science as yet has taken little cognizance. It obeys the same laws. It builds up an organism into its own form. It is the Christ-Life. As the Bird-Life builds up a bird, the image of itself, so the Christ-Life builds up a Christ, the image of Himself, in the inward nature of man. When a man becomes a Christian the natural process is this: The Living Christ enters into his soul. Development begins. The quickening Life seizes upon the soul, assimilates surrounding elements, and begins to fashion it. According to the great Law of Conformity to Type this fashioning takes a specific form. It is that of the Artist who fashions. And all through Life this wonderful, mystical, glorious, yet perfectly definite process, goes on "until Christ be formed" in it.

The Christian Life is not a vague effort after righteousness—an ill-defined pointless struggle for an ill-defined pointless end. Religion is no dishevelled mass of aspiration, prayer, and faith. There is no more mystery in Religion as to its processes than in Biology. There is much mystery in Biology. We know all but nothing of Life yet, nothing of development. There is the same mystery in the spiritual Life. But the great lines are the same, as decided, as luminous; and the laws of natural and spiritual are the same, as unerring, as simple. Will everything else in the natural world unfold its order, and yield to Science more and more a vision of harmony and Religion, which should complement and perfect all, remain a chaos? From the standpoint of Revelation no truth is more obscure than Conformity to Type. If Science can furnish a companion phenomenon from an every-day process of the natural life, it may at least throw this most mystical doctrine of Christianity into thinkable form. Is there any fallacy in speaking of the Embryology of the New Life? Is the analogy invalid? Are there not vital processes in the Spiritual as well as in the Natural world? The Bird being an incarnation of the Bird-Life, may not the Christian be a spiritual incarnation of the Christ-Life? And is here not a real justification in the processes of the New Birth for such a parallel?

Let us appeal to the record of these processes.

In what terms does the New Testament describe them? The answer is sufficiently striking. It uses everywhere the language of Biology. It is impossible that the New Testament writers should have been familiar with these biological facts. It is impossible that their views of this great truth should have been as clear as Science can make them now. But they had no alternative. There was no other way of expressing this truth. It was a biological question. So they struck out unhesitatingly into the new fields of words, and, with an originality which commands both reverence and surprise, stated their truth with such light, or darkness, as they had. They did not mean to be scientific, only to be accurate, and their fearless accuracy has made them scientific.

What could be more original, for instance, than the Apostle's reiteration that the Christian was a new creature, a new man, a babe?[90] Or that this new man was "begotten of God," God's workmanship?[91] And what could be a more accurate expression of the law of Conformity to Type than this: "Put on the new man, which is renewed in knowledge after the image of Him that created him?"[92] Or this, "We are changed into the same image from glory to glory?"[93] And elsewhere we are expressly told by the same writer that this Conformity is the end and goal of the Christian life. To work this Type in us is the whole purpose of God for man. "Whom He did foreknow He also did predestinate to be conformed to the image of His Son."[94]

One must confess that the originality of this entire New Testament conception is most startling. Even for the nineteenth century it is the most startling. But when one remembers that such an idea took form in the first, he cannot fail to be impressed with a deepening wonder at the system which begat and cherished it. Men seek the origin of Christianity among philosophies of that age. Scholars contrast it still with these philosophies, and scheme to fit it in to those of later growth. Has it never occurred to them how much more it is than a philosophy, that it includes a science, a Biology pure and simple? As well might naturalists contrast zoology with chemistry, or seek to incorporate geology with botany—the living with the dead—as try to explain the spiritual life in terms of mind alone. When will it be seen that the characteristic of the Christian Religion is its Life, that a true theology must begin with a Biology? Theology is the Science of God. Why will men treat God as inorganic?

If this analogy is capable of being worked out, we should expect answers to at least three questions.

First: What corresponds to the protoplasm in the spiritual sphere?
Second: What is the Life, the Hidden Artist who fashions it?
Third: What do we know of the process and the plan?

First: The Protoplasm

We should be forsaking the lines of nature were we to imagine for a moment that the new creature was to be found out of nothing. *Ex nihilo nihil*—nothing can be made out of nothing. Matter is uncreatable and indestructible; Nature and man can only form and transform. Hence when a new animal is made, no new clay is made. Life merely enters into already existing matter, assimilates more of the same sort and re-builds it. The spiritual Artist works in the same way. He must have a peculiar kind of protoplasm, a basis of life, and that must be already existing.

Now we find this in the materials of character with which the natural man is previously provided. Mind and character, the will and the affections, the moral nature—these form the bases of spiritual life. To look in this direction for the protoplasm of the spiritual life is consistent with all analogy. The lowest or mineral world mainly supplies the material—and this is true even for insectivorous species—for the vegetable kingdom. The vegetable supplies the material for the animal. Next in turn, the animal furnishes material for the mental, and lastly, the mental for the spiritual. Each member of the series is complete only when the steps below it are complete; the highest demands all. It is not necessary for the immediate purpose to go so far into the psychology either of the new creature or of the old as to define more clearly what these moral bases are. It is enough to discover that in this womb the new creature is to be born, fashioned out of the mental and moral parts, substance, or essence of the natural man. The only thing to be insisted upon is that in the natural man this mental and moral substance or basis is spiritually lifeless. However active the intellectual or moral life may be, from the point of view of this other Life it is dead. That which is flesh is flesh. It wants, that is to say, the kind of Life which constitutes the difference between the Christian and the not-a-Christian. It has not yet been "born of the Spirit."

To show further that this protoplasm possesses the necessary properties of a normal protoplasm it will be necessary to examine in passing what these properties are. They are two in number, the capacity for life and plasticity. Consider first the capacity for life. It is not enough to find an adequate supply of material. That must be of the right kind. For all kinds of matter have not the power to be the vehicle of life—all kinds of matter are not even fitted to be the vehicle of electricity. What peculiarity there is in Carbon, Hydrogen, Oxygen, and Nitrogen, when combined in a certain way, to receive life, we cannot tell. We only know that life is always associated in Nature with this particular physical basis and never with any other. But we are not in the same darkness with regard to the moral protoplasm. When we look at this complex combination which we have predicted as the basis of spiritual life, we do find something which gives it a peculiar qualification for being the protoplasm of the Christ-Life. We discover one strong reason at least, not only why this kind of life should be associated with this kind of protoplasm, but why it should never be associated with other kinds which seem to resemble it—why, for instance, this spiritual life should not be engrafted upon the intelligence of a dog or the instincts of an ant.

The protoplasm in man has a something in addition to its instincts or its habits. It has a capacity for God. In this capacity for God lies its receptivity; it is the very protoplasm that was necessary. The chamber is not only ready to receive the new Life, but the Guest is expected, and, till He comes, is missed. Till then the soul longs and yearns, wastes and pines, waving its tentacles piteously in the empty air, feeling after God if so be that it may find Him. This is not peculiar to the protoplasm of the Spiritual man's soul. In every land and in every age there have been altars to the Known or Unknown God. It is now agreed as a mere question of anthropology that the universal language of the human soul has always been "I perish with hunger." This is what fits it for Christ. There is a grandeur in this cry from the depths which makes its very unhappiness sublime.

The other quality we are to look for in the soul is mouldableness, plasticity. Conformity demands conformability. Now plasticity is not only a marked characteristic of all forms of life, but in a special sense of the highest forms. It increases steadily as we rise in the scale. The inorganic world, to begin with, is rigid. A crystal of silica dissolved and redissolved a thousand times will never assume any other form than the hexagonal. The plant next, though plastic in its elements, is comparatively insusceptible of change. The very fixity of its sphere, the imprisonment for life in a single spot of earth, is the symbol of a certain degradation. The animal in all parts is mobile, sensitive, free; the highest animal, man, is the most mobile, the most at leisure from routine, the most impressionable, the most open for change. And when we reach the mind and soul, this mobility is found in its most developed form. Whether we regard its susceptibility to impressions, its lightning-like response even to influences the most impalpable and subtle, its power of instantaneous adjustment, or whether we regard the delicacy and variety of its moods, or its vast powers of growth, we are forced to recognize in this the most perfect capacity for change. This marvellous plasticity of mind contains at once the possibility and prophecy of its transformation. The soul, in a word, is made to be *converted*.

SECOND, THE LIFE

The main reason for giving the Life, the agent of this change, a separate treatment, is to emphasize the distinction between it and the natural man on the one hand, and the spiritual man on the other. The natural man is its basis, the spiritual man is its product, the Life itself is something different. Just as in an organism we have these three things—formative matter, formed matter, and the forming principle or life; so in the soul we have the old nature, the renewed nature, and the transforming Life.

This being made evident, little remains here to be added. No man has ever seen this Life. It cannot be analyzed, or weighed, or traced in its essential nature. But this is just what we expected. This invisibility is the same property which we found to be peculiar to the natural life. We saw no life in the first embryos, in oak, in palm, or in bird. In the adult it likewise escapes us. We shall not wonder if we cannot see it in the Christian. We shall not expect to see it. *A fortiori* we shall not expect to see it, for we are further removed from the coarser matter—moving now among ethereal and spiritual things. It is because it conforms to the law of this analogy so well that men, not seeing it, have denied its being. Is it hopeless to point out that one of the most recognizable characteristics of life is its unrecognizableness, and that the very token of its spiritual nature lies in its being beyond the grossness of our eyes?

We do not pretend that Science can define this Life to be Christ. It has no definition to give even of its own life, much less of this. But there are converging lines which point, at least, in the direction that it is Christ.

There was One whom history acknowledges to have been the Truth. One of His claims was this, "I am the Life." According to the doctrine of Biogenesis, life can only come from life. It was His additional claim that His function in the world was to give men Life. "I am come that ye might have Life, and that ye might have it more abundantly." This could not refer to the natural life, for men had that already. He that hath the Son hath another Life. "Know ye not your own selves how that Jesus Christ is in you."

Again, there are men whose characters assume a strange resemblance to Him who was the Life. When we see the bird-character appear in an organism we assume that the Bird-Life has been there at work. And when we behold Conformity to Type in a Christian, and know moreover that the type-organization can be produced by the type-life alone does this not lend support to the hypothesis that the Type-Life also has been here at work? If every effect demands a cause, what other cause is there for the Christian? When we have a cause, and an adequate cause, and no other adequate cause; when we have the express statement of that Cause that he is that cause, what more is possible? Let not Science, knowing nothing of its own life, go further than to say it knows nothing of this Life. We shall not dissent from its silence. But till it tells us what it is, we wait for evidence that it is not this.

THIRD, THE PROCESS

It is impossible to enter at length into any details of the great miracle by which this protoplasm is to be conformed to the Image of the Son. We enter that province now only so far as this Law of Conformity compels us. Nor is it so much the nature of the process we have to consider as its general direction and results. We are dealing with a question of morphology rather than of physiology.

It must occur to one on reaching this point, that a new element here comes in which compels us, for the moment, to part company with zoology. That element is the conscious power of choice. The animal in following the type is blind. It does not only follow the type involuntarily and compulsorily, but does not know that it is following it. We might certainly have been made to conform to the Type in the higher sphere with no more knowledge or power of choice than animals or automata. But then we should not have been men. It is a possible case, but not possible to the kind of protoplasm with which men are furnished. Owing to the peculiar characteristics of this protoplasm an additional and exceptional provision is essential.

The first demand is that being conscious and having this power of choice, the mind should have an adequate knowledge of what it is to choose. Some revelation of the Type, that is to say, is necessary. And as that revelation can only come from the Type, we must look there for it.

We are confronted at once with the Incarnation. There we find how the Christ-Life has clothed Himself with matter, taken literal flesh, and dwelt among us. The Incarnation is the Life revealing the Type. Men are long since agreed that this is the end of the Incarnation—the revealing of God. But why should God be revealed? Why, indeed, but for man? Why but that "beholding as in a glass the glory of the only begotten he should be changed into the same image?"

To meet the power of choice, however, something more was necessary than the mere revelation of the Type—it was necessary that the Type should be the highest conceivable Type. In other words, the Type must be an Ideal. For all true human growth, effort, and achievement, an ideal is acknowledged to be indispensable. And all men accordingly whose lives are based on principle, have set themselves an ideal, more or less perfect. It is this which first deflects the will from what is base, and turns the wayward life to what is holy. So much is true as mere philosophy. But philosophy failed to present men with their ideal. It has never been suggested that Christianity has failed. Believers and unbelievers have been compelled to acknowledge that Christianity holds up to the world the missing Type, the Perfect Man.

The recognition of the Ideal is the first step in the direction of Conformity. But let it be clearly observed that it is but a step. There is no vital connection between merely seeing the Ideal and being conformed to it. Thousands admire Christ who never become Christians.

But the great question still remains, How is the Christian to be conformed to the Type, or as we should now say, dealing with consciousness, to the Ideal? The mere knowledge of the Ideal is no more than a motive. How is the process to be practically accomplished? Who is to do it? Where, when, how? This is the test question of Christianity. It is here that all theories of Christianity, all attempts to explain it on natural principles, all reductions of it to philosophy, inevitably break down. It is here that all imitations of Christianity perish. It is here, also, that personal religion finds its most fatal obstacle. Men are all quite clear about the Ideal. We are all convinced of the duty of mankind regarding it. But how to secure that willing men shall attain it—that is the problem of religion. It is the failure to understand the dynamics of Christianity that has most seriously and most pitifully hindered its growth both in the individual and in the race.

From the standpoint of biology this practical difficulty vanishes in a moment. It is probably the very simplicity of the law regarding it that has made men stumble. For nothing is so invisible to most men as transparency. The law here is the same biological law that exists in the natural world. For centuries men have striven to find out ways and means to conform themselves to this type. Impressive motives have been pictured, the proper circumstances arranged, the direction of effort defined, and men have toiled, struggled, and agonized to conform themselves to the Image of the Son. Can the protoplasm *conform itself* to its type? Can the embryo *fashion itself*? Is Conformity to Type produced by the matter *or by the life*, by the protoplasm or by the Type? Is organization the cause of life or the effect of it? It is the effect of it. Conformity to Type, therefore, is secured by the type. Christ makes the Christian.

Men need only reflect on the automatic processes of their natural body to discover that this is the universal law of Life. What does any man consciously do, for instance, in the matter of breathing? What part does he take in circulating the blood, in keeping up the rhythm of his heart? What control has he over growth? What man by taking thought can add a cubit to his stature? What part voluntarily does man take in secretion, in digestion, in the reflex actions? In point of fact is he not after all the veriest automaton, every organ of his body given him, every function arranged for him, brain and nerve, thought and sensation, will and conscience, all provided for him ready made? And yet he turns upon his soul and wishes to organize that himself! O preposterous and vain man, thou who couldest not make a finger nail of thy body, thinkest thou to fashion this wonderful, mysterious, subtle soul of thine after the ineffable Image? Wilt thou ever permit thyself *to be* conformed to the Image of the Son? Wilt thou, who canst not add a cubit to thy stature, submit *to be* raised by the Type-Life within thee to the perfect stature of Christ?

This is a humbling conclusion. And therefore men will resent it. Men will still experiment "by works of righteousness which they have done" to earn the Ideal life. The doctrine of Human Inability, as the Church calls it, has always been objectionable to men who do not know themselves. The doctrine itself, perhaps, has been partly to blame. While it has been often affirmed in such language as rightly to humble men, it has also been stated and cast in their teeth with words which could only insult them. Merely to assert dogmatically that man has no power to move hand or foot to help himself toward Christ, carries no real conviction. The weight of human authority is always powerless, and ought to be, where the intelligence is denied a rationale. In the light of modern science, when men seek a reason for every thought of God or man, this old doctrine with its severe and almost inhuman aspect—till rightly understood—must presently have succumbed. But to the biologist it cannot die. It stands to him on the solid ground of Nature. It has a reason in the laws of life which must resuscitate it and give it another lease of years. Bird-Life makes the Bird. Christ-Life makes the Christian. No man by taking thought can add a cubit to his stature.

So much for the scientific evidence. Here is the corresponding statement of the truth from Scripture. Observe the passive voice in these sentences: "*Begotten* of God;" "The new man which *is renewed* in knowledge after the Image of Him that created him;" or this, "We *are changed* into the same Image;" or this, "Predestinate *to be* conformed to the Image of His Son;" or again, "Until Christ *be formed* in you;" or "Except a man *be born again* he cannot see the Kingdom of God;" "Except a man *be born* of water and of the Spirit he cannot enter the Kingdom of God." There is one outstanding verse which seems at first sight on the other side: "Work out your own salvation with fear and trembling;" but as one reads on he finds, as if the writer dreaded the very misconception, the complement, "For it is God which worketh in you both to will and to do of His good pleasure."

It will be noticed in these passages, and in others which might be named, that the process of transformation is referred indifferently to the agency of each Person of the Trinity in turn. We are not concerned to take up this question of detail. It is sufficient that the transformation is wrought. Theologians, however, distinguish thus: the indirect agent is Christ, the direct influence is the Holy Spirit. In other words, Christ by his Spirit renews the souls of men.

Is man, then, out of the arena altogether? Is he mere clay in the hands of the potter, a machine, a tool, an automaton? Yes and No. If he were a tool he would not be a man. If he were a man he would have something to do. One need not seek to balance what God does here and what man does. But we shall attain to a sufficient measure of truth on a most delicate problem if we make a final appeal to the natural life. We find that in maintaining this natural life Nature has a share and man has a share. By far the larger part is done for us—the breathing, the secreting, the circulating of the blood, the building up of the organism. And although the part which man plays is a minor part, yet, strange to say, it is not less essential to the well being, and even to the being, of the whole. For instance, man has to take food. He has nothing to do with it after he has once taken it, for the moment it passes his lips it is taken in hand by reflex actions and handed on from one organ to another, his control over it, in the natural course of things, being completely lost. But the initial act was his. And without that nothing could have been done. Now whether there be an exact analogy between the voluntary and involuntary functions in the body, and the corresponding processes in the soul, we do not at present inquire. But this will indicate, at least, that man has his own part to play. Let him choose Life; let him daily nourish his soul; let him for ever starve the old life; let him abide continuously as a living

branch in the Vine, and the True-Vine Life will flow into his soul, assimilating, renewing, conforming to Type, till Christ, pledged by His own
law, be formed in him.

We have been dealing with Christianity at its most mystical point.
Mark here once more its absolute naturalness. The pursuit of the Type
is just what all Nature is engaged in. Plant and insect, fish and reptile,
bird and mammal—these in their several spheres are striving after the
Type. To prevent its extinction, to ennoble it, to people earth and sea
and sky with it; this is the meaning of the Struggle for Life. And this is
our life—to pursue the Type, to populate the world with it.

Our religion is not all a mistake. We are not visionaries. We are not
"unpractical," as men pronounce us, when we worship. To try to follow
Christ is not to be "righteous overmuch." True men are not rhapsodizing when they preach; nor do those waste their lives who waste
themselves in striving to extend the Kingdom of God on earth. This is
what life is for. The Christian in his life-aim is in strict line with
Nature. What men call supernatural is quite natural.

Mark well also the splendor of this idea of salvation. It is not merely
final "safety," to be forgiven sin, to evade the curse. It is not, vaguely, "to
get to heaven." It is to be conformed to the Image of the Son. It is for
these poor elements to attain to the Supreme Beauty. The organizing
Life being Eternal, so must this Beauty be immortal. Its progress toward
the Immaculate is already guaranteed. And more than all there is here
fulfilled the sublimest of all prophecies; not Beauty alone but Unity is
secured by the Type—Unity of man and man, God and man, God and
Christ and man till "all shall be one."

Could Science in its most brilliant anticipations for the future of its
highest organism ever have foreshadowed a development like this? Now
that the revelation is made to it, it surely recognizes it as the missing
point in Evolution, the climax to which all Creation tends. Hitherto
Evolution had no future. It was a pillar with marvelous carving, growing
richer and finer toward the top, but without a capital; a pyramid, the vast
base buried in the inorganic, towering higher and higher, tier above tier,
life above life, mind above mind, ever more perfect in its workmanship,

more noble in its symmetry, and yet withal so much the more mysterious in its aspiration. The most curious eye, following it upward, saw nothing. The cloud fell and covered it. Just what men wanted to see was hid. The work of the ages had no apex. But the work begun by Nature is finished by the Supernatural—as we are wont to call the higher natural. And as the veil is lifted by Spirituality it strikes men dumb with wonder. For the goal of Evolution is Jesus Christ.

The Christian life is the only life that will ever be completed. Apart from Christ the life of man is a broken pillar, the race of Men an unfinished pyramid. One by one in sight of Eternity all human Ideals fall short, one by one before the open grave all human hopes dissolve. The Laureate sees a moment's light in Nature's jealousy for the Type; but that too vanishes.

> "'So careful of the type?'" but no.
> From scarpèd cliff and quarried stone
> She cries, 'A thousand types are gone:
> I care for nothing, all shall go.'"

All shall go? No, one Type remains. "Whom He did foreknow He also did predestinate to be conformed to the Image of His Son." And "when Christ who is our life shall appear, then shall ye also appear with Him in glory."

VI

GROWTH

Is not the evidence of Ease on the very front of all the greatest works in existence? Do they not say plainly to us, not "there has been a great effort here," but "there has been a great power here"? It is not the weariness of mortality but the strength of divinity, which we have to recognise in all mighty things; and that is just what we now never recognise, but think that we are to do great things by help of iron bars and perspiration; alas! we shall do nothing that way, but lose some pounds of our own weight.
Ruskin

Consider the lilies of the field how they grow.
The Sermon on the Mount

Nunquam aliud natura, aliud sapientia dicit.
Juvenal

What gives the peculiar point to this object-lesson from the lips of Jesus is, that He not only made the illustration, but made the lilies. It is like an inventor describing his own machine. He made the lilies and He made me—both on the same broad principle. Both together, man and flower, He planted deep in the Providence of God; but as men are dull at studying themselves He points to this companion-phenomenon to teach us how to live a free and natural life, a life which God will unfold for us, without our anxiety, as He unfolds the flower. For

Christ's words are not a general appeal to consider nature. Men are not to consider the lilies simply to admire their beauty, to dream over the delicate strength and grace of stem and leaf. The point they were to consider was *how they grew*—how without anxiety or care the flower woke into loveliness, how without weaving these leaves were woven, how without toiling these complex tissues spun themselves, and how without any effort or friction the whole slowly came ready-made from the loom of God in its more than Solomon-like glory. "So," He says, making the application beyond dispute, "you care-worn, anxious men must grow. You, too, need take no thought for your life, what ye shall eat or what ye shall drink or what ye shall put on. For if God so clothe the grass of the field, which to-day is, and to-morrow is cast into the oven, shall He not much more clothe you, O ye of little faith?"

This nature-lesson was a great novelty in its day; but all men now who have even a "little faith" have learned this Christian secret of a composed life. Apart even from the parable of the lily, the failures of the past have taught most of us the folly of disquieting ourselves in vain, and we have given up the idea that by taking thought we can add a cubit to our stature.

But no sooner has our life settled down to this calm trust in God than a new and graver anxiety begins. This time it is not for the body we are in travail, but for the soul. For the temporal life we have considered the lilies, but how is the spiritual life to grow? How are we to become better men? How are we to grow in grace? By what thought shall we add the cubits to the spiritual stature and reach the fullness of the Perfect Man? And because we know ill how to do this, the old anxiety comes back again and our inner life is once more an agony of conflict and remorse. After all, we have but transferred our anxious thoughts from the body to the soul. Our efforts after Christian growth seem only a succession of failures, and instead of rising into the beauty of holiness our life is a daily heartbreak and humiliation.

Now the reason of this is very plain. We have forgotten the parable of the lily. Violent efforts to grow are right in earnestness, but wholly wrong in principle. There is but one principle of growth both for the natural and spiritual, for animal and plant, for body and soul. For all growth is an organic thing. And the principle of growing in grace is once more this, "Consider the lilies *how they grow*."

In seeking to extend the analogy from the body to the soul there are two things about the lilies' growth, two characteristics of all growth, on which one must fix attention. These are—

First, Spontaneousness.

Second, Mysteriousness.

I. Spontaneousness. There are three lines along which one may seek for evidence of the spontaneousness of growth. The first is Science. And the argument here could not be summed up better than in the words of Jesus. The lilies grow, He says, of themselves; they toil not, neither do they spin. They grow, that is, automatically, spontaneously, without trying, without fretting, without thinking. Applied in any direction, to plant, to animal, to the body or to the soul this law holds. A boy grows, for example, without trying. One or two simple conditions are fulfilled, and the growth goes on. He thinks probably as little about the condition as about the result; he fulfils the conditions by habit, the result follows by nature. Both processes go steadily on from year to year apart from himself and all but in spite of himself. One would never think of *telling* a boy to grow. A doctor has no prescription for growth. He can tell me how growth may be stunted or impaired, but the process itself is recognised as beyond control—one of the few, and therefore very significant, things which Nature keeps in her own hands. No physician of souls, in like manner, has any prescription for spiritual growth. It is the question he is most often asked and most often answers wrongly. He may prescribe more earnestness, more prayer, more self-denial, or more Christian work. These are prescriptions for something, but not for growth. Not that they may not encourage growth; but the soul grows as the lily grows, without trying, without fretting, without ever thinking. Manuals of devotion, with complicated rules for getting on in the Christian life, would do well sometimes to return to the simplicity of nature; and earnest souls who are attempting sanctification by struggle instead of sanctification by faith might be spared much humiliation by learning the botany of the Sermon on the Mount. There *can* indeed be no other principle of growth than this. It is a vital act. And to try to *make* a thing grow is as absurd as to help the tide to come in or the sun rise.

Another argument for the spontaneousness of growth is universal experience. A boy not only grows without trying, but he cannot grow if he tries. No man by taking thought has ever added a cubit to his stature; nor has any man by mere working at his soul ever approached nearer to the stature of the Lord Jesus. The stature of the Lord Jesus was not itself reached by work, and he who thinks to approach its mystical height by anxious effort is really receding from it. Christ's life unfolded itself from a divine germ, planted centrally in His nature, which grew as naturally as a flower from a bud. This flower may be imitated; but one can always tell an artificial flower. The human form may be copied in wax, yet somehow one never fails to detect the difference. And this precisely is the difference between a native growth of Christian principle and the moral copy of it. The one is natural, the other mechanical. The one is a growth, the other an accretion. Now this, according to modern biology, is the fundamental distinction between the living and the not living, between an organism and a crystal. The living organism grows, the dead crystal increases. The first grows vitally from within, the last adds new particles from the outside. The whole difference between the Christian and the moralist lies here. The Christian works from the centre, the moralist from the circumference. The one is an organism, in the center of which is planted by the living God a living germ. The other is a crystal, very beautiful it may be; but only a crystal—it wants the vital principle of growth.

And one sees here also, what is sometimes very difficult to see, why salvation in the first instance is never connected directly with morality. The reason is not that salvation does not demand morality, but that it demands so much of it that the moralist can never reach up to it. The end of Salvation is perfection, the Christlike mind, character and life. Morality is on the way to this perfection; it may go a considerable distance towards it, but it can never reach it. Only Life can do that. It requires something with enormous power of movement, of growth, of overcoming obstacles, to attain the perfect. Therefore the man who has within himself this great formative agent, Life, is nearer the end than the man who has morality alone. The latter can never reach perfection; the former *must*. For the Life must develop out according to its type; and being a germ of the Christ-life, it must unfold into a *Christ*. Morality, at the utmost, only develops the character in one or two directions. It may perfect a single virtue here and there, but it cannot perfect all. And especially it fails always to give that rounded harmony of parts, that perfect tune to the whole orchestra, which is the marked characteristic of life. Perfect life is not merely the possessing of perfect functions, but of perfect functions perfectly adjusted to each other and all conspiring to a single result, the perfect working of the whole organism. It is not said that the character will develop in all its fulness in this life. That were a time too short for an Evolution so magnificent. In this world only the cornless ear is seen; sometimes only the small yet still prophetic blade. The sneer at the godly man for his imperfections is ill-judged. A blade is a small thing. At first it grows very near the earth. It is often soiled and crushed and downtrodden. But it is a living thing. That great dead stone beside it is more imposing; only it will never be anything else than a stone. But this small blade—*it doth not yet appear what it shall be.*

Seeing now that Growth can only be synonymous with a living automatic process, it is all but superfluous to seek a third line of argument from Scripture. Growth there is always described in the language of physiology. The regenerate soul is a new creature. The Christian is a new man in Christ Jesus. He adds the cubits to his stature just as the old man does. He is rooted and built up in Christ; he abides in the vine, and so abiding, not toiling or spinning, brings forth fruit. The Christian in short, like the poet, is born not made; and the fruits of his character are not manufactured things but living things, things which have grown from the secret germ, the fruits of the living Spirit. They are not the produce of this climate, but exotics from a sunnier land.

II. But, secondly, besides this Spontaneousness there is this other great characteristic of Growth—Mysteriousness. Upon this quality

depends the fact, probably, that so few men ever fathom its real character. We are most unspiritual always in dealing with the simplest spiritual
things. A lily grows mysteriously, pushing up its solid weight of stem
and leaf in the teeth of gravity. Shaped into beauty by secret and invisible fingers, the flower develops we know not how. But we do not
wonder at it. Every day the thing is done; it is Nature, it is God. We are
spiritual enough at least to understand that. But when the soul rises
slowly above the world, pushing up its delicate virtues in the teeth of
sin, shaping itself mysteriously into the image of Christ, we deny that
the power is not of man. A strong will, we say, a high ideal, the reward
of virtue, Christian influence—these will account for it. Spiritual character is merely the product of anxious work, self-command, and
self-denial. We allow, that is to say, a miracle to the lily, but none to the
man. The lily may grow; the man must fret and toil and spin.

Now grant for a moment that by hard work and self-restraint a
man may attain to a very high character. It is not denied that this can be
done. But what is denied is that this is growth, and that this process is
Christianity. The fact that you can account for it proves that it is not
growth. For growth is mysterious; the peculiarity of it is that you
cannot account for it. Mysteriousness, as Mozley has well observed, is
"the test of spiritual birth." And this was Christ's test. "The wind
bloweth where it listeth. Thou hearest the sound thereof, but canst not
tell whence it cometh or whither it goeth, *so is every one that is born of
the Spirit.*" The test of spirituality is that you cannot tell whence it
cometh or whither it goeth. If you can tell, if you can account for it on
philosophical principles, on the doctrine of influence, on strength of
will, on a favourable environment, it is not growth. It may be so far a
success, it may be a perfectly honest, even remarkable, and praiseworthy
imitation, but it is not the real thing. The fruits are wax, the flowers
artificial—you can tell whence it cometh and whither it goeth.

The conclusion is, then, that the Christian is a unique phenome-
non. You cannot account for him. And if you could he would not be a
Christian. Mozley has drawn the two characters for us in graphic words:
"Take an ordinary man of the world—what he thinks and what he

does, his whole standard of duty is taken from the society in which he lives. It is a borrowed standard: he is as good as other people are; he does, in the way of duty, what is generally considered proper and becoming among those with whom his lot is thrown. He reflects established opinion on such points. He follows its lead. His aims and objects in life again are taken from the world around him, and from its dictation. What it considers honourable, worth having, advantageous and good, he thinks so too and pursues it. His motives all come from a visible quarter. It would be absurd to say that there is any mystery in such a character as this, because it is formed from a known external influence—the influence of social opinion and the voice of the world. 'Whence such a character cometh' we see; we venture to say that the source and origin of it is open and palpable, and we know it just as we know the physical causes of many common facts."

Then there is the other. "There is a certain character and disposition of mind of which it is true to say that 'thou canst not tell whence it cometh or whither it goeth.' . . . There are those who stand out from among the crowd, which reflects merely the atmosphere of feeling and standard of society around it, with an impress upon them which bespeaks a heavenly birth. . . . Now, when we see one of those characters, it is a question which we ask ourselves, How has the person become possessed of it? Has he caught it from society around him? That cannot be, because it is wholly different from that of the world around him. Has he caught it from the inoculation of crowds and masses, as the mere religious zealot catches his character? That cannot be either, for the type is altogether different from that which masses of men, under enthusiastic impulses, exhibit. There is nothing gregarious in this character; it is the individual's own; it is not borrowed, it is not a reflection of any fashion or tone of the world outside; it rises up from some fount within, and it is a creation of which the text says, We know not whence it cometh."[53]

Now we have all met these two characters—the one eminently respectable, upright, virtuous, a trifle cold perhaps, and generally, when critically examined, revealing somehow the mark of the tool; the other with God's breath still upon it, an inspiration; not more virtuous, but differently virtuous; not more humble, but different, wearing the meek and quiet spirit artlessly as to the manner born. The other-worldliness of such a character is the thing that strikes you; you are not prepared for what it will do or say or become next, for it moves from a far-off centre, and in spite of its transparency and sweetness, that presence fills you always with awe. A man never feels the discord of his own life, never hears the jar of the machinery by which he tries to manufacture his own good points, till he has stood in the stillness of such a presence. Then he discerns the difference between growth and work. He has considered the lilies, how they grow.

We have now seen that spiritual growth is a process maintained and secured by a spontaneous and mysterious inward principle. It is a spontaneous principle even in its origin, for it bloweth where it listeth; mysterious in its operation, for we can never tell whence it cometh; obscure in its destination, for we cannot tell whence it goeth. The whole process therefore transcends us; we do not work, we are taken in hand—"it is God which worketh in us, both to will and to do of His good pleasure." We do not plan—we are "created in Christ Jesus unto good works, which God hath before ordained that we should walk in them."

There may be an obvious objection to all this. It takes away all conflict from the Christian life? It makes man, does it not, mere clay in the hands of the potter? It crushes the old character to make a new one, and destroys man's responsibility for his own soul?

Now we are not concerned here in once more striking the time-honored "balance between faith and works." We are considering how lilies grow, and in a specific connection, namely, to discover the attitude of mind which the Christian should preserve regarding his spiritual growth. That attitude, primarily, is to be free from care. We are not lodging a plea for inactivity of the spiritual energies, but for the tranquility of the spiritual mind. Christ's protest is not against work, but against anxious thought; and rather, therefore, than complement the lesson by showing the other side, we take the risk of still further extending the plea in the original direction.

What is the relation, to recur again to analogy, between growth and work in a boy? Consciously, there is no relation at all. The boy never thinks of connecting his work with his growth. Work in fact is one thing and growth another, and it is so in the spiritual life. If it be asked therefore, Is the Christian wrong in these ceaseless and agonizing efforts after growth? the answer is, Yes, he is quite wrong, or at least, he is quite mistaken. When a boy takes a meal or denies himself indigestible things, he does not say, "All this will minister to my growth"; or when he runs a race he does not say, "This will help the next cubit of my stature." It may or it may not be true that these things will help his stature, but, if he thinks of this, his idea of growth is morbid. And this is the point we are dealing with. His anxiety here is altogether irrelevant and superfluous. Nature is far more bountiful than we think. When she gives us energy she asks none of it back to expend on our own growth. She will attend to that. "Give your work," she says, "and your anxiety to others; trust me to add the cubits to your stature." If God is adding to our spiritual stature, unfolding the new nature within us, it is a mistake to keep twitching at the petals with our coarse fingers. We must seek to let the Creative Hand alone. "It is God which giveth the increase." Yet we never know how little we have learned of the fundamental principle of Christianity till we discover how much we are all bent on supplementing God's free grace. If God is spending work upon a Christian, let him be still and know that it is God. And if he wants work, he will find it there—in the being still.

Not that there is no work for him who would grow, to do. There is work, and severe work—work so great that the worker deserves to have himself relieved of all that is superfluous during his task. If the amount of energy lost in trying to grow were spent in fulfilling rather the conditions of growth, we should have many more cubits to show for our stature. It is with these conditions that the personal work of the Christian is chiefly concerned. Observe for a moment what they are, and their exact relation. For its growth the plant needs heat, light, air, and moisture. A man, therefore, must go in search of these, or their spiritual equivalents, and this is his work? By no means. The Christian's work is not yet. Does the plant go in search of its conditions? Nay, the conditions come to the plant. It no more manufactures the heat, light, air, and moisture, than it manufactures its own stem. It finds them all around it in Nature. It simply stands still with its leaves spread out in unconscious prayer, and Nature lavishes upon it these and all other bounties, bathing it in sunshine, pouring the nourishing air over and over it, reviving it graciously with its nightly dew. Grace, too, is as free as the air. The Lord God is a Sun. He is as the Dew to Israel. A man has no more to manufacture these than he has to manufacture his own soul. He stands surrounded by them, bathed in them, beset behind and before by them. He lives and moves and has his being in them. How then shall he go in search of them? Do not they rather go in search of him? Does he not feel how they press themselves upon him? Does he not know how unweariedly they appeal to him? Has he not heard how they are sorrowful when he will not have them? His work, therefore, is not yet. The voice still says, "Be still."

The conditions of growth, then, and the inward principle of growth being both supplied by Nature, the thing man has to do, the little junction left for him to complete, is to apply the one to the other. He manufactures nothing; he earns nothing; he need be anxious for nothing; his one duty is *to be in* these conditions, to abide in them, to allow grace to play over him, to be still therein and know that this is God.

The conflict begins and prevails in all its life-long agony the moment a man forgets this. He struggles to grow himself instead of struggling to get back again into position. He makes the church into a workshop when God meant it to be a beautiful garden. And even in his closet, where only should reign silence—a silence as of the mountains whereon the lilies grow—is heard the roar and tumult of machinery. True, a man will often have to wrestle with his God—but not for growth. The Christian life is a composed life. The Gospel is Peace. Yet the most anxious people in the world are Christians—Christians who misunderstand the nature of growth. Life is a perpetual self-condemning because they are not growing. And the effect is not only the loss of tranquillity to the individual. The energies which are meant to be spent on the work of Christ are consumed in the soul's own fever. So long as the Church's activities are spent on growing there is nothing to spare for the world. A soldier's time is not spent in earning the money to buy his armour, in finding food and raiment, in seeking shelter. His king provides these things that he may be the more at liberty to fight his battles. So, for the soldier of the Cross all is provided. His Government has planned to leave him free for the Kingdom's work.

The problem of the Christian life finally is simplified to this—man has but to preserve the right attitude. To abide in Christ, to be in position, that is all. Much work is done on board a ship crossing the Atlantic. Yet none of it is spent on making the ship go. The sailor but harnesses his vessel to the wind. He puts his sail and rudder in position, and lo, the miracle is wrought. So everywhere God creates, man utilizes. All the work of the world is merely a taking advantage of energies already there.[54] God gives the wind, and the water, and the heat; man but puts himself in the way of the wind, fixes his water-wheel in the way of the river, puts his piston in the way of the steam; and so holding himself in position before God's Spirit, all the energies of Omnipotence course within his soul. He is like a tree planted by a river whose leaf is green and whose fruits fail not. Such is the deeper lesson to be learned from considering the lily. It is the voice of Nature echoing the whole evangel of Jesus, "Come unto Me, and I will give you rest."

VII

THE GREATEST THING IN THE WORLD

Though I speak with the tongues of men and of angels,
and have not love, I am become as a sounding brass, or a tinkling cymbal.
And though I have the gift of prophecy, and understand all mysteries,
and all knowledge; and though I have all faith, so that I could remove
mountains, and have not LOVE I am nothing. And though I bestow
all my goods to feed the poor, and though I give my body
to be burned, and have not Love, it profiteth me nothing.
Love suffereth long, and is kind;
Love envieth not;
Love vaunteth not itself is not puffed up,
Doth not behave itself unseemly,
Seeketh not her own,
Is not easily provoked,
Thinketh no evil;
Rejoiceth not in iniquity, but rejoiceth in the truth;
Beareth all things, believeth all things, hopeth all things, endureth all things.

Love never faileth: but whether there be prophecies, they shall fail;
whether there be tongues, they shall cease; whether there be knowledge,
it shall vanish away. For we know in part, and we prophesy in part.
But when that which is perfect is come, then that which is in part shall
be done away. When I was a child, I spake as a child, I understood as
a child, I thought as a child: but when I became a man, I put away
childish things. For now we see through a glass, darkly; but then
face to face: now I know in part; but then shall I know even as also

I am known. And now abideth faith, hope, Love, these three;
but the greatest of these is Love.
1 Corinthians 13

Every one has asked himself the great question of antiquity as of the modern world: What is the *summum bonum*—the supreme good? You have life before you. Once only you can live it. What is the noblest object of desire, the supreme gift to covet?

We have been accustomed to be told that the greatest thing in the religious world is Faith. That great word has been the key-note for centuries of the popular religion; and we have easily learned to look upon it as the greatest thing in the world. Well, we are wrong. If we have been told that, we may miss the mark. I have taken you, in the chapter which I have just read, to Christianity at its source; and there we have seen, "The greatest of these is love." It is not an oversight. Paul was speaking of faith just a moment before. He says, "If I have all faith, so that I can remove mountains, and have not love, I am nothing." So far from forgetting, he deliberately contrasts them, "Now abideth Faith, Hope, Love," and without a moment's hesitation, the decision falls, "The greatest of these is Love."

And it is not prejudice. A man is apt to recommend to others his own strong point. Love was not Paul's strong point. The observing student can detect a beautiful tenderness growing and ripening all through his character as Paul gets old; but the hand that wrote, "The greatest of these is love," when we meet it first, is stained with blood.

Nor is this letter to the Corinthians peculiar in singling out love as the *summum bonum*. The masterpieces of Christianity are agreed about it. Peter says, "Above all things have fervent love among yourselves." *Above all things.* And John goes farther, "God is love." And you remember the profound remark which Paul makes elsewhere, "Love is the fulfilling of the law." Did you ever think what he meant by that? In those days men were working their passage to Heaven by keeping the Ten Commandments, and the hundred and ten other commandments which they had manufactured out of them. Christ said, I will show you a more simple way. If you do one thing, you will do these hundred and ten things, without ever thinking about them. If you love, you will unconsciously fulfil the whole law. And you can readily see for yourselves how that must be so. Take any of the commandments. "Thou shalt have no other gods before Me." If a man loves God, you will not require to tell him that. Love is the fulfilling of that law. "Take not His name in vain." Would he ever dream of taking His name in vain if he loved Him? "Remember the Sabbath day to keep it holy." Would he not be too glad to have one day in seven to dedicate more exclusively to the object of his affection? Love would fulfil all these laws regarding God. And so, if he loved Man, you would never think of telling him to honor his father and mother. He could not do anything else. It would be preposterous to tell him not to kill. You could only insult him if you suggested that he should not steal—how could he steal from those he loved? It would be superfluous to beg him not to bear false witness against his neighbor. If he loved him it would be the last thing he would do. And you would never dream of urging him not to covet what his neighbors had. He would rather they possessed it than himself. In this way "Love is the fulfilling of the law." It is the rule for fulfilling all rules, the new commandment for keeping all the old commandments, Christ's one secret of the Christian life.

❝ ❝ ❝

THE CONTRAST

Paul begins by contrasting Love with other things that men in those days thought much of. I shall not attempt to go over those things in detail. Their inferiority is already obvious.

He contrasts it with eloquence. And what a noble gift it is, the power of playing upon the souls and wills of men, and rousing them to lofty purposes and holy deeds. Paul says, "If I speak with the tongues of men and of angels, and have not love, I am become as sounding brass, or a tinkling cymbal." And we all know why. We have all felt the brazenness of words without emotion, the hollowness, the unaccountable unpersuasiveness, of eloquence behind which lies no Love.

He contrasts it with prophecy. He contrasts it with mysteries. He contrasts it with faith. He contrasts it with charity. Why is Love greater than faith? Because the end is greater than the means. And why is it greater than charity? Because the whole is greater than the part. Love is greater than faith, because the end is greater than the means. What is the use of having faith? It is to connect the soul with God. And what is the object of connecting man with God? That he may become like God. But God is Love. Hence Faith, the means, is in order to Love, the end. Love, therefore, obviously is greater than faith. It is greater than charity, again, because the whole is greater than a part. Charity is only a little bit of Love, one of the innumerable avenues of Love, and there may even be, and there is, a great deal of charity without Love. It is a very easy thing to toss a copper to a beggar on the street; it is generally an easier thing than not to do it. Yet Love is just as often in the withholding. We purchase relief from the sympathetic feelings roused by the spectacle of misery, at the copper's cost. It is too cheap—too cheap for us, and often too dear for the beggar. If we really loved him we would either do more for him, or less.

Then Paul contrasts it with sacrifice and martyrdom. And I beg the little band of would-be missionaries and I have the honor to call some of you by this name for the first time—to remember that though you give your bodies to be burned, and have not Love, it profits nothing—nothing! You can take nothing greater to the heathen world than the impress and reflection of the Love of God upon your own character. That is the universal language. It will take you years to speak in Chinese, or in the dialects of India. From the day you land, that language of Love, understood by all, will be pouring forth its unconscious eloquence. It is the man who is the missionary, it is not his words. His character is his message. In the heart of Africa, among the great Lakes, I have come across black men and women who remembered the only white man they ever saw before—David

Livingstone; and as you cross his footsteps in that dark continent, men's faces light up as they speak of the kind Doctor who passed there years ago. They could not understand him; but they felt the Love that beat in his heart. Take into your new sphere of labor, where you also mean to lay down your life, that simple charm, and your lifework must succeed. You can take nothing greater, you need take nothing less. It is not worth while going if you take anything less. You may take every accomplishment; you may be braced for every sacrifice; but if you give your body to be burned, and have not Love, it will profit you and the cause of Christ nothing.

THE ANALYSIS

After contrasting Love with these things, Paul, in three verses, very short, gives us an amazing analysis of what this supreme thing is. I ask you to look at it. It is a compound thing, he tells us. It is like light. As you have seen a man of science take a beam of light and pass it through a crystal prism, as you have seen it come out on the other side of the prism broken up into its component colours—red, and blue, and yellow, and violet, and orange, and all the colours of the rainbow—so Paul passes this thing, Love, through the magnificent prism of his inspired intellect, and it comes out on the other side broken up into its elements. And in these few words we have what one might call the Spectrum of Love, the analysis of Love. Will you observe what its elements are? Will you notice that they have common names; that they are virtues which we hear about every day; that they are things which can be practised by every man in every place in life; and how, by a multitude of small things and ordinary virtues, the supreme thing, the *summum bonum*, is made up?

The Spectrum of Love has nine ingredients:

Patience . . . . "Love suffereth long."
Kindness . . . . "And is kind."
Generosity . . . . . "Love envieth not."

Humility . . . . "Love vaunteth not itself, is not puffed up."
Courtesy . . . . "Doth not behave itself unseemly."
Unselfishness . . . . "Seeketh not her own."
Good Temper . . . "Is not easily provoked."
Guilelessness . . . . "Thinketh no evil."
Sincerity . . . . . . "Rejoiceth not in iniquity, but rejoiceth
in the truth."

Patience; kindness; generosity; humility; courtesy; unselfishness; good temper; guilelessness; sincerity—these make up the supreme gift, the stature of the perfect man. You will observe that all are in relation to men, in relation to life, in relation to the known to-day and the near to-morrow, and not to the unknown eternity. We hear much of love to God; Christ spoke much of love to man. We make a great deal of peace with heaven; Christ made much of peace on earth. Religion is not a strange or added thing, but the inspiration of the secular life, the breathing of an eternal spirit through this temporal world. The supreme thing, in short, is not a thing at all, but the giving of a further finish to the multitudinous words and acts which make up the sum of every common day.

There is no time to do more than make a passing note upon each of these ingredients. Love is *Patience*. This is the normal attitude of Love; Love passive, Love waiting to begin; not in a hurry; calm; ready to do its work when the summons comes, but meantime wearing the ornament of a meek and quiet spirit. Love suffers long; bears all things; believeth all things; hopes all things. For Love understands, and there - fore waits.

Kindness. Love active. Have you ever noticed how much of Christ's life was spent in doing kind things—in *merely* doing kind things? Run over it with that in view and you will find that He spent a great proportion of His time simply in making people happy, in doing good turns to people. There is only one thing greater than happiness in the world, and that is holiness; and it is not in our keeping; but what God *has* put in our power is the happiness of those about us, and that is largely to be secured by our being kind to them.

"The greatest thing," says some one, "a man can do for his Heavenly Father is to be kind to some of His other children." I wonder why it is that we are not all kinder than we are? How much the world needs it. How easily it is done. How instantaneously it acts. How infallibly it is remembered. How superabundantly it pays itself back—for there is no debtor in the world so honourable, so superbly honourable, as Love. "Love never faileth." Love is success, Love is happiness, Love is life. "Love," I say, with Browning, "is energy of Life."

For life, with all it yields of joy and woe
And hope and fear,
Is just our chance o' the prize of learning love—
How love might be, hath been indeed, and is.

Where Love is, God is. He that dwelleth in Love dwelleth in God. God is love. Therefore *love*. Without distinction, without calculation, without procrastination, love. Lavish it upon the poor, where it is very easy; especially upon the rich, who often need it most; most of all upon our equals, where it is very difficult, and for whom perhaps we each do least of all. There is a difference between *trying to please* and *giving pleasure*. Give pleasure. Lose no chance of giving pleasure. For that is the ceaseless and anonymous triumph of a truly loving spirit.

"I shall pass through this world but once. Any good thing therefore that I can do, or any kindness that I can show to any human being, let me do it now. Let me not defer it or neglect it, for I shall not pass this way again."

Generosity. "Love envieth not" This is Love in competition with others. Whenever you attempt a good work you will find other men doing the same kind of work, and probably doing it better. Envy them not. Envy is a feeling of ill-will to those who are in the same line as ourselves, a spirit of covetousness and detraction. How little Christian work even is a protection against un-Christian feeling. That most despicable of all the unworthy moods which cloud a Christian's soul assuredly waits for us on the threshold of every work, unless we are fortified with this grace of magnanimity. Only one thing truly need the Christian envy, the large, rich, generous soul which "envieth not."

And then, after having learned all that, you have to learn this further thing, *Humility*—to put a seal upon your lips and forget what you have done. After you have been kind, after Love has stolen forth into the world and done its beautiful work, go back into the shade again and say nothing about it. Love hides even from itself. Love waives even self-satisfaction. "Love vaunteth not itself, is not puffed up."

The fifth ingredient is a somewhat strange one to find in this *summum bonum: Courtesy.* This is Love in society, Love in relation to etiquette. "Love doth not behave itself unseemly." Politeness has been defined as love in trifles. Courtesy is said to be love in little things. And the one secret of politeness is to love. Love cannot behave itself unseemly. You can put the most untutored person into the highest society, and if they have a reservoir of love in their heart, they will not behave themselves unseemly. They simply cannot do it. Carlyle said of Robert Burns that there was no truer gentleman in Europe than the ploughman-poet. It was because he loved everything—the mouse, and the daisy, and all the things, great and small, that God had made. So with this simple passport he could mingle with any society, and enter courts and palaces from his little cottage on the banks of the Ayr. You know the meaning of the word "gentleman." It means a gentle man—a man who does things gently, with love. And that is the whole art and mystery of it. The gentleman cannot in the nature of things do an ungentle, an ungentlemanly thing. The un-gentle soul, the inconsiderate, unsympathetic nature cannot do anything else. "Love doth not behave itself unseemly."

Unselfishness. "Love seeketh not her own." Observe: Seeketh not even that which is her own. In Britain the Englishman is devoted, and rightly, to his rights. But there come times when a man may exercise even the higher right of giving up his rights. Yet Paul does not summon us to give up our rights. Love strikes much deeper. It would have us not seek them at all, ignore them, eliminate the personal element altogether from our calculations. It is not hard to give up our rights. They are often external. The difficult thing is to give up ourselves. The more difficult thing still is not to seek things for ourselves at all. After we have sought them, bought them, won them, deserved them, we have taken the cream off them for ourselves already. Little cross then, perhaps, to give them up. But not to seek them, to look every man not on his own things, but on the things of others—*id opus est.* "Seekest thou great things for thyself?" said the prophet; "*seek them not.*" Why? Because there is no greatness in things. Things cannot be great. The only greatness is unselfish love. Even self-denial in itself is nothing, is almost a mistake. Only a great purpose or a mightier love can justify the waste. It is more difficult, I have said, not to seek our own at all, than, having sought it, to give it up. I must take that back. It is only true of a partly selfish heart. Nothing is a hardship to Love, and nothing is hard. I believe that Christ's yoke is easy. Christ's "yoke" is just His way of taking life. And I believe it is an easier way than any other. I believe it is a happier way than any other. The most obvious lesson in Christ's teaching is that there is no happiness in having and getting anything, but only in giving. I repeat, *there is no happiness in having or in getting, but only in giving.* And half the world is on the wrong scent in the pursuit of happiness. They think it consists in having and getting, and in being served by others. It consists in giving, and in serving others. He that would be great among you, said Christ, let him serve. He that would be happy, let him remember that there is but one way—it is more blessed, it is more happy, to give than to receive.

The next ingredient is a very remarkable one: *Good Temper.* "Love is not easily provoked." Nothing could be more striking than to find this here. We are inclined to look upon bad temper as a very harmless weakness. We speak of it as a mere infirmity of nature, a family failing, a matter of temperament, not a thing to take into very serious account in estimating a man's character. And yet here, right in the heart of this analysis of love, it finds a place; and the Bible again and again returns to condemn it as one of the most destructive elements in human nature.

The peculiarity of ill temper is that it is the vice of the virtuous. It is often the one blot on an otherwise noble character. You know men who are all but perfect, and women who would be entirely perfect, but for an easily ruffled, quick-tempered, or "touchy" disposition. This compatibility of ill temper with high moral character is one of the strangest and saddest problems of ethics.... No form of vice, not worldliness, not greed of gold, not drunkenness itself, does more to un-Christianize society than evil temper. For embittering life, for breaking up communities, for destroying the most sacred relationships, for devastating homes, for withering up men and women, for taking the bloom off childhood; in short, for sheer gratuitous misery-producing power, this influence stands alone.

❛ ❛ ❛

Jealousy, anger, pride, uncharity, cruelty, self-righteousness, touchiness, doggedness, sullenness—these are the ingredients of this dark and love-less soul. In varying proportions, also, these are the ingredients of all ill temper. Judge if such sins of the disposition are not worse to live in, and for others to live with, than sins of the body. Did Christ indeed not answer the question Himself when He said, "I say unto you, that the publicans and the harlots go into the Kingdom of Heaven before you." There is really no place in Heaven for a disposition like this. A man with such a mood could only make Heaven miserable for all the people in it. Except, therefore, such a man be born again, he cannot, he simply cannot, enter the Kingdom of Heaven. For it is perfectly certain—and you will not misunderstand me—that to enter Heaven a man must take it with him.

You will see then why Temper is significant. It is not in what it is alone, but in what it reveals. This is why I take the liberty now of speaking of it with such unusual plainness. It is a test for love, a symp-tom, a revelation of an unloving nature at bottom. It is the intermittent fever which bespeaks unintermittent disease within; the occasional bub-ble escaping to the surface which betrays some rottenness underneath; a sample of the most hidden products of the soul dropped involuntarily when off one's guard; in a word, the lightning form of a hundred

hideous and un-Christian sins. For a want of patience, a want of kindness, a want of generosity, a want of courtesy, a want of unselfishness,
are all instantaneously symbolised in one flash of Temper.

Hence it is not enough to deal with the temper. We must go to the
source, and change the inmost nature, and the angry humours will die
away of themselves. Souls are made sweet not by taking the acid fluids
out, but by putting something in—a great Love, a new Spirit, the Spirit
of Christ. Christ, the Spirit of Christ, interpenetrating ours, sweetens,
purifies, transforms all. This only can eradicate what is wrong, work
a chemical change, renovate and regenerate, and rehabilitate the inner
man. Will-power does not change men. Time does not change men.
Christ does. Therefore "Let that mind be in you which was also
in Christ Jesus." Some of us have not much time to lose. Remember,
once more, that this is a matter of life or death. I cannot help speaking
urgently, for myself, for yourselves. "Whoso shall offend one of these
little ones, which believe in me, it were better for him that a millstone
were hanged about his neck, and that he were drowned in the depth of
the sea." That is to say, it is the deliberate verdict of the Lord Jesus that it
is better not to live than not to love. *It is better not to live than not to love.*

Guilelessness and *Sincerity* may be dismissed almost with a word.
Guilelessness is the grace for suspicious people. And the possession of it
is the great secret of personal influence. You will find, if you think for a
moment, that the people who influence you are people who believe in
you. In an atmosphere of suspicion men shrivel up; but in that atmosphere they expand, and find encouragement and educative fellowship. It
is a wonderful thing that here and there in this hard, uncharitable world
there should still be left a few rare souls who think no evil. This is the
great unworldliness. Love "thinketh no evil," imputes no motive, sees
the bright side, puts the best construction on every action. What a
delightful state of mind to live in! What a stimulus and benediction
even to meet with it for a day! To be trusted is to be saved. And if we
try to influence or elevate others, we shall soon see that success is in
proportion to their belief of our belief in them. For the respect of
another is the first restoration of the self-respect a man has lost; our

ideal of what he is becomes to him the hope and pattern of what he may become.

"Love rejoiceth not in iniquity, but rejoiceth in the truth." I have called this *Sincerity* from the words rendered in the Authorised Version by "rejoiceth in the truth." And, certainly, were this the real translation, nothing could be more just. For he who loves will love Truth not less than men. He will rejoice in the Truth—rejoice not in what he has been taught to believe; not in this Church's doctrine or in that; not in this ism or in that ism; but "in *the Truth*." He will accept only what is real; he will strive to get at facts; he will search for Truth with a humble and unbiased mind, and cherish whatever he finds at any sacrifice. But the more literal translation of the Revised Version calls for just such a sacrifice for truth's sake here. For what Paul really meant is, as we there read, "Rejoiceth not in unrighteousness, but rejoiceth with the truth," a quality which probably no one English word—and certainly not *Sincerity*—adequately defines. It includes, perhaps more strictly, the self-restraint which refuses to make capital out of others' faults; the charity which delights not in exposing the weakness of others, but "covereth all things"; the sincerity of purpose which endeavours to see things as they are, and rejoices to find them better than suspicion feared or calumny denounced.

So much for the analysis of Love. Now the business of our lives is to have these things fitted into our characters. That is the supreme work to which we need to address ourselves in this world, to learn Love. Is life not full of opportunities for learning Love? Every man and woman every day has a thousand of them. The world is not a playground; it is a schoolroom. Life is not a holiday, but an education. And the one eternal lesson for us all is *how better we can love*. What makes a man a good cricketer? Practice. What makes a man a good artist, a good sculptor, a good musician? Practice. What makes a man a good linguist, a good stenographer? Practice. What makes a man a good man? Practice. Nothing else. There is nothing capricious about religion. We do not get the soul in different ways, under different laws, from those in which we get the body and the mind. If a man does not exercise his arm he develops no biceps muscle; and if a man does not exercise his soul, he acquires no muscle in his soul, no strength of character, no vigour of moral fibre, nor beauty of spiritual growth. Love is not a thing of enthusiastic emotion. It is a rich, strong, manly, vigorous expression of the whole round Christian character—the Christlike nature in its fullest development. And the constituents of this great character are only to be built up by ceaseless practice.

What was Christ doing in the carpenter's shop? Practising. Though perfect, we read that He *learned* obedience, He *increased* in wisdom and in favour with God and man. Do not quarrel therefore with your lot in life. Do not complain of its never-ceasing cares, its petty environment, the vexations you have to stand, the small and sordid souls you have to live and work with. Above all, do not resent temptation; do not be perplexed because it seems to thicken round you more and more, and ceases neither for effort nor for agony nor prayer. That is the practice which God appoints you; and it is having its work in making you patient, and humble, and generous, and unselfish, and kind, and courteous. Do not grudge the hand that is moulding the still too shapeless image within you. It is growing more beautiful though you see it not, and every touch of temptation may add to its perfection. Therefore keep in the midst of life. Do not isolate yourself. Be among men, and among things, and among troubles, and difficulties, and obstacles. You remember Goethe's words: *Es bildet ein Talent sich in der Stille, Doch ein Character indem Strom der Welt.* "Talent develops itself in solitude; character in the stream of life." Talent develops itself in solitude—the talent of prayer, of faith, of meditation, of seeing the unseen; Character grows in the stream of the world's life. That chiefly is where men are to learn love.

How? Now, how? To make it easier, I have named a few of the elements of love. But these are only elements. Love itself can never be defined. Light is a something more than the sum of its ingredients—a glowing, dazzling, tremulous ether. And love is something more than all its elements—a palpitating, quivering, sensitive, living thing. By synthesis of all the colours, men can make whiteness, they cannot make light. By synthesis of all the virtues, men can make virtue, they cannot make love. How then are we to have this transcendent living whole conveyed into our souls? We brace our wills to secure it. We try to copy those who have it. We lay down rules about it. We watch. We pray. But these things alone will not bring Love into our nature. Love is an *effect*. And only as we fulfil the right condition can we have the effect produced. Shall I tell you what the *cause* is?

If you turn to the Revised Version of the First Epistle of John you will find these words: "We love, because He first loved us." . . . Look at that word "because." It is the cause of which I have spoken. "Because He first loved us," the effect follows that we love, we love Him, we love all men. We cannot help it. Because He loved us, we love, we love everybody. Our heart is slowly changed. Contemplate the love of Christ, and you will love. Stand before that mirror, reflect Christ's character, and you will be changed into the same image from tenderness to tenderness. There is no other way. You cannot love to order. You can only look at the lovely object, and fall in love with it, and grow into likeness to it. . . . Love begets love. It is a process of induction. Put a piece of iron in the presence of a magnetised body, and that piece of iron for a time becomes magnetised. It is charged with an attractive force in the mere presence of the original force, and as long as you leave the two side by side, they are both magnets alike. Remain side by side with Him who loved us, and gave Himself for us, and you too will become a centre of power, a permanently attractive force; and like Him you will draw all men unto you, like Him you will be drawn unto all men. That is the inevitable effect of Love. Any man who fulfils that cause must have that effect produced in him. Try to give up the idea that religion comes to us by chance, or by mystery, or by caprice. It comes to us by natural law, or by supernatural law, for all law is Divine. Edward Irving went to see a dying boy once, and when he entered the room he just put his hand on the sufferer's head, and said, "My boy, God loves you," and went away. And the boy started from his bed, and called out to the people in the house, "God loves me! God loves me!" It changed that boy. The sense that God loved him overpowered him, melted him down, and began the creating of a new heart in him. And that is how the love of God melts down the unlovely heart in man, and begets in him the new creature, who is patient and humble and gentle and unselfish. And there is no other way to get it. There is no mystery about it. We love others, we love everybody, we love our enemies, because He first loved us.

THE DEFENCE

Now I have a closing sentence or two to add about Paul's reason for singling out love as the supreme possession. It is a very remarkable reason. In a single word it is this: *it lasts.* "Love," urges Paul, "never faileth."

Can you tell me anything that is going to last? Many things Paul did not condescend to name. He did not mention money, fortune, fame; but he picked out the great things of his time, the things the best men thought had something in them, and brushed them peremptorily aside. Paul had no charge against these things in themselves. All he said about them was that they would not last. They were great things, but not supreme things. There were things beyond them. What we are stretches past what we do, beyond what we possess. Many things that men denounce as sins are not sins; but they are temporary. And that is a favorite argument of the New Testament. John says of the world, not that it is wrong, but simply that it "passeth away." There is a great deal in the world that is delightful and beautiful; there is a great deal in it that is great and engrossing; but it will not last. All that is in the world, the lust of the eye, the lust of the flesh, and the pride of life, are but for a little while. Love not the world therefore. Nothing that it contains is worth the life and consecration of an immortal soul. The immortal soul must give itself to something that is immortal.

❦ ❦ ❦

To love abundantly is to live abundantly, and to love for ever is to live for ever. Hence, eternal life is inextricably bound up with love. We want to live forever for the same reason that we want to live tomorrow. Why do you want to live tomorrow? It is because there is some one who loves you, and whom you want to see tomorrow, and be with, and love back. There is no other reason why we should live on than that we love and are beloved. It is when a man has no one to love him that he commits suicide. So long as he has friends, those who love him and whom he loves, he will live; because to live is to love. Be it but the love of a dog, it will keep him in life; but let that go and he has no contact with life, no reason to live. The "energy of life" has failed. Eternal life also is to know God, and God is love. This is Christ's own definition. Ponder it. "This is life eternal, that they might know Thee the only true God, and Jesus Christ whom Thou hast sent." Love must be eternal. It is what God is. On the last analysis, then, love is life. Love never faileth, and life never faileth, so long as there is love. That is the philosophy of what Paul is showing us; the reason why in the nature of things Love should be the supreme thing—because it is going to last; because in the nature of things it is an Eternal Life. That Life is a thing that we are living now, not that we get when we die; that we shall have a poor chance of getting when we die unless we are living now. No worse fate can befall a man in this world than to live and grow old alone, unloving, and unloved. To be lost is to live in an unregenerate condition, loveless and unloved; and to be saved is to love; and he that dwelleth in love dwelleth already in God. For God is love.

Notes (Abridged)

Preface

2. Bacon, Sir Francis, "Meditationes Sacræ," x c. 1600c.e.

INTRODUCTION—PART I: A New Science

3. "Reign of Law," chap. ii.
4. "Animal Kingdom."
5. "Sartor Resartus," 1858 Ed., p. 43.
6. Even parable, however, has always been considered to have attached to it a measure of evidential as well as of illustrative value. Thus: "The parable or other analogy to spiritual truth appropriated from the world of nature or man, is not merely illustrative, but also in some sort proof. It is not merely that these analogies assist to make the truth intelligible or, if intelligible before, present it more vividly to the mind, which is all that some will allow them. Their power lies deeper than this, in the harmony unconsciously felt by all men, and which all deeper minds have delighted to trace, between the natural and spiritual worlds, so that analogies from the first are felt to be something more than illustrations happily but yet arbitrarily chosen. They are arguments, and may be alleged as witnesses; the world of nature being throughout a witness for the world of spirit, proceeding from the same hand, growing out of the same root, and being constituted for that very end."—(Archbishop Trench: "Parables," pp. 12, 13.)

INTRODUCTION—PART II: One Law

19. "First Principles," p. 161.
24. The Duke of Argyll: *Contemporary Review*, Sept, 1880, p. 358.
26. 6th edition p. 235.
27. Ibid. p. 286.
31. Hinton's "Philosophy and Religion," p. 40.

BIOGENESIS

33. "Beginnings of Life." By H. C. Bastian, M.A., M.D., F.R.S. Macmillan, vol. ii. p. 633.
34. "Critiques and Addresses." T. H. Huxley. F.R.S., p. 239.
35. Nineteenth Century, 1878, p. 507.
36. This being the crucial point it may not be inappropriate to supplement the quotations already given in the text with the following—

"We are in the presence of the one incommunicable gulf—the gulf of all gulfs—that gulf which Mr. Huxley's protoplasm is as powerless to efface as any other material expedient that has ever been suggested since the eyes of men first looked into it—the mighty gulf between death and life."—"As Regards Protoplasm." By J. Hutchinson Stirling, LL.D., p. 42.

"The present state of knowledge furnishes us with no link between the living and the not-living."—Huxley, "Encyclopædia Britannica" (new Ed.). Art. "Biology."

"Whoever recalls to mind the lamentable failure of all the attempts made very recently to discover a decided support for the *generatio æquivoca* in the lower forms of transition from the inorganic to the organic world, will feel it doubly serious to demand that this theory, so utterly discredited, should be in any way accepted as the basis of all our views of life."—Virchow, Rudolf, "The Freedom of Science in the Modern State."

"All really scientific experience tells us that life can be produced from a living antecedent only."—"The Unseen Universe," 6th Ed., p. 229.
37. John iii.
38. Rom. viii. 6.
39. Rev. iii. 1.
40. 1 Tim. v. 6.
41. Eph. ii. 1, 5.
42. 1 Cor. ii. 14.
43. "First Principles," 2nd Ed., p. 17.

44. 2 Cor. xii. 5.
45. 1 Cor. vi. 15.
46. John xiv. 20.
47. John xiv. 21-23.
48. John xv. 4.
49. Gal. ii. 20.
50. One must not be misled by popular statements in this connection, such as this of Professor Owen's: "There are organisms which we can devitalize and revital-ize—devive and revive—many times." (*Monthly Microscopical Journal*, May, 1869, p. 294.) The reference is of course to the extraordinary capacity for *resuscitation* possessed by many of the Protozoa and other low forms of life.
51. Acts ix. 5.

ENVIRONMENT

81. *Vide* Karl Semper's "The Natural Conditions of Existence as They Affect Animal Life;" Wallace's "Tropical Nature;" Weismann's "Studies in the Theory of Descent;" Darwin's "Animals and Plants under Domestication."
82. "Principles of Biology," p. 57.
83. Ps. cxlii. 4, 5.
84. "Unseen Universe," 6th Ed., p. 100.

CONFORMITY TO TYPE

85. "There is, indeed, a period in the development of every tissue and every living thing known to us when there are actually no *structural* peculiarities whatever—when the whole organism consists of transparent, structureless, semi-fluid living bioplasm—when it would not be possible to distinguish the growing moving matter which was to evolve the oak from that which was the germ of a verte-brate animal. Nor can any difference be discerned between the bioplasm matter of the lowest, simplest, epithelial scale of man's organism and that from which the nerve cells of our brain are to be evolved. Neither by studying bioplasm under the microscope nor by any kind of physical or chemical investigation known, can we form any notion of the nature of the substance which is to be formed by the bioplasm, or what will be the ordinary results of the living."—Beale, F.R.S., Lionel S., "Bioplasm," pp. 17, 18.
86. Huxley "Lay Sermons," 6th Ed., pp. 127, 129.
87. Huxley "Lay Sermons," 6th Ed., p. 261.
88. "Origin of Species," p. 166.

89. There is no intention here to countenance the old doctrine of the permanence of species. Whether the word species represent a fixed quantity or the reverse does not affect the question. The facts as stated are true in contemporary zoology if not in palæontology. It may also be added that the general conception of a definite Vital Principle is used here simply as a working hypothesis. Science may yet have to give up what the Germans call the "ontogenetic directive Force." But in the absence of any proof to the contrary, and especially of any satisfactory alternative, we are justified in working still with the old theory.
90. 2 Cor. v. 17.
91. 1 John v. 18; 1 Pet. i. 3.
92. Col. iii. 9, 10.
93. 2 Cor. iii. 18.
94. Rom. viii. 29.

GROWTH

53. University Sermons, pp. 234–241.
54. See Bushnell's "New Life."

READER'S GROUP GUIDE

enry Drummond was a late-nineteenth-century professor of natural sciences and an evangelical Christian who spent much of his life reconciling those two ways of thinking. While studying at the University of Edinburgh, Drummond was most interested in the physical and mathematical sciences. He began to form a library, starting with a volume of extracts from John Ruskin's works. These writings taught Drummond to see the world around him in a new way, as one full of charm and loveliness. He next acquired the writings of Ralph Waldo Emerson, who powerfully affected both Drummond's teaching and his writing style. Both these authors were optimists with no belief in evil. They taught Drummond to find a joy in Nature that carried over into his religion.

After studying these works, Drummond thought that practical religion might be treated as an exact science. His book *Natural Law in the Spiritual World* was immediately seen as a godsend to thinking people around the world. And one of his last "little books," *The Greatest Thing in the World*, remains a popular gift of love today.

In *One Law*, Dr. Ruth Miller has brought Drummond's merging of the scientific with the spiritual into today's world of multiple sciences and many faith traditions. The questions below are based on passages from her interpretation of Drummond's text.

QUESTIONS FOR DIALOGUE

1. In the opening sentence of the book, Drummond noted, "Books and articles dealing with science and spirituality receive more suspicion—more derision, even—than any other body of work." Why do you think this is? What examples support this statement? Name some scientists who believe that spirituality and science shouldn't mix. Why do you think they hold this belief?

2. Drummond then asked, "Is there reason to believe that, even though we think of them as separate, the laws of the spiritual world are simply extensions of the laws of the natural world?" Why would you consider your spiritual life an extension of your natural, physical life? Should we consider the ongoing spiritual life of those who've passed on as extensions of their bodily life? Why?

3. Drummond later noted that "educated young people find it hard to accept or retain the forms of religion they grew up with, and this is especially true of those trained in the sciences." Was it hard to reconcile your faith with what you were learning in school? Did you find a way for your beliefs and learning to coexist? If you know people who have not yet reconciled them, what challenges do they face?

4. Drummond assured readers that "it's not possible for science to overthrow a faith based on understanding. . . . rather than blind adherence to the voices of authority from our childhood." What does "a faith based on understanding" mean? How did the tradition you grew up in encourage that kind of faith, or how did it require you to accept what others told you? Is there an advantage to either approach?

5. Drummond's solution was to "extend the scientific method into spirituality." The scientific method is a set of steps designed to answer a question and raise new ones. The steps are as follows: (1) observe something; (2) consider different explanations; (3) form a hypothesis that might explain it; (4) test that hypothesis as rigorously as possible, so that nothing else might be affecting the results; (5) observe and analyze the results; and (6) share the results so that others can replicate them and explore the questions they raise. Who do you know of has done or is doing this kind of work with spirituality and consciousness? How have they done this work, and what was the result? How would you use this method to answer some of your own spiritual questions?

6. The Law of Continuity tells us we can expect the same sort of processes to happen at many levels of life. (For example, the cell takes in nutrients and excretes waste, as does the body comprising many cells and the community comprising many bodies.) What are some other examples of the Law of Continuity? Drummond described a children's book titled *The Chance World*, in

which there is no Continuity. *Alice in Wonderland* is another example of such a book. What are some others? How do they illustrate the lack of Continuity?

7. Drummond then told us we should be able to apply the Law of Continuity to the spiritual world as well. He went on to note that "as the upward thrust of the growing plant appears to overcome gravity, which is the primary defining law of the mineral realm, any new laws of the spiritual realm would appear to overcome the laws of the lower kingdoms." As you think about spiritual life, what kind of new laws might appear? How are some of today's events that we call "miracles" actually those laws at work?

8. One way Drummond helped us understand miracles was by explaining that "the great thinkers across time—both scientific and spiritual—have declared that all that we see and hear—all the phenomena of Nature—has no reality apart from our thought. They are symbols, metaphors, and analogies demonstrating our individual and collective thought." The world of quantum physics and the world of New Thought come together in this idea, and the concept of synchronicities is related to it. What are some ways the world around you has reflected your thoughts and feelings? Have you thought about someone and had that person show up or call or thought of an issue that was explained soon after? How would you live your life if you knew that everything you see, hear, and touch is reflecting what you're thinking and feeling?

9. Regarding the world around us, Drummond said, "Our environment is that in which we live and move and have our being. Without it, we would neither live nor move nor have any being." Could any of us live without air? Without water? Where do our clothes and cars and food come from? If our environment were to change radically, how would we change? What might the environment of our spiritual being be, and how might it support our spiritual lives? What is the role of prayer, or communing with the divine, in how it supports us? What is the source and power of Life?

10. Drummond told us that "as the mineral cannot enter the plant kingdom and the plant cannot enter the animal kingdom without being pulled 'from above,' unless we human beings are born 'from above,' we cannot enter the kingdom just above us." Minerals from the soil are pulled into the plant and converted into living cells. Plants we eat are digested and converted into living, moving tissue in our bodies. Is it possible that we may be pulled into the spiritual realm and converted into spiritual beings? If so, would we still be "us" or something else? What would you be if you realized you were part of something more than your physical self? How does that relate to your idea of divinity?

11. We often feel the need to behave like "good people," but Drummond said that "moralistic behavior is not the same as blossoming spirituality" What is the difference between the naturally good behavior of someone who has developed

spiritually and one who has developed moralistic behavior? Have you ever "faked it till you made it?" What does it feel like? Can you think of a more effective way to be the best you can be?

12. What do you believe is the greatest good there is? The Greek and Latin term for what is usually translated as "love" or "charity," which the apostle Paul called "the greatest of these" is caritas. It's based on a root word meaning "heart" and might be literally translated as "heart action" or "coming from the heart." What does it feel like to have a thought or action come from the heart? Think about a difficult relationship you have. How would you deal with it if your thoughts and actions came from the heart? What would the world be like if we all lived by caritas?

ENHANCE YOUR EXPERIENCE

1. Watch the film *The Living Matrix* (available on DVD and online at www .thelivingmatrix.com). Take a close look at the first and last sections, which describe how the little boy was healed, and the section titled The Field. Consider the idea of a "miracle" in this context.

2. Watch the video *What the Bleep do We Know!?* (available on DVD and online at www.whatthebleep.com). Consider how what they're saying may explain some of the miracles in our world.

3. Ask someone in your group to study the description of an interesting experiment in a scientific journal such as *Science, The New England Journal of Medicine*, and Nature, and make a step-by-step outline of how the experimenter followed the scientific method described in question 5 in the previous section. Then design a simple experiment your group can do, using materials you already have at home. (You can get ideas from an internet search if you have difficulties designing one.)

4. Watch *What Dreams May Come*, with Robin Williams. Explore how the thoughts and images his character focused on early in the film affected his later experience. Then talk about how his "mentor" first appeared, while Williams's character was still confused, and what happened later. Compare this film to your ideas about the spiritual life we've been told we will be born into as we pass from this earthly life. Does this explain anything for you?

5. Make a joint commitment to take the twenty-eight-day challenge outlined in the exercises at the end of the modern interpretation. Compare experiences and ideas that come up in the process. Find ways to support each other in caritas.